D1599443

A Union Woman

in

Civil War Kentucky

A Union Woman in Civil War Kentucky

The Diary of Frances Peter

EDITED BY
JOHN DAVID SMITH
AND
WILLIAM COOPER JR.

THE UNIVERSITY PRESS OF KENTUCKY

Publication of this volume was made possible in part
by a grant from the National Endowment for the Humanities.

Scholarly publisher for the Commonwealth,
serving Bellarmine College, Berea College, Centre College
of Kentucky, Eastern Kentucky University, The Filson Club
Historical Society, Georgetown College, Kentucky Historical
Society, Kentucky State University, Morehead State University,
Murray State University, Northern Kentucky University,
Transylvania University, University of Kentucky, University of
Louisville, and Western Kentucky University.

Editorial and Sales Offices: The University Press of Kentucky
663 South Limestone Street, Lexington, Kentucky 40508-4008

04 03 02 01 00   5 4 3 2 1

E
601
.P48
2000

Library of Congress Cataloging-in-Publication Data

Peter, Frances Dallam, 1843-1864.
    A Union woman in Civil War Kentucky : the diary of Frances Peter /
edited by John David Smith and William Cooper, Jr. — Expanded ed.
        p.   cm.
    Rev. ed. of: Window on the war. c1976.
    Includes bibliographical references (p.   ) and index.
    ISBN 0-8131-2144-2 (alk. paper)
    1. Peter, Frances Dallam, 1843-1864 Diaries. 2. United States—History—
Civil War, 1861-1865 Personal narratives. 3. Kentucky—History—Civil War,
1861-1865 Personal narratives. 4. Lexington (Ky.)   Biography. 5. Women—
Kentucky—Lexington Diaries. I. Smith, John David, 1949-   . II. Cooper,
William, 1933-   . III. Peter, Frances Dallam, 1843-1864. Window on the
war. IV. Title.
E601.P48   1999
976.9'4703'092—dc21
[B]   99-23203

Manufactured in the United States of America

Contents

Illustrations

For the Rousells—Leslie, Charles,
David, Jonathan, Cinder, and Forest
J.D.S.

For Norma, Suzanne, and Gregory
W.C.

Acknowledgments

The editors have accumulated many debts to scholars and friends over the long history of editing Frances Dallam Peter's diary. Ron Alexander's Ph.D. dissertation, "Central Kentucky During the Civil War" (University of Kentucky, 1976), first alerted us to the richness and significance of the diary when the editors were graduate students at the University of Kentucky. E.I. Thompson, Richard S. DeCamp, Ed Houlihan, Burton Milward, and Holman Hamilton encouraged the Lexington-Fayette County Historic Commission to publish a small portion of the diary as *Window on the War*. The editors are grateful to Bill Marshall, head of the Division of Special Collections and Archives, Margaret I. King Library, University of Kentucky, for permission to publish the Peter diary, and to Bettie L. Kerr, Historic Preservation Officer, Lexington-Fayette Urban County Government, for permission to draw upon material from *Window on the War*.

A Union Woman in Civil War Kentucky benefited immeasurably from the assistance of Christopher A. Graham. Mr. Graham conducted extensive research, drafted annotations, and assisted the editors in conceptualizing and editing the introduction. Norene Miller of the Department of History, North Carolina State University, entered the text of *Window on the War* into a word processor. Daniel J. Salemson edited the revised transcription. Richard Costello provided his usual computer expertise and good cheer. Troy Burton, Susan Lyons Hughes, Ann B. Ward, and Leila May offered additional research assistance.

Introduction

Frances Dallam Peter, barely eighteen years old when the Civil War began, wrote one of the most perceptive eyewitness accounts of the conflict in Kentucky. Her diary, the only extant published recollection of a female Kentucky Unionist, records descriptions of daily life in Lexington and observations on the war from January 1862 to April 1864. Miss Peter's pages not only include routine stories of rumor, gossip, and military affairs, but also provide a clear view of a community severely divided by internecine war.

The Peter diary, portions of which were first published in a limited edition in 1976, brims with insights into the meaning of the war for Lexingtonians in particular and Kentuckians in general. Frances Peter's account of the war as seen through her window facing the Little College Lot[1] (now called Gratz Park) also offers us the unique reflections of a young woman whose world was circumscribed by a physical handicap and by the Victorian middle-class gender system that defined women as delicate and helpless.[2]

Writing in 1978, historian William C. Davis remarked that Frances's diary contains "much of social history . . . and to anyone interested in how a

An 1855 engraving in *Ballou's* (Boston) depicting Lexington as seen from Morrison Hall looking south. (Audio-Visual Archives, Special Collections and Archives, University of Kentucky Libraries)

Introduction

divided border community functioned during the war, this will prove invaluable." He added that though "'Home front' diaries for most of the North and South are not all that scarce, . . . there is not that much from Kentucky diarists, and particularly from Lexingtonians. This is made all the more unfortunate by the fact that, although Frankfort may have been the capital, Lexington was really the center of interest in Civil War Kentucky."[3]

This edition of Frances Dallam Peter's Lexington Civil War diary includes a new interpretive introduction that frames her life and text, more than two hundred additional diary entries, and hundreds of new annotations. Collectively, this new material adds much fresh military and civilian detail and considerable social context to that contained in the 1976 edition. In addition to expanding the breadth and depth of *Window on the War*, the opportunity to publish a new edition has enabled the editors to correct errors in the first edition, to integrate new sources and interpretations, and to prepare the text and annotations in line with modern editorial practice. The last two decades have witnessed significant changes not only in documentary editing, but in the writing of local, social, and women's history as well.

Born in Lexington on January 28, 1843, Miss Peter lived with her parents, Dr. Robert Peter and Frances Paca Dallam, and never married. The Peters were prominent residents of the Bluegrass. A native of Cornwall, England, Dr. Peter (1805–1894) migrated to Baltimore in 1817, then to Pittsburgh, and in 1832 moved to Lexington, where he emerged as one of America's most respected chemists, geologists, and physicians. He was a pioneer in the field of public health. Awarded the M.D. degree from Transylvania University in 1834, he was promptly appointed chair of chemistry in Morrison College. In 1838 Dr. Peter was named chair of chemistry and pharmacy at Transylvania University's Medical Department, serving in that capacity until shortly before the Civil War. During much of this time Dr. Peter also was dean and librarian of the medical school, which ranked among the nation's best in the antebellum years. Once the war began, he served as U.S. Army surgeon for troops stationed in Lexington. His wife, Frances, was born near Lexington in 1815 and descended from the famous Henry, Preston, and Breckinridge families of Virginia and Kentucky. Mrs. Peter's great-uncle, William Paca of Maryland, was among those who signed the Declaration of Independence. Dr. and Mrs. Peter had eleven children.[4]

The Peters lived in wartime Lexington, one of Kentucky's two urban centers and a city of approximately 9,500 citizens with sharply divided loyalties. Dr. Peter's responsibilities as medical officer for Lexington's U.S. military hospitals and the proximity of the family's home on the corner of Market

Two daguerreotypes taken in September 1846 of Dr. Robert Peter and family. The children (above, left to right) are William, Ben, Frances and Lettie and (below, left to right) Lettie, Frances, and Ben. (Audio-Visual Archives, Special Collections and Archives, University of Kentucky Libraries)

Dr. Robert Peter in the 1840s. (Transylvania University Library)

Introduction

Street and Mechanics Alley to bivouacking troops on the Little College Lot afforded Frances unusual opportunities to observe the movements of both Union and Confederate forces as they passed through and occupied Lexington. Described by a relative as "a talented, charming girl," Frances (or "Frank" as her family called her) enjoyed drawing, reading, and writing.[5] Surviving examples of her poetry, short stories, and sketches illustrate a fertile and creative mind. Her diary entries suggest that she was a keen observer and outspoken social critic as well.

Unfortunately, Miss Peter was an epileptic and her illness somewhat curtailed her social activities. However, she did attend Sayre Female Institute, a respected Lexington academy. The 1850s was a period of transition in the medical understanding of epilepsy. Heretofore, the medical profession attributed the affliction to one of various causes—fright, masturbation, drunkenness, and other mental frailties. As the Civil War approached, researchers in Europe developed theories that epilepsy resulted from problems in the central nervous system and the brain. By 1861 physicians had begun trephining (drilling the skull) in an attempt to find a cure. One report in the United States asserted that trephining was practiced as far west as St. Louis. Actually, Dr. Benjamin Dudley, a colleague and close friend of Dr. Peter, had performed this operation with some success as early as the 1820s. Dr. Dudley left the Transylvania Medical School about 1850, however, when Frances was still very young.[6] With little hope of finding a cure, most epileptics lived with families or extended families and were unable to integrate into their communities. Because she was a member of an educated and relatively enlightened family, Frances was not subjected to the degree of seclusion that many epileptics experienced.

Frances Peter's epilepsy, however, may have contributed to her introspection and her determination to understand the world beyond her family. To an important degree, the diary served as her means of responding to and interacting with the outside world. The pages of her diary—scrap paper composed of military hospital supply sheets stitched together with thread—connected Frances to wartime Lexington, a city caught in the midst of dramatic social change. Her diary succinctly chronicles Kentucky's invasion by Confederates under General Braxton Bragg in August 1862, Lexington's month-long occupation by General Edmund Kirby Smith, the trials and tribulations of her hated "secesh" neighbors, and the emancipation of their black slaves. But the diary also served as a means for Frances to extend her world, to negotiate the boundaries of a mid-nineteenth-century middle-class woman with a serious disease that left her marginalized on the fringes of Lexington society.

Lines
on the Oak Tree at Winton

Oh, dear to my heart are the scenes of my childhood
Those loved scenes where often, how often I've strayed
The meadow, the spring, and the thick tangled wildwood
Where often in Life's merry morn I have played.

Of all these fair scenes which my heart hath kept treasured
And which oft to my thought, fond Remembrance will bring
The one which is uppermost still 'mong my pleasures
Is the stately old "Oak Tree" that grew at the spring.

Beneath its green branches how oft have I sported
And played with the fruit which its wide arms had strown
Or seated upon its roots, gnarled and wide spreading,
List the splash of the spring, when I threw in the stone.

And when with advancing time, years had flown by,
And the joy of these childish amusements had fled,
'Twas my greatest delight to read 'neath its branches,
Or list to the songs of the birds overhead.

But once in my visit Oh sad is the story!
The Oak Tree had fallen, the monarch lieas low
Like the greatest of empires that history tells us
'Twas fallen in an instant, so strong was the blow.

A poem by Frances Peter (continued on next page) about her favorite oak tree at Winton, the ancestral estate of her mother's family. (Evans Collection, Special Collections and Archives, University of Kentucky Libraries)

I was like to a friend whom we've many years cherish'd
With the memory of whom the thoughts of childhood are rife
By the hands of some deadly blight snatched from among us
And never to return to the scenes of this life.

———

Oh' long I lament thee, thou "King of the forrest"!
No more in thy branches the gay birds do sing,
But though thou wilt pass from the mind of another
I'll remember the 'Oak Tree' that grew at the spring.

Frances D Peter

Lexington, February 14th 1857.

7

The Sayre Female Institute,

LEXINGTON, KY.

REPORT OF MISS _____

Nov. 16th 186?

Reading, ...	9	Chemistry, ...
Spelling, _deficient_	9	Botany, ...
Writing, ...	9	Geology, ...
Geography, . . .	8½	Ancient Geography, .
Arithmetic . . .	9½	Mythology, ...
History, ...	9½	Geometry, ...
Natural History, . .		Trigonometry, . . .
English Grammar, . .	9	Rhetoric, ...
Physiology, ...		Composition, . . . 9½
Latin, ...		Greek, ...
French, ...		Logic, ...
Algebra, ...		Biblical Study,
Natural Philosophy, .		Alexander's Evidences, .
Astronomy, . . .		Butler's Analogy, . .
Music, ...		Mental Philosophy, . .
Drawing, ...		Moral Philosophy, . .

No. 10 is the maximum rarely reached. These Nos. do not denote the *absolute* attainments in a study, but the average merit of the recitations and the relative proficiency since last Report.

N. B. Circulars to be had at the Book Stores.

DEMERIT MARKS.

General Deportment _much improved_

Order in School _good_

Keeping of Books and Desks _"_

Punctuality in attendance _"_

Neatness of Bed Room, &c.

These marks of discredit affect the pupils claim to a premium and demand inquisition by parents.

H. V. D. NEVIUS.

A report card for Frances Peter at age twelve. (Evans Collection, Special Collections and Archives, University of Kentucky Libraries)

Introduction

Though Frances's epilepsy restricted her world beyond her home, she nevertheless expressed no regrets or self-pity. Her diary contains no evidence of envy or resentment, for example, when her sisters attended the Amateur Musical Association benefits, promenaded on the sidewalks, or exchanged gossip with other Union women. Frances's diary quite amazingly contains nothing that might be perceived as frustration or disappointment at her malady. A diary entry suggesting that she actually left her home—her March 7, 1863, report on the decorations at the Aid Society Tableaux—was no more descriptive or sentimental than other diary entries.[7] Frances took advantage of the time afforded by confinement to read newspapers, which allowed her to contribute information to the gossip of the day and to share knowledge of the war's events.

Frances Peter's text offers a relatively unobscured view of the world she watched closely but from afar on the Little College Lot. Though an outsider, she wrote from the perspective, and with the voice, of an insider. In their valuable anthology of American diaries, Randall M. Miller and Linda Patterson Miller maintain that the majority of American "diarists . . . wrote to tell about themselves." "Regardless of its content," they explain, "a diary is a way to assert individuality." Michael O'Brien, who reminds us that we know surprisingly little about the roughly 20 to 25 percent of adult white women who remained single in the Old South, maintains that journals or diaries provided women in general, but unmarried women in particular, crucial voices. They "answered varying needs," he explains. Frances's diary speaks to her need to interpret, explain, reach out, and comprehend the complex world around her. Like other diarists, Frances could control what she described and chose to comment upon. In doing so, she merged the dramatic events of Civil War Lexington with her own *Weltanschauung*.[8]

In clear and precise language, Frances recorded her daily observations of men, women, and events that literally unfolded outside her window. Her diary is marked by a general sense of restraint and decorum, and she usually refrained from recording rumors that may have been considered socially unacceptable. Nevertheless, her strong opinions, concerns, and biases do frequently emerge. While Frances Peter, as a participant in her own diary, is less than dominant, her personal hopes and fears are not entirely missing. Her frequent militancy and biting remarks about the local "secesh" and Confederates give voice to the private ruminations of other female Kentucky Unionists.

Frances's reports of daily life in Lexington were generally brief and restrained. She wrote in simple narrative style to relay facts and kept her comments on each subject to a sentence or two (see, for example, her comments on the efficacy of U.S. Colored Troops as soldiers on February 4, 1863).[9] Her major interest, of course, pertained to events in and around Lexington and central Kentucky, especially the activities of her neighbors, local authorities, and Confederate sympathizers. Frances, too, was concerned with military affairs, especially the comings and goings of her neighbor, Confederate General John Hunt Morgan, the invasion of Kentucky by Confederate Generals Edmund Kirby Smith and Braxton Bragg, and the efforts of the U.S. Army to delay or pursue the Confederate advance. Perhaps because Frances was unattached, she found vicarious pleasure in focusing on exciting events beyond the confines of her home. Significantly, she expressed little fear or excitement in her reports of the entrance of Confederate forces into Kentucky in 1862 and 1863. In a straightforward style she noted Kirby Smith's 1862 invasion and observed that other Lexingtonians exhibited higher states of anxiety than she did.

Curiously, Frances's family members remain relatively minor players in her diary. Occasionally she mentioned sisters Lettie and Johanna, her mother, and her brothers. But of all family members, it is Dr. Peter, the family patriarch, who appears most often within her pages, primarily because he was engaged in those activities outside the home that most interested her. Frances expressed considerable interest in Kentucky politics, and the degree to which the commonwealth remained loyal to the Union. In fact, the issue of Kentucky's loyalty became Frances's abiding passion. She supported the Union unflaggingly and resisted the temptation to turn against its cause because of her differences of opinion with President Abraham Lincoln's administration. Frances considered the disloyalty of Kentucky Unionists most grievous, and this spirited her extended outbursts at such figures as Judge Richard A. Buckner Jr. (March 14, 1863), antislavery clergyman Henry Ward Beecher (November 20, 1863), U.S. Senator Garrett Davis (January 16, 1864), and Colonel Frank Wolford (March 10 and 14, 1864). Frances was most incensed by Wolford's disloyal attacks on President Lincoln in March 1864. She considered him a former Kentucky Unionist and war hero gone bad.

Frances articulated themes common to Kentucky Unionists. For example, she vehemently supported the war against the Confederacy but was extremely wary of perceived or real excesses of constitutional authority by Lincoln. Like many other Kentucky Unionists, Frances objected initially to the Emancipation Proclamation, the blacks' emerging sense of freedom and independence, and the enlistment of blacks in the U.S. Army. Her racial views thus approximated those of her "secesh" foes and were consistent with the attitudes of most whites, northern and southern, in the 1860s. Her derisive comments about "abolitionists" make this point abundantly clear. Gradually, however, Frances accepted slavery's dissolution and the reality of emancipation. "I for one," she noted on October 19, 1863, "would not be at all disgusted at having Ky slaves emancipated." She added "that we are much nearer emancipation now, than even last year[.] People are getting more accustomed to the idea, and do not think it near so terrible as they used to. It is rather significant that at the present writing it is considered nearly if not quite as cheap to buy negroes as to hire them." Frances also expressed particular disdain for Copperheads (northern Democrats conciliatory toward the Confederacy). Writing, for example, on November 20, 1863, she remarked: "I think with Gov Bramlette that a man who wont have the Union, unless the negroes are out of it, is just as bad and as much an enemy to the union cause, as the secessionist who wont have the Union unless he can have the negro too." Though Frances offers us few clues as to the source of her slow acceptance of emancipation, she nonetheless came to regard Lincoln's freeing of the slaves as a necessary war measure.

Frances's descriptions of daily events in divided Lexington are the most vivid of her text and rank among the most salient contributions of this edition. In a succinct and clear style, she made detailed comments on the interactions of women and men of Lexington's networks of both "secesh" and Unionists. They chronicle interactions with various authorities, incidents at the military hospitals, stories from the countryside, and descriptions of Union and Confederate soldiers in town, particularly in the vicinity of the Little College Lot.

Frances's narrative, of course, reflected her biases. She disdainfully described the "secesh" as uniformly conniving and spiteful. On November 7, 1862, for example, Frances blasted Lexington women who sided with the Confederates for failing to care for wounded soldiers. "The secesh ladies Consciences (if they have any)," she wrote, "doubtless reproach them for their own neglect." Frances described Jack Keiser as "the meanest man in town" (October 17, 1862), remarked that "Mrs. Basil Duke hissed" (March 21, 1862), and that Lu Robb and Theo Curd hid secrets about Confederate maneuvers (September 20, 1862). She routinely accused other local "secesh" of passing letters through the lines and possessing advance knowledge of Confederate offensives (November 16, 1862).

But Frances reserved her most vituperative remarks and most scathing judgments for the Morgans—Mrs. Henrietta Morgan and her son John Hunt Morgan—whose home was barely a block away from hers. Before the war the Peter and Morgan families were good friends and neighbors, but the start of hostilities severed the once cordial ties. Frances seemed almost obsessed with the Morgans, speculating about the comings and goings at their

Introduction

residence close to the Peters' home. Not surprisingly, like other Unionists, she viewed General Morgan as a coward and scoundrel. Writing on January 27, 1864, Frank remarked that Morgan's "character . . . was always that of a gambler and libertine, and before this war no gentleman in Lexington would associate with him." She wondered "what loyal Kentuckians are there that would be delighted at the escape of the traitor who pillaged their families, destroyed their homes, and persecuted them in every way. The outlaw whom they so often pursued to bring to justice, and who could never be called a brave man." Gawking no doubt from her window to observe activities in the Morgans' home, Frances recorded the exchange of letters, the secreting of rebel soldiers, and the response of the Morgans to news of Confederate setbacks.

But Frances Peter observed many soldiers, not just Lexington's most colorful Confederate. Her observations of rebel soldiers in Lexington during September 1862, for example, rival the oft-quoted descriptions by U.S. Sanitary Commission Officer Lewis Steiner and the English observer Lt. Colonel Arthur Fremantle.[10] Miss Peter described Kirby Smith's men as "the tag, rag & bobtail of the earth" and complained that they apparently "hadnt been near water since Fort Sumter fell." She compared the Confederates unfavorably to "our men . . . so clean & gentlemanly looking & looking so well fed" (September 18, 1862). Though Frances occasionally sympathized with individual southern soldiers, she overwhelmingly held them in contempt, blasting the "chivalry" who "expect to have a 'nigger' to do everything & if they can't get one will do without washing & every thing else rather than help themselves" (October 7, 1862). Her diary documents stealing by Confederates as well as a great deal of deprivation and hardship within their ranks.

Frances Peter's diary also provides a window to Federal troops stationed in Lexington. Union troops encamped in the Little College Lot close to the Peters' home nearly the entire time that Frances kept her diary. In her opinion, the Peters considered most U.S. troops, especially Missourians, Ohioans, Indianans, Pennsylvanians, and Rhode Islanders, to be friendly. She noted, however, that "the men belonging to the Michigan regiment are not near as nice. . . . There are so many mean fellows among them and more Abolitionists than in all the Ohio & Indiana regiments put together. In fact I have never seen an Ohio Abolitionist yet" (November 15, 1862). In addition to her commentary on the men she observed, Frances also recorded troop movements in and around Lexington. Her entries provide a ground-level view of larger military operations and should remind historians that most citizens caught in the path of the war understood the sweeping campaigns and battles as a series of small, locally defined skirmishes.

Frances's comments and analyses suggest that, despite her affliction, she was not totally isolated from Lexington's community of women. Significantly, Miss Peter participated fully in a decidedly female network in Lexington that sustained friendships, provided support in times of anxiety, offered humor to release tension, and monitored the activities of enemies. If viewed from the interpretive framework of recent writings on women in the Civil War, divided Lexington contained two such networks: one pro-Confederate and the other pro-Union. Close reading of Frances's diary unveils these networks. In fact, her unintended description of the activities of these competing communication systems is Frances's foremost contribution to the study of Civil War women.[11]

Over the last decade historians such as Catherine Clinton, George Rable, Nina Silber, Elizabeth D. Leonard, Lee Ann Whites, Drew Gilpin Faust, and others have argued most convincingly that the Civil War altered not only antebellum notions of politics, economics, and "race" but the role of white women as well. Modern historians underscore the adaptability of "gender systems," the fact that gender roles, socially constructed concepts of appropriate behavior, may and do change over time. War, feminist theorists argue, is not only an extreme expression of these roles (particularly male) but also a critical period when existing concepts of acceptable gender roles and gendered behavior may be questioned and tested. The Civil War, they explain, was a dynamic period of social change for white women.[12]

Though most Civil War combatants were male (postwar polemicists indeed dubbed it the "Brothers' War"), the conflict nonetheless introduced gender as an important issue and provides historians with a new category of analysis.[13] Historical understanding of the role of Confederate women has received the greatest attention from scholars. Before the 1980s, historians of southern white women in the Civil War generally celebrated their loyalty, enthusiasm, and determination to the "cause." Though clearly in the shadows of their men, white southern women nevertheless served the Confederacy heroically in many auxiliary capacities—as nurses, producers of war materiel, farm and plantation managers, and employees of the Confederate War Department, Post Office, Quartermaster Department, Clothing Bureau, and the offices of the Commissary General and Treasury Department. Until recently, scholars have interpreted the wartime service of southern women as an extension of the Victorian gender system of "separate spheres" for men and women and the "cult of domesticity," which Barbara Welter has described as incorporating "piety, purity, submissiveness and domesticity." According to the traditional view, southern white women accepted death, defeat, and destitution without complaint.[14]

Introduction

The important work of Clinton, Rable, and Faust began a major revision of this interpretation and launched a vital reexamination of women's impact on the war as well as the ways that women defined the war's effect on them. The "new" Civil War women's history questions the degree to which southern elite women supported the Confederacy and, in doing so, tested gender boundaries and limits. As the Confederacy crumbled around them, southern women, forced to accept new and not always comfortable roles, became disillusioned and disappointed. Their men let them down by failing to protect them. Lee Ann Whites calls this process the disruption of "the antebellum gender quid pro quo between white men and women, in which men had promised to 'protect' and women had agreed to 'obey.'" But the war overturned these assumptions dramatically. Abandoned and left unprotected by their men in an increasingly "lost cause," after 1863 southern white women demanded a return to the safe confines of the antebellum period. They lost faith and confidence in the Confederacy, the world their men had made. Though scholars disagree about the influence of female discontent on the Confederate war effort, the war unquestionably served as a crucible of change for white women. It forced them to develop new skills, to accept new responsibilities and, ultimately, to redefine traditional gender roles.[15]

Northern women have received less attention than their southern sisters from historians, primarily because the war provided northerners fewer challenges than southerners. Most of the battles occurred in the South and, of course, white southerners alone experienced their unique "burden" of history—the traumas of defeat, emancipation, and Reconstruction. Because northern women endured fewer wartime hardships caused by shortages and proximity to military campaigns, historians generally have interpreted them, according to Leonard, as "the weeping widows of the dead." Yet northern women experienced the same fundamental disruption caused by the war as southern women did: the widespread exodus of husbands, sons, and lovers to the army, in thousands of cases never to return. And like southern females, northern women assumed new wartime roles, emerging as leaders and managers and as newly empowered heads-of-households. They assumed newfound roles, Leonard explains, and entered the public sphere. "Above all," Leonard writes, they "challenged spatial boundaries in an unprecedented manner," thereby expanding their worlds "by travelling far from home to the front, or by linking in various ways their community undertakings on behalf of the soldiers to organizations national in scope." The appearance of northern women as businesspeople, managers, organizers, and leaders tested Victorian gender assumptions in ways unique to the North. The full significance of this transformation has yet to be examined by historians. And because of

Introduction

her particular circumstances, Frances Peter falls between the interpretive cracks of extant gender studies. Her experiences thus fit poorly into the "new" Civil War women's history.[16]

Unmarried, Frances apparently had no significant relationship with a male besides her father, Dr. Robert Peter. Ironically, historians of women in the Civil War have used women's relationships with their menfolk as frames of reference, as barometers of the gender battles wrought by the war. Men, after all, provided economic support, protection, and a public face for the family, while women ostensibly reciprocated by reproducing, maintaining households, and overseeing a moral and nurturing atmosphere for the growth of children. Frances's significant male relationship, her father, did not change as a result of the conflict. Throughout the war Dr. Peter remained an ever-present protective figure within her home. Nor does evidence suggest that the war significantly challenged Lexington's patriarchy. Conditions never required Frances (or provided her with opportunities) to assume new responsibilities. While the war liberated many women—enabling them to leave their domiciles and perform war-related work—Frances's physical condition blocked her entry into the public world.

Unable to venture far beyond her home and participate fully, along with sister Lettie, in the Soldier's Aid Society, at hospitals, and at social functions sponsored by the military, Frances never had the opportunity to engage in activities that tested her assumptions about the place of women in society. Though she never questioned traditional gender roles (or if she did so, they remain unrecorded in her diary), Frances nonetheless noted the assertiveness and empowerment of women necessitated by wartime conditions.

Frances described mothers and wives defending their homes and property against marauding guerrillas and foragers. Mrs. Martin used a gun to save her husband's wagon and to drive Confederates from her home (October 9, 1862). Mrs. J. Wilgus wrestled a weapon from the hands of intruding soldiers (October 19, 1862). Mrs. Hart Gibson and Miss Ella Duncan interrupted a Unionist political meeting, where the governor was present, with hisses and disorderly conduct (April 7, 1863). And in the only incident whereby a woman assumed the power of a man, Frances recorded the case of Mrs. Breshears, the wife of a Union army surgeon, who reportedly had been given authority to punish men under her husband's charge during his absence (January 26, 1862).

Frances, however, unlike many Confederate female diarists, never suffered overt physical hardships, shortages, or undue emotional trauma from the war. Aside from the brief mention of her brother's impulse to enlist in the U.S. Army (September 18, 1862), she had no known relatives in the service and none of her loved ones were in immediate danger of death in battle. Lack of a close male figure to whom she could express maternal or spousal concern probably permitted Frances to distance herself from the worst reality of war: separation by death of a loved one. This possibly accounts for the rather cavalier narrative voice that she maintained throughout her diary.

Yet even without immediate family in the ranks, the war obviously was central to Frances's life in these years. Evidence of the war and its impact were all around her. Kentucky, Lexington, even the Little College Lot, were divided in loyalties and were centers of military activity. At different times from her window Frances observed both U.S. and Confederate troops in camp and on the march. Though the guns of battle occasionally rang in and around Lexington, she more commonly defined the war by the presence of the local "secesh," the passing of troops in transit, and the movement of the wounded and sick in and out of the city's hospitals. Frances's diary reported on all of this—and more—but makes little reference to its young author and none to her disease.

Yet even in her confinement, Frances remained fully aware of local gossip and news. Indeed, neither she nor any of her circle of friends in Lexington was isolated from current information. Lexington women continued to build upon an informal network for the discussion of news and the calming of anxieties. While this network had diverse sources, including newspapers and local authorities, the grapevine remained strictly informal in operation and largely feminine in origin. Through her network Frances obtained news about military campaigns, conflicts between local Unionists and "secesh," activities at the military headquarters, political conventions in Frankfort and Louisville, stories of guerrilla attacks, and events in the more remote Kentucky countryside.

The primary sources that fed Frances's network apparently were gossip and stories passed between women as they met in the street, stopped by for visits, or attended functions together. Frances gathered most of her information at home, either at the front door or inside the residence. Her references to "*We* heard . . . ," "A woman told *us* . . . ," and "Mrs. Williams related an incident to *us*..." (October 14 and 15, 1862, emphasis added), indicated that she was part of a group, probably composed of her mother and sisters, who received information from visitors. When strangers, or passersby, stopped at the front door of the Peter home, Frances's father or mother spoke to them while she listened in (September 18, 1862). On one occasion Frances recorded speaking from the doorstep, in a highly uncharacteristic outburst directed at a Confederate prisoner (March 31, 1862). From time to time she also reported gathering information by innocent eavesdropping: "I overheard

Introduction

..." (September 18, 1862), and "A lady overheard Dr Major say . . ." (March 23, 1863).

Newspapers provided Frances her second most important source of information for her diary. She favored the Cincinnati papers and, after the Lexington *Observer and Reporter* began to endorse "copperhead" ideas, Miss Peter lamented the lack of any staunchly Unionist paper in the commonwealth. On August 31, 1863, while commenting on newspapers, she recorded her only statement that might be regarded as an observation on sexual differences: "[W]e didn't get the [Cincinnati] Times, not that I expected it would have anything in it, but the gentlemen always seem to think so and throw away many a five cents upon it, and dont get much satisfaction."

There were still other sources of information for Frances's diary. Upon returning home from social gatherings that she could not attend, her sisters promptly reported the details of dances, fundraisers, and events at the hospitals (May 22, 1863). Lexington's black population formed another interesting part of Frances's communication network. Informants for Frances included the slave girl who belonged to Mrs. Curd, a "secesh" neighbor (October 10, 1862), and an anonymous "black man" (Ocober 12, 1862). Finally, Frances's father served as a convenient and rich source for stories and local gossip. Each night Dr. Peter regaled his family with his own gossip: stories from the hospitals, military headquarters, and the city administration.

Frances's network, and the information it communicated to her diary, thus reveals that Lexington women were neither isolated from nor uninterested in the larger world around them. From Frances's vantage point on the Little College Lot, she viewed the frequent assemblage of "secesh" ladies at Mrs. Morgan's home when news of her son's triumphs or tragedies were received. Frances described the workings of her own network on the occasion of General Morgan's Ohio Raid (July 2–26, 1863) that threatened Lexington. Miss Peter explained, "As for us we did nothing but sit in the front door. Annie & Miriam Gratz and ourselves and talk about the news and what we would do if they did come, and had a deal of fun" (July 6, 1863).

Not surprisingly, the "secesh" ladies did the same thing. Frances in fact was almost as obsessed with the activities of the "secesh" women as she was with the comings and goings of Mrs. Morgan. The rival "secesh" used their network not only for gossip but, more importantly, to pass official information, news, and personal letters between themselves and loved ones unable to return home to Union-occupied Kentucky. Their network often provided the greatest source of strength for Confederate sympathizers whose intimate relations were away. When news of a potential southern victory or defeat was expected, the Unionist and Confederate networks convened. After some "secesh" were rounded up by U.S. troops and forced to leave Lexington, Miss Peter remarked, "The secesh ladies were very much excited and walked the streets a great deal" (March 14, 1863).

Lizzie Hardin, a "secesh" lady and Confederate sympathizer from Harrodsburg, noted in her diary the actions of her own network. "Our gloom though was somewhat enlivened by a great abundance of what was familiarly called 'grapevine.' That is, secret Southern intelligence." The "secesh" network in Harrodsburg relied heavily on information brought by letters from the Confederacy and from close readings of sympathetic northern newspapers, particularly the *Cincinnati Enquirer*. In Harrodsburg and Lexington, the two competing networks rarely interacted. Commenting on relations between the "secesh" and Unionists, Lizzie observed that she had "never seen such bitter feelings as there was between the two parties. Social intercourse had almost ceased."[17]

While the two rival female networks rarely spoke, and never looked to each other for support, in Lexington lines did cross and Frances Peter was aware of news within the "secesh" camp, sometimes within hours after it hit the streets. Frances commented frequently on the rude behavior of "secesh" ladies and noticed that they were often privy to advance warning (whether true, or not) of a Confederate assault on the city. Despite the intensity of her animus against the "secesh" ladies, she recorded only one incident of open violence upon a pro-Confederate woman. When a "secesh" lady or, as Frances remarked, "rather a rebel individual of the feminine gender, for she disgraced the name of lady," confronted a Union guard with "insolent language," loyal Lexingtonians gathered and began to throw stones at the woman. They almost mobbed her (September 21, 1863).

Unfortunately historians have paid insufficient attention to the kind of informal female networks that supplied Frances with information for her diary. Assessing antebellum southern white women's culture, Joan E. Cashin has explained that while historians "still know little about how white Southern women experienced the self," her research suggests "how crucial it was for them to share their emotions with other white women. The exchanges alleviated loneliness, comforted the weary and the grief-stricken, and afforded them many moments of joy." Wartime conditions no doubt exacerbated the need for such contact.[18]

Examining women in the Confederacy, Faust uncovered "thousands of women's voluntary organizations that appeared in the South for the first time in response to the demands of war." In her opinion, these female associations "represent a significant locus in the formation of female self-consciousness, for here women saw themselves in groups; here they explored the meanings of gender in a way they had not previously been impelled to." Important to women's emerging gender identity, such groups no doubt provided means for women to share information and provide mutual support. Frances's more informal network served much the same functions. Women, northern and southern, no doubt constructed similar systems of informal communication.[19]

Drawing upon her female network of Unionists for information, comradeship, and support, Frances Peter observed life in war-torn central Kentucky. Her diary provides considerable detail and insight into the Civil War in a hotly contested border state. With a sophistication beyond her years, Frances recorded her day-to-day impressions of Lexington and rendered shrewd assessments of men and women caught in the throes of dramatic social, economic, and political change. From her window, Frances Peter watched events around her unfold and no doubt pondered her future. Regrettably, Frances succumbed to an epileptic seizure before the war's end and died on August 5, 1864, at age twenty-one.

Though Frances Peter lost her battle with epilepsy, during her short life she drew upon her female network to triumph over the limitations of her confinement. Her insightful diary, which recorded her impressions of life as a staunch Unionist, underscores the impact of the war on a Kentucky community. Writing her diary enabled Frances to participate symbolically in the war, even as just an observer. It provides us with a strategically positioned window to that war through the gaze of a young woman of intelligence and substance.

THE TRUSTEES OF THE LEXINGTON CEMETERY COMPANY,

Do Certify, That *Robt Peter* on this day purchased of them at the price of *One Hundred* Dollars $\frac{00}{100}$ which have been paid in full, **A BURIAL LOT,** being part of their **Cemetery Grounds** in and near the City of Lexington, which Lot contains *Four hundred* Square Feet of Ground, and *is known and designated as Lot No 109 of Section C* according to the Plot of said Ground. The Title to which Burial Lot is hereby conveyed to said *Robt Peter* to be held by *him* and *his* heirs and assigns forever, subject to such regulations as may from time to time be made in pursuance of the Charter of said Company.

In Testimony Whereof, said Trustees have caused the Corporate Seal of the Lexington Cemetery Company, and the signature of *R. Higgins* Chairman of the Trustees to be hereunto affixed, this *8th* day of *August* 1864.

R Higgins

Lexington Cemetery, *August 9* 1864

To Robt Peter

TO LEXINGTON CEMETARY COMPANY,

To 1 Grave opening and closing, $ 4.00
" Vault " " ....
" Single Grave Lot, No ....

Received payment,

C V Bell

For Lexington Cemetery Co.

Frances Dallam Peter died August 5, 1864, eight months before Lee's surrender at Appomattox. (Evans Collection, Special Collections and Archives, University of Kentucky Libraries)

Dr. Robert Peter's letter to his brother Arthur in Louisville concerning the death of Frances and asking him to place a notice in the *Journal*. (Evans Collection, Special Collections and Archives, University of Kentucky Libraries)

Introduction

NOTES

1. A helpful map of the Little College Lot including many of the sites mentioned in Miss Peter's diary appeared in "Gratz Park Bids You Welcome," *Louisville Courier-Journal Magazine*, May 25, 1958. The original map, drawn by Howard Evans in 1933, is found in the Evans Papers, Division of Special Collections and Archives, University of Kentucky.

2. Gail Bederman argues that "Gender was central" to middle class "self-definition." It "celebrated true women as pious, maternal guardians of virtue and domesticity." See *Manliness and Civilization: A Cultural History of Gender and Race in the United States, 1880–1917* (Chicago: Univ. of Chicago Press, 1995), 11.

3. Davis, review of *Window on the War: Frances Dallam Peter's Lexington Civil War Diary*, eds. John David Smith and William Cooper Jr., in *Register of the Kentucky Historical Society* 76 (January 1978): 54–55. In his review of the first edition of the Peter diary in 1979, Robert D. Hoffsommer commented that it was "only the second diary that I have seen in the past dozen or so more years on life behind the fighting lines in war-divided Kentucky." See *Civil War Times Illustrated* 17 (January 1979): 50. *Lexington Herald-Leader* columnist Don Edwards described the Peter diary as "good reading, a very human little book of glimpses of a city at war." See issue of January 23, 1977. Garold L. Cole included a useful summary of the first edition in *Civil War Eyewitnesses: An Annotated Bibliography of Books and Articles, 1955–1986* (Columbia: Univ. of South Carolina Press, 1988), 135–36. Claudia Lynn Lady relied on *Window on the War* in three works: "Six Tri-State Women During the Civil War" (M.A. thesis, Marshall University, 1981); "Five Tri-State Women During the Civil War: Day-to-Day Life," *West Virginia History* 43 (spring 1982): 189–226; and "Five Tri-State Women During the Civil War: Views on the War," ibid. (summer 1982): 303–21.

4. Biographical information on Miss Peter and her parents is contained throughout the Evans Papers, Special Collections, University of Kentucky Library. See especially "Description of the Civil War Diary" by Mrs. Catherine Peter Evans; and memorials to Dr. Robert Peter by William Benjamin Smith, August 1928, and Charles E. Snow, February 17, 1954. Also see John D. Wright Jr., "Robert Peter and Early Science in Kentucky" (Ph.D. diss., Columbia University, 1955).

5. This description is by Mrs. Evans, a niece of Miss Peter, cited above.

6. F. Garvin Davenport, *Ante-Bellum Kentucky: A Social History, 1800–1860* (Oxford, Ohio: Mississippi Valley Press, 1943), 97–98; Robert Peter, *History of the Medical Department of Transylvania University* (Louisville: John P. Morton & Co., 1905), 21–22. Institutions for the housing of severe epileptics emerged after the Civil War. The most notable of such facilities opened in Gallipolis, Ohio, in 1891. (See Owsei Temkin, *The Falling Sickness: A History of Epilepsy from the Greeks to the Beginnings of Modern Neurology* [Baltimore: Johns Hopkins Univ. Press, 1971], 255–95).

7. The entry of March 7, 1863 ("I only went the first night, so I can say nothing of those shown last night") suggested that Frances did venture out from time to time, but that she held this one occasion of no special significance.

8. Miller and Miller, eds., *The Book of American Diaries: From Heart and Mind to Pen to Paper; Day-by-Day Personal Accounts Through the Centuries* (New York: Avon Books, 1995), xiv; O'Brien, ed., *An Evening When Alone: Four Journals of Single Women in the South, 1827–67* (Charlottesville: Univ. Press of Virginia, 1993), 2–3. On the

Introduction

special circumstances of unmarried women in the Old South, see Victoria E. Bynum, *Unruly Women: The Politics of Social & Sexual Control in the Old South* (Chapel Hill: Univ. of North Carolina Press, 1992), 42, 44–45, 89–90, 110. For samples from other wartime Kentucky female diarists, see Susan Lyons Hughes, "My Old Kentucky Home—At War" (unpublished paper delivered at the Conference on Women and the Civil War, Hood College, Frederick, Maryland, June 27, 1998, copy in possession of the editors).

9. In contrast, see the diary entries of Rachel Cormany, whose remarks during the Confederate occupation of Chambersburg, Pennsylvania, in July 1864, revealed distress and anxiety. James C. Mohr and Richard E. Winslow, eds., *The Cormany Diaries: A Northern Family in the Civil War* (Pittsburgh: Univ. of Pittsburgh Press, 1982).

10. Lewis Steiner's comments appear in Richard B. Harwell, ed., *The Union Reader* (New York: Longmans, Green and Company, 1958), 156–74. Fremantle recorded his observations in the travel diary, *Three Months in the Southern States, April–June, 1863* (New York: J. Bradburn, 1864).

11. In *The Enclosed Garden: Women and Community in the Evangelical South, 1830–1900* (Chapel Hill: Univ. of North Carolina Press, 1985), Jean E. Friedman notes the presence of female networks in urban rather than rural environments. See pages 19, 32, 129.

12. See Clinton, *The Other Civil War: American Women in the Nineteenth Century* (New York: Hill and Wang, 1984); Rable, *Civil Wars: Women and the Crisis of Southern Nationalism* (Urbana: Univ. of Illinois Press, 1989); Clinton and Silber, eds., *Divided Houses: Gender and the Civil War* (New York: Oxford Univ. Press, 1992); Leonard, *Yankee Women: Gender Battles in the Civil War* (New York: W.W. Norton, 1994); idem, *All the Daring of the Soldier: Women of the Civil War Armies* (New York: W. W. Norton, 1999); Whites, *The Civil War as a Crisis in Gender: Augusta, Georgia, 1860–1890* (Athens: Univ. of Georgia Press, 1995). Faust's *Mothers of Invention: Women of the Slaveholding South in the American Civil War* (Chapel Hill: Univ. of North Carolina Press, 1996), is the most complete statement of the "new" history of southern white women in the Civil War. See also her "Trying to Do a Man's Business: Gender, Violence, and Slave Management in Civil War Texas," *Gender and History* 4 (summer 1992): 197–214; *Southern Stories: Slaveholders in Peace and War* (Columbia: Univ. of Missouri Press, 1992); and Faust, Thavolia Glymph, and Rable, "A Woman's War: Southern Women in the Civil War," in Edward D.C. Campbell Jr., and Kym S. Rice, eds., *A Woman's War: Southern Women, Civil War, and the Confederate Legacy* (Charlottesville: Univ. Press of Virginia, 1996), 1–28. For an insightful critique of Faust and others, see Margaret Ripley Wolfe, *Daughters of Canaan: A Saga of Southern Women* (Lexington: Univ. Press of Kentucky, 1995), 83–85. Two recent articles on women in the Civil War include Alice Fahs, "The Feminized Civil War: Gender, Northern Popular Literature, and the Memory of the War, 1861–1900," *Journal of American History* 85 (March 1999): 1461–94, and S. J. Kleinberg, "Review Essay: Race, Region, and Gender in American History," *Journal of American Studies* 33 (April 1999): 83–88.

13. For an interesting exception, see Lauren Cook Burgess, *An Uncommon Soldier: The Civil War Letters of Sarah Rosetta Wakeman, alias Pvt. Lyons Wakeman, 153rd Regiment, New York State Volunteers, 1862–1864* (New York: Oxford Univ. Press, 1994).

14. Faust, "Altars of Sacrifice: Confederate Women and the Narratives of War," *Journal of American History* 76 (March 1990): 1200–1228; idem, *Mothers of Inven-*

tion, 80–113; Manisha Sinha, "Louisa Susanna McCord: Spokeswoman of the Master Class in Antebellum South Carolina," in Susan Ostrov Weisser and Jennifer Fleischner, eds., *Feminist Nightmares: Women at Odds, Feminism and the Problem of Sisterhood* (New York: New York Univ. Press, 1994), 62–63; Nancy F. Cott, *The Bonds of Womanhood: "Woman's Sphere" in New England, 1780–1835* (New Haven: Yale Univ. Press, 1977), 61–62; Welter, "The Cult of True Womanhood, 1820–1860," *American Quarterly* 18 (summer 1966): 152. For some of the best early scholarship on women and the war, see Francis Butler Simkins and James Welch Patton, *Women of the Confederacy* (Richmond: Garrett and Massie, 1936); Mary Elizabeth Massey, *Bonnet Brigades* (New York: Alfred A. Knopf, 1966); Anne Firor Scott, *The Southern Lady: From Pedestal to Politics, 1830–1930* (Chicago: Univ. of Chicago Press, 1970); and Bell Irvin Wiley, *Confederate Women* (Westport: Greenwood Press, 1975). For a contextual analysis of this work, see Jean V. Berlin, "Introduction to the Bison Book Edition," Mary Elizabeth Massey, *Women in the Civil War* (Lincoln: Univ. of Nebraska Press, 1994), vii–xvi.

15. Whites, *The Civil War as a Crisis in Gender*, 4. Despite the current trend of women's historians to emphasize gender-based discontent, two recent works—Daniel E. Sutherland, ed., *A Very Violent Rebel: The Civil War Diary of Ellen Renshaw House* (Knoxville: Univ. of Tennessee Press, 1996), and Gary Gallagher, *The Confederate War* (Cambridge: Harvard Univ. Press, 1997)—remind us that a significant portion of the southern populace, women included, remained faithful to the Confederacy until 1865.

16. Leonard, *Yankee Women*, xv, 198. For similar themes, see Nancy Huston, "Tales of War and Tears of Women," *Women's Studies International Forum* 5 (summer 1982): 271–82; Nancy Grey Osterud, "Rural Women During the Civil War: New York's Nanticoke Valley, 1861–1865," *New York History* 72 (October 1990): 357–85; Jane E. Schultz, "The Inhospitable Hospital: Gender and Professionalism in Civil War Medicine," *Signs* 17 (winter 1992): 363–92; Rachel Filene Seidman, "Beyond Sacrifice: War and Politics on the Pennsylvania Homefront During the Civil War" (Ph.D. diss., Yale University, 1996). For the merger of gender and nationalism in the Civil War North, see Jeanie Attie, "Warwork and the Crisis of Domesticity in the North," in Clinton and Silber, eds., *Divided Houses*, 247–59.

17. G. Glenn Clift, ed., *The Private War of Lizzie Hardin: A Kentucky Confederate Girl's Diary of the Civil War in Kentucky, Virginia, Tennessee, Alabama, and Georgia* (Frankfort: Kentucky Historical Society, 1963), 59, 66, 67, 59.

18. Cashin, ed., *Our Common Affairs: Texts from Women in the Old South* (Baltimore: Johns Hopkins Univ. Press, 1996), 18–19.

19. Faust, *Mothers of Invention*, 24.

NOTE ON THE TEXT

The Peter diary, located in Box 7 of the Evans Papers, Division of Special Collections and Archives, Margaret I. King Library, University of Kentucky, covers the period, January 19, 1862–April 4, 1864. The original diary was written in eight small booklets made of scrap paper—mainly hospital supply sheets—stitched together with thread. Entries selected for inclusion in this volume represent, in the opinion of the editors, the most significant portions of the total diary. Lengthy accounts of military activities and battles, which the diarist generally copied verbatim from newspapers, have been omitted. Mundane matters have been included when those activities either had some bearing on the war or revealed attitudes of Lexington residents toward that conflict.

The editors have made every effort to transcribe Miss Peter's diary faithfully. Unlike many nineteenth-century diarists, she was quite literate. Her spelling and grammar generally conform to modern practice and are intelligible. As a result the editors largely have retained her wording, spelling, and punctuation. To assist the reader, however, in some cases they have made minor emendations to the text. Specifically, throughout the diary they have capitalized first letters of sentences and occasionally added letters, words, and punctuation in square brackets to correct spelling or to make passages more intelligible. Especially long entries have been divided into paragraphs. No other changes have been made; even Miss Peter's tendency to omit punctuation in titles and throughout sentences has been retained to preserve the original flavor and intent of her diary.

The Diary
of
Frances Peter

The Diary
of
Frances Peter

SUNDAY JAN. 19TH 1862

. . . We heard this morning of the arrest of a secessionist. He had been
taken up before the house of Mr. Viley of this city for carrying the
Southern mail but had made his escape. Last night an officer of Mundy's
regiment[1] with a squad of not more than six men went to the house of
Mrs. Morgan[2] a secessionist and informed her that the man was in her
house and must be given up immediately. Mrs. Morgan came out with her
daughter & protested that she knew nothing about the man that he was
not in her house. The officer persisted, his orders were peremptory & if
she did not give him up he would have to search the premises, but said he
should be sorry to be driven to that measure.

A good many of the neighbors had assembled (mostly southern
sympathizers) and Mr. Cally Morgan also came out, and said he would
give his word of honor. The officer intimated that the last was not to be
relied on, but the neighbors said he ought to believe Mrs. Morgan as she
was a lady and her word might be relied on. The officer again protested he
could take no ones word, that his information was certain, dispatched a
man for reinforcement in order to search the house & stationed his men so
as to guard the premises as well as possible. Not having quite enough men
he called a negro who was standing by and placed him to watch one part
and told him to be sure and shout if he saw any one attempt to escape
from the house.

It was not long before the negro was heard shouting "Here him be
massa here him be." The man had jumped out into the negro's very arms
not having seen him perhaps and was secured, the black holding him tight
in his embrace until he was secured & taken out to camp. . . . Mrs. Morgan
said the man had come there for protection and she did not think it would

be kind to betray him. This lady is the mother of the notorious rebel Capt John Morgan. . . .

1. Colonel Marcellus Mundy recruited and organized the 23rd Kentucky Infantry Regiment at Camp King, near Covington, in late 1861. See Thomas Speed, *The Union Regiments of Kentucky* (Louisville: Courier-Journal Job Printing, 1877), 513–17.
2. Mrs. Henrietta Morgan (1805–1891) resided at the corner of Second and Mill Streets. The daughter of John Wesley Hunt, a wealthy Lexington merchant, she was married to Calvin C. Morgan of Huntsville, Alabama, in 1823. Mrs. Morgan was the mother of six sons and two daughters. All her sons and both sons-in-law (Generals A.P. Hill and Basil W. Duke) served in the Confederate army. John Hunt Morgan (the eldest son), Thomas H., and Hill were killed during the Civil War. Calvin C., Richard C., Charlton H., and Frank Key, along with Duke, were all wounded. Basil Duke, *History of Morgan's Cavalry* (Cincinnati: Miami Printing and Publishing, 1867), 18. The *Louisville Courier-Journal*, September 9, 1891, contains an obituary of Mrs. Morgan.

TUESDAY JAN 21ST 1862

. . . Another arrest was made today by Mundy's men. Dr. Steele[1] and Will Dudley Jr. were arrested at the house of the secessionist Dr. Desha. Dr. Steele has been acting as surgeon to the rebels at Bowling Green,[2] and was taken up as a spy. He said he only came to see his wife and child whom he left here but who are now at Danville,[3] but he of course had a better reason than that for making such a journey. The guard at the door was standing with his musket pointing in the passage while the rest went in to take the prisoners when he heard the window above him violently thrown up. Thinking some one was going to fire on him he raised his musket & looking up saw Mrs. Desha who poured forth a volley of abuse in the most refined & chivalric terms . . . no resistance was offered & the men were marched off & Dr. Steele sent to Camp Chase[4] Ohio for his health. Col. Mundy is a sharp fellow and just the man that was wanting here for he does not stand upon ceremony with traitors.

1. Major Theophilus Steele, M.D., of Woodford County, Kentucky, entered Confederate service as a surgeon in Colonel Roger Hanson's 2nd Kentucky Regiment. He later served in Gano's Regiment of Morgan's Cavalry. Although a doctor, Steele apparently preferred inflicting wounds to healing them. See William E. Mickle, *Well Known Confederate Veterans and Their War Records* (New Orleans: W.E. Mickle, 1907), 74, and Duke, *History of Morgan's Cavalry*, 228.
2. Bowling Green, in south central Kentucky, marked the center of the Confederate defenses that stretched the length of the Kentucky-Tennessee border in the winter and spring of 1861–1862. See Thomas Lawrence Connelly, *Army of the Heartland: The Army of Tennessee, 1861–1862* (Baton Rouge: Louisiana State Univ. Press, 1967), 65–77.

3. Danville, the Boyle County seat, is southwest of Lexington. See John E. Kleber, ed., *The Kentucky Encyclopedia* (Lexington: Univ. Press of Kentucky, 1992), 252.
4. First used as a training camp, this place (located west of Columbus, Ohio) was later more important as a Federal prison camp. In 1863 about 8,000 Confederate prisoners were confined there. See Mark Boatner, *The Civil War Dictionary* (New York: David McKay Company, 1969), 117.

WEDNESDAY JAN 22ND 1862

. . . Col. Mundys cavalry leaves here today for London.[1] There are five companies, & in leaving the city they passed through Main Street. As each company passed the Wheeler & Wilson[2] machine shop where the ladies of the Aid Society were sitting sewing they hurrad for them. One old fellow was very drunk & shouted & pulled out his pistol flourishing it about in a dangerous manner. The man next to him got the weapon from him but he still continued to behave in an uproarious manner. The commanding officer Col. Mundy rode up to him on hearing the noise he made, took him by the collar & belabored him well. They are a rough looking set, & ride very mean horses but I suppose they will fight well enough. Lieut. Green Clay one of Shoepff's[3] Aide de camps passed through here this evening on his way to Gen. Buell[4] & brought with him a company flag taken from Zollicoffers Army. The secessionists will not believe a word of the late battle, but put it off by saying that Zollicoffer has whipped Thomas.[5]

1. London, the seat of Laurel County, is south of Lexington. See Kleber, ed., *The Kentucky Encyclopedia*, 570.
2. The Wheeler & Wilson sewing machine shop was located at Number 5, Higgins' Block. See *Williams' Lexington City Directory for 1864–1865* (Lexington: Williams and Company, 1864), 91 (hereafter cited *Williams' Lexington City Directory*).
3. Albin Francisco Schoepf, a Polish born refugee of the Hungarian Revolution, received a commission as Brigadier General in the United States Army in September 1861. His brigade was engaged at the battle of Mill Springs, Kentucky. After Perryville, Schoepf commanded the prisoner of war camp, Fort Delaware. See Ezra Warner, *Generals in Blue* (Baton Rouge: Louisiana State Univ. Press, 1964), 424–25.
4. General Don Carlos Buell (1818–1898) was a native of Ohio, an 1841 graduate of West Point, and a Mexican War hero. In November 1861, he assumed command of the Department of the Ohio; in January 1862, he advanced upon Nashville, Tennessee. See Patricia L. Faust, ed., *Historical Times Illustrated Encyclopedia of the Civil War* (New York: Harper Perennial, 1991), 88.
5. Tennessean Felix Zollicoffer commanded Confederates at the battle of Mill Springs, January 19, 1862. In the clash with General George H. Thomas's Federal troops, Zollicoffer mistakenly rode into the Federal line and was fatally shot by Colonel Speed Fry of the 4th Kentucky Infantry (U.S.). The defeat marked the collapse of a Confederate presence in eastern Kentucky. See Connelly, *Army of the Heartland*, 86–99, and Faust, ed., *Historical Times Illustrated Encyclopedia of the Civil War*, 495.

THURSDAY JAN 23RD 1862

Our victory is more complete than was thought. Thomas is still in pursuit. The rebels had very fine entrenchments with huts & every thing suitable for winter quarters but were so confused they did not think of falling back to them. Zollicoffer evidently supposed that Thomas had fewer men than was the case and as the river was flooded by the late rains so as to cut off his retreat thought he would fall an easy prey. . . .
Zollicoffer met his death in this manner, he rode up to Col. S.S. Fry[1] of the 4th Kentucky[2] and said "you had better not shoot your own men" (trying to play the old secesh dodge of making our men believe they were friends) Col Fry replied he was not doing so, Fry's horse was shot under him, he fired mortally wounding Zollicoffer who now lies in a tent under a flag of truce to see if the rebels will claim his body. But I don't think they will, it is more likely they will put another in his place & call him Zollicoffer to prevent the secesh from knowing the truth. . . .
We heard this morning that Mr. Cally Morgan was taken up in Louisville. He left Lex in a hurry after that man was arrested at his mother's & went to Louisville very likely in order to carry the southern mail, in place of the man who was taken up.

1. Speed Smith Fry (1817–1892) was born in Boyle County, Kentucky, and attended Centre College and Wabash College. Fry commanded a division of General William S. Rosecrans' army at the battle of Murfreesboro in January 1863. For much of the remainder of the war he was in charge of training black recruits at Camp Nelson, Kentucky. See Victor B. Howard, *Black Liberation in Kentucky: Emancipation and Freedom, 1862–1884* (Lexington: Univ. Press of Kentucky, 1983), 113, 115.
2. President Abraham Lincoln authorized the enlistment of three regiments for the Union cause while Kentucky attempted to remain neutral. William Nelson, a Kentucky native and former captain in the United States Navy, raised the three regiments, including the 4th Kentucky. See Speed, *The Union Regiments of Kentucky*, 302.

FRIDAY JAN 24TH 1862

. . . the secesh persist in saying there is no battle & Mr. Frank Waters[1] declares that he has been down to the battlefield & that no battle has been fought & Zollicoffer is not dead.

1. An attorney, Frank Waters was a Lexington native and an 1837 graduate of Transylvania University. See William H. Perrin, *History of Fayette County, Kentucky* (Chicago: O.L. Baskin, 1882), 745.

SATURDAY JAN 25TH 1862

Zollicoffers body has been embalmed and is to be taken to Nashville by way of Louisville of course it will pass through here. The secesh always boasted that Zollicoffer would come here and he will, but not by any means in the way they expected.

SUNDAY JAN 26 1862

Two of the soldiers from De Courcy's hospital spent the day here, & in the evening Mrs. Breshears (wife of the surgeon of the 16th Ohio who is now at Somerset with his regiment) came to get Lettie[1] to go to some of the hospitals with her. She is a strapping woman & has a commission as nurse in the regiment and has followed it during the time they were in Virginia. When the Col left here he gave her full power over the men he left sick and authority to punish those who were unruly. Lately she had a man put in jail for getting drunk.

1. Letitia, oldest of the Peter children, was born on July 21, 1836. The diarist's other brothers and sisters and their years of birth were: William (1838), Benjamin (1840), Johanna (1845), Robert (1847), Sarah (1849), Arthur (1852), Hugh (1854), Alfred (1857), and Alice (1859). See Evans Papers.

FRIDAY JANUARY 31ST 1862

Tonight the ladies and gentlemen of this city gave an amateur concert, the third one they have given this winter for the benefit of the Soldiers Aid Society.[1] Mr. Chas. Shultze[2] is manager, and the performance was assisted by Mundy's band. Several patriotic songs were sung by the company & Lieut. Jacob Kessler[3] of the 23rd Ky regiment (Col Mundy) sang. He has a fine tenor voice & sings very well. It reminds one of the days when the British army was quartered at New York & Philadelphia when the soldiers had amateur concerts & theatres. There will be another concert in about a week & we are going to have some of Cobans[4] men to sing. The Col Mark Mundy & his wife were present & a great many soldiers. The Col is handsome but looks rather pale & careworn.

1. Organized by Union sympathizers in October 1861, this society provided assistance for sick and wounded Federal soldiers. See Perrin, *History of Fayette County, Kentucky*, 454.
2. A native of Germany, Schultze came to Lexington in 1860. After giving private music lessons for two years, he became an instructor of music at the Sayre Female Academy and later taught at the Baptist Female Seminary and the Kentucky Agricultural and Mechanical College. See Perrin, *History of Fayette County, Kentucky*, 713–14.
3. Miss Peter may be referring to Jacob Keesler of the 23rd Kentucky band. See Speed, *The Union Regiments of Kentucky*, 517.
4. Probably Colonel John Coburn, who commanded the 33rd Indiana Infantry stationed in Lexington at this time. See Boatner, *The Civil War Dictionary*, 161.

[THURSDAY] FEBRUARY 6TH 1862

Report says that a skirmish took place between Capt John Morgan & our troops between Lebanon & Green River the other day & Morgan & 40 of his men taken prisoners.[1] About 25 army wagons leave here daily. Zollicoffers body did not pass through here but was sent to Nashville from Munfordville.

1. Captain John Hunt Morgan, accompanied by nine of his troopers, raided and scouted around Greensburg and Lebanon, Kentucky, between January 28 and February 1, 1862. Morgan captured Federal soldiers and horses. Portions of the 1st Ohio Cavalry pursued, but never made contact with the raider. See U.S. Congress, *The War of the Rebellion: A Compilation of the Official Records of the Union and Confederate Armies* (Washington, D.C.: Government Printing Office, 1880–1901), ser. 1, vol. 7, 116–118 (hereafter cited *OR*).

[SATURDAY] FEBRUARY 8TH 1862

. . . Gen Schoeff has been here for a day or two. The report of the capture of Morgan is unfounded.

[TUESDAY] FEBRUARY 18TH [1862]

. . . A salute of 40 guns was fired this evening on the receipt of the additional news that Nashville is taken.[1]

1. The celebration was probably held to commemorate the capture of the Confederates' Fort Donelson on Feburary 16, 1862, leaving the road to Nashville open. Pressure by Federal armies under Ulysses S. Grant and Buell caused Confederate General Albert Sidney Johnston to evacuate the politically and industrially important city on February 23. See James M. McPherson, *Battle Cry of Freedom: The Civil War Era* (New York: Oxford Univ. Press, 1988), 401–3.

WENSDAY FEBUARY 19TH 1862

Last evening a short time after the salute was fired a large crowd was seen to assemble at Mrs Morgan's . . . & several soldiers were seen to search the house. We learnt to day that the occasion was this. While the guns were firing Frank Key or as he is called Key Morgan[1] with two or three other boys went to the janitor of the college [Transylvania] and got the key to the door leading on the roof on pretext that a ball had been thrown up there, & hoisted a secession flag on the college. The janitor saw it and cut it down & by order of the teacher Mr. Patterson[2] put it in a cellar till it could be delivered to the authorities, but a Mrs John Dudley[3] who lives near the college told Morgan who got the flag & took it home & having secreted it made the best of his way off. Some soldiers however had seen the flag on the college and came to inquire the cause of its being there, which having learnt they searched Mrs Morgans house found the flag which they tore up and divided among themselves. They got the names of the boys concerned & will probably arrest them. Mr. Patterson this morning suspended them until a faculty meeting could be held when they (the boys) will probably be expelled.

1. The youngest Morgan son, Frank Key, enlisted in the Confederate army on September 10, 1862, at the age of fifteen. See *Report of the Adjutant General of the State of Kentucky Confederate Kentucky Volunteers*, 2 vols. (Frankfort: The State Journal Company, [1951]), 1:582.
2. James Kennedy Patterson (1833–1922) was born in Glasgow, Scotland, but immigrated to America at the age of ten. In 1861 he came to Lexington as principal of Transylvania High School and, when it was merged into Kentucky University in 1865, became professor of Latin and literature. Patterson was named president of the Kentucky Agricultural and Mechanical College in 1869, was re-elected to that position when the school became an independent state institution in 1880, and served until his retirement in 1910. See Perrin, *History of Fayette County, Kentucky*, 684–85, and James F. Hopkins, *The University of Kentucky: Origins and Early Years* (Lexington: Univ. of Kentucky Press, 1951), 123, 268.
3. Wife of a prominent grocer in Lexington. See George W. Ranck, *History of Lexington, Kentucky: Its Early Annals and Recent Progress* (Cincinnati: Robert Clarke and Co., 1872), 397.

FRIDAY FEB. 21ST 1862

Last night the bells were tolled for the death of Dr. Ethelbert L. Dudley,[1] Col of the 21st reg. K.V. who died at Columbia, Adair Co. of typhoid fever.

1. A Lexington native, Dr. Ethelbert Dudley was educated at Harvard and Transylvania University before becoming a member of Transylvania's medical school faculty. He died of typhoid fever, February 20, 1862, while commanding his regiment. See Perrin, *History of Fayette County, Kentucky*, 450–51.

SATURDAY FEB. 22ND [1862]

Washington's birthday has dawned dark & cloudy as if the elements sympathized with the loss that Dr. Dudley's death will be to Lexington. His body is expected here Monday. Coburn's regiment has received marching orders.

TUESDAY FEB. 25TH [1862]

Col. E. Dudley's body arrived here Sunday and was attended from the cars to the Oddfellows Hall[1] by the Mayor, Councilmen and crowd of citizens. The funeral oration was pronounced by Mr. Brank[2] today at the Oddfellows Hall where the body lay in state. The 33rd Indiana,[3] Col

Coburn, the Lex Blues, Cap Wilgris,[4] Odd fellows & masons, with some of the old Infantry Chasseurs,[5] formed part of the procession with some of Dr. Dudleys men who came with him & a great many carriages. It was the largest funeral ever seen here (except Henry Clay's)

1. The Oddfellows Hall was located on the southeast corner of Broadway and Main. See *Williams' Lexington City Directory*, 19.
2. Reverend Robert G. Brank, a Kentucky native and graduate of Centre College, was pastor of the Second Presbyterian Church. Following the war, Brank represented the Southern Assembly faction in a church dispute and then resigned in 1869. See Ranck, *History of Lexington, Kentucky*, 284.
3. The 33rd Indiana Infantry was raised in Indianapolis in September 1861, and served at the battles of Wild Cat and Mill Springs. The regiment was in Lexington as part of the 1st Brigade, 1st Division, Army of Ohio. See Frederick H. Dyer, *A Compendium of the War of the Rebellion, Compiled and Arranged from Official Records of the Federal and Confederate Armies, Reports of the Adjutant Generals of the Several States* (Des Moines, Iowa: Dyer Publishing Company, 1908), 3:1132.
4. John B. Wilgus, captain of the Lexington Blues and prominent grocer and merchant, reportedly freed his slaves two months after Fort Sumter as an expression of support for the Union cause. See Perrin, *History of Fayette County, Kentucky*, 734–36.
5. Here Miss Peter confuses the names of two organizations. The Old Infantry was a Lexington militia company that dated to the eighteenth century, and the Lexington Chasseurs, a militia company raised in Lexington in May 1860, had a reputation for ornate uniforms and proficiency in drill. At the outbreak of war the company split and its members fought for both the Union and the Confederacy. Both companies were noted for stylish dress, drill, and for the social standing of their members. See Perrin, *History of Fayette County, Kentucky*, 442–44, 448–49, and Ranck, *History of Lexington, Kentucky*, 383–385.

WENSDAY FEB 26TH [1862]

We have certain intelligence that Nashville is ours. The rebels left with out resistance but burnt the state library. The Louisville Journal of today was suppressed & there is some talk of suppressing all the papers but I don't think they will do it. Col. S.S. Fry, the Mill Spring hero was in town today. He visited the sewing society & talked with the ladies. He said he intended to make it his business to come back here when the war was over & let the ladies ask him as many questions as they pleased. The report that Coburn's regiment had received marching orders is unfounded. The wound Col. Fry gave Zollicoffer was not it seems the one that killed him for on examination [it was found] that a minie ball had passed through the heart, whereas Fry's ball went through the head, consequently the real honor belongs to a private soldier.

THURSDAY MARCH 20 [1862]

. . . The secesh are getting pretty high here. The other day when some rebel prisoners passed through here, a great crowd of them went down to the cars & hurrad for Jeff Davis and made a great fuss over the scamps. It is said they expected them for some days & had even got a dinner ready for them. . . . The secesh ladies have also had a sewing society and have been supplying the rebel prisoners Gen Halleck[1] sent an order here that hurraing for Jeff. was not to be allowed.

1. Henry Wager Halleck (1815–1872), a native of New York, was named commander of Union armies in the West in March 1862. Failing to defeat the Confederates decisively at Corinth, Mississippi, in April 1862, Halleck was placed in an administrative position as general-in-chief of all Union armies. In March 1864, when Grant assumed chief command, Halleck was demoted to chief of staff. See T. Harry Williams, *Lincoln and His Generals* (New York: Alfred A. Knopf, 1952), 300–301, and Stephen E. Ambrose, *Halleck: Lincoln's Chief of Staff* (Baton Rouge: Louisiana State Univ. Press, 1962).

FRIDAY MARCH 21ST [1862]

Today the much talked of funeral of the rebel Lieut Edward Keen[1] was to take place. The secesh have said they were going to make a great display and even threatened to have military (although where they would get the last article is more than I can say unless they thought the rebels would take Cincinnati as they have been lately excusing themselves for their defeats by saying that their retreating is only a part of their strategy to get into the northern states) but the young mans family said it should be a private funeral. Before the funeral was ready to start about 300 or 400 men under command of Major Manguer? Manquer? were sent in by Col. Coburn. The procession came down Broadway & by the Medical Hall was met by a squad of soldiers who allowed the hearse & 20 carriages to pass & cut off the remainder (there were about 33). Such a scattering as there was then! The carriages & the followers on foot who had been cut off hastened away in all directions and endeavored to reach the cemetary by other routes but every where they were met by armed soldiers who guarded every approach till the major and three companies of men had conducted the remainder of the funeral to the cemetery. It is said that none of the carriages were permitted to enter the cemetary but I cannot be sure. The major said there was only one thing he regretted not to have done & that was to have cut off Mrs. Morgan's carriage for all the way to the cemetery Mrs. Basil Duke[2] hissed at him or his men. It seems the soldiers thought they would have a secesh flag for Mr. J. Elliot[3] had been heard to say they would have one at the cemetary. They did not however. It is against the law now for secesh to have more than 20 carriages at funerals. A good

many union people friends of the family were at the funeral. I don't think
they ought to have let them bring Ed Keen here anyhow. He had one
funeral & been buried with military honors down in "Dixie" & I think
they might have let him stay there instead of putting him near Henry Clay
& other good union men. The incident I have related goes generally by the
euphorious name of "Skeedadle". . . .

1. A former member of the Lexington Chasseurs, Edward Keen was mortally wounded
at Ft. Donelson while serving with the 2nd Kentucky Cavalry (C.S.). See Perrin,
History of Fayette County, Kentucky, 450.
2. Henrietta, John Hunt Morgan's sister, was the wife of Basil Duke, a trusted Morgan subordinate. See Duke, *History of Morgan's Cavalry*, 579.
3. This may be J.M. Elliot, a Lexington dry goods merchant who had a store on the
south side of Main Street opposite the courthouse. See *Williams' Lexington City Directory*, 47, and Eighth Census of the United States for Fayette County, 1860, Schedule 1, 518.

SATURDAY MAR 22 [1862]

A notorious fellow named Columbus Gilreath one of Morgan's[1]
cavalry was taken up here today.

1. Born in Huntsville, Alabama, in 1825, John Hunt Morgan was educated at
Transylvania University. After serving in the Mexican War, Morgan operated the
general merchandising business of his grandfather, John Wesley Hunt, in Lexington.
In 1857 he organized the Lexington Rifles, most of whom joined the forces of General Simon B. Buckner at the outbreak of the war. Morgan's series of raids into Tennessee, Kentucky, Indiana, and Ohio made him a legendary figure in the
commonwealth and the Confederacy. Captured in Ohio in 1863, Morgan escaped
and later commanded the Department of Southwestern Virginia. He was killed by
Union cavalry in September 1864, at Greenville, Tennessee. See James A. Ramage,
Rebel Raider: The Life of General John Hunt Morgan (Lexington: Univ. Press of Kentucky, 1986).

MONDAY MAR. 24 [1862]

Old Mr John Gilbert was taken up in Scott county so we heard today
for carring the southern mail A good many letters were found on him. The
Gilberts have always borne the name of underhand people Report accused
them of hiring negroes to work all night, & trading with the negros for
stolen things Some even went so far as to say that Mr Gilbert used to stop
the wagons of hemp that passed his house and forcing the drivers to give
him some. The credit of his arrest is said to belong to Adjutant Durham of
the 33rd Indiana. . . .

John Morgan & wife

Brigadier General John Hunt Morgan and his second wife, Mattie Ready, shortly after their marriage in December 1862. (Audio-Visual Archives, Special Collections and Archives, University of Kentucky Libraries)

MONDAY MAR 31ST [1862]

Today a flag was presented to the 33rd Indiana. The presentation took place in the College lawn. Mr. Carmichael Wickliffe addressed the soldiers from the College steps & was replied to by Col. Coburn. The whole regiment was not present as 2 or 3 companies were left behind on guard. They passed by our house both going & coming down & wore the uniforms they had worn at Wild Cat.[1] The flag was of dark blue silk with gold fringe & eagle on it with the words "Wild Cat" in a cloud in reference to the battle of Wild Cat in which the regiment took so large a part. When the people were coming down we saw Mr. John Dudley coming down with a stranger. Pa said "that is one of the rebel officers who are on parole here." He was dressed in a suit of what is called "rebel gray" with no shoulder straps on his coat or stripes of any kind on his breeches or badge on his cap. But the last was embroidered somewhat like a smoking cap with narrow gold braid in a fancy pattern. As he passed ma who had been talking to Pa remarked I shall always say "down with secession." How he did stare!

1. In a prelude to the battle of Mill Springs, General Albin Schoepf's Federal troops clashed with General Felix Zollicoffer's Confederates at Camp Wild Cat in southeast Kentucky. See Kleber, ed., *The Kentucky Encyclopedia*, 952.

THURSDAY APRIL 10TH [1862]

. . . A terrible battle has been fought at Pittsburg Tenn. We do not know as yet the loss on both sides; Our troops had the worst the first day & Gen. Prentiss & a number of men prisoners. But we beat in the end. The rebel Gen. A. Sidney Johnston killed. Dr's James & Dudley Bush went down this evening to help attend the wounded.

. . . The Amateur Society will give another concert shortly for the purpose of raising funds to assist the hospitals. A meeting of citizens will be held tomorrow for the same purpose.

FRIDAY APRIL 11TH [1862]

. . . There are 300 sick at hospital here.

MONDAY APRIL 14TH [1862]

. . . 300 more soldiers expected at the hospital from Cumberland Ford.

WENSDAY APRIL 16TH [1862]

They have taken the house near the college that was used for a hospital by De Courcy for a hospital for some of the soldiers here & Mr. John Dudley who occupied one half of the place received orders to move & left this morning, a good riddance. The 42 Ohio Col Shelton & the 18th Ky.[1] Col Warner are here at the fairground.[2] It was discovered the other day that one of Lindsay's[3] [22nd Ky.] men who was left at the hospital had the smallpox & there has been no end to the trouble that was had getting a place to put him.

1. The 42nd Ohio served in western (West) Virginia and eastern Kentucky. The 18th Kentucky, commanded by Colonel William A. Warner and headquartered at Lexington, guarded the Lexington and Covington Railroad. See Dyer, *A Compendium of the War of the Rebellion*, 3:1516; Speed, *The Union Regiments of Kentucky*, 463; and Thomas Speed, *The Union Cause in Kentucky, 1860–1865* (New York: G.P. Putnam's Sons, 1907), 463–64.
2. The Lexington Fairground was first occupied as a campground for soldiers in September 1861, and remained a favorite spot for troops garrisoned in Lexington. See Perrin, *History of Fayette County, Kentucky*, 453–55.
3. Miss Peter referred to Daniel W. Lindsay, colonel of the 22nd Kentucky Infantry (U.S.). See Speed, *The Union Cause*, 146.

FRIDAY APRIL 18TH [1862]

Doctor Bush[1] has returned from Pittsburg Landing[2] bringing a great many memorials of the battle in the shape of shells, Minnie balls, etc. Tom Monroe[3] the late editor of the Kentucky Statesman[4] is undoubtedly dead for Tom Bush[5] who is on Gen Buell's staff buried him. Jno. Hogan[6] the other editor of the [Lex.] Observer & Reporter[7] is also said to be dead.

1. Doctor James Bush, a Kentucky native, was professor of Surgery and Anatomy at Transylvania University. See Perrin, *History of Fayette County, Kentucky*, 305.
2. The battle of Shiloh, or Pittsburg Landing, took place April 6–7, 1862, in southwest Tennessee. See Faust, ed., *Historical Times Encyclopedia of the Civil War*, 684, and Larry J. Daniel, *Shiloh: The Battle That Changed the Civil War* (New York: Simon and Schuster, 1997).
3. Thomas B. Monroe Jr., former editor of the *Kentucky Statesman*, served as Governor Beriah Magoffin's secretary of state before his death at Shiloh while serving as major of the 4th Kentucky Infantry. See Perrin, *History of Fayette County, Kentucky*, 372.
4. The *Kentucky Statesman*, a Democratic, pro-Confederate newspaper, suspended publication in September 1861. It published briefly in September and October 1862 during the Confederate occupation of Lexington. See Perrin, *History of Fayette County, Kentucky*, 372.
5. Corporal Thomas J. Bush, a former member of the Lexington Chasseurs, was an aide-de-camp to General Buell. See Perrin, *History of Fayette County, Kentucky*, 449.

6. John T. Hogan edited the *Lexington Observer and Reporter* from 1855 to 1859. See Ranck, *History of Lexington*, 237.
7. The *Lexington Observer and Reporter*, edited and published semi-weekly by D.C. Wickliffe, was one of the most influential newspapers in the state.

MONDAY APRIL 28TH [1862]

One of Warner's men named Watson was shot the other night while passing from Broadway to camp, supposed by a secesh. The man was drunk at the time. He is from Grant Co., Ky. & leaves a wife & six children. Pa has got a place as assistant surgeon at one of the hospitals.

THURSDAY MAY 1ST [1862]

Mr. Parker Craig[1] was arrested today for harboring a southern emissary named Clarke, who had letters & papers concealed about him.

1. Parker Craig ran a livery stable on the north side of Short Street between Mulberry and Upper. See *Williams' Lexington Directory, City Guide, and Business Mirror, 1859–1860* (Lexington: Hitchcock and Searles, 1859), 49 (hereafter cited *Williams' Lexington City Guide*).

SUNDAY MAY 4 [1862]

About 150 sick soldiers have been sent here lately from Cumberland Ford. A battle is expected there and the hospitals in the neighborhood are sending back such of the sick as can be moved to make room for the wounded. Some of the young secesh here attempted to join the rebel forces. Several arrests have been made among those concerned. . . .

THURSDAY MAY 8TH [1862]

Yesterday the ladies gave the soldiers at the Short Street hospital a dinner. Capt Lanphiger's[1] Michigan battery is here. They have some pretty large guns with them. Two of them looked like Parrotts.[2] They are going to Cumberland Ford.

1. Miss Peter probably meant Captain Charles H. Lanphere's Battery G, 1st Michigan Light Artillery, which served in Kentucky during this time. See John Robertson, comp., *Michigan in the War* (Lansing: W.S. George & Company, 1882), 532–34.
2. Named for its inventor, Robert Parker Parrott, this type of cannon was recognizable by the iron reinforcing band around the gun's breech. See Faust, ed., *Historical Times Illustrated Encyclopedia of the Civil War*, 558.

FRIDAY MAY 9TH [1862]

Tonight the Amateur Musical Association gave their 5th concert for the benefit of the Aid Society. Some very pretty tableaux were exhibited in

addition to the usual performance & everything went off very well u..
the performance was over, when several members of the battery appeared
upon the stage headed by an officer from one of the regiments here, who
introduced them by name to the audience & announced that they had
been requested to sing their new Dixie. He then stepped aside & the men
commenced. They had hardly finished the first verse when Mr. George
Didlake[1] came out & stopped them. They were evidently offended by what
he said for the officer said that Capt. Lanphiger had at the request of
several citizens allowed these men to stay in town for the express purpose
of singing at this concert, but that they did not wish to intrude. The house
was immediately in an uproar. Cries of Battery! battery! sing! go on! were
heard from every side. Many got upon the seats & waved their hats &
hankerchiefs & the crowd barred every avenue of escape. The excitement
was extreme. At last the men were compelled to sing. The audience were
delighted & showed their appreciation of the Dixie by uproarious applause
& furious waving of scarfs & hankerchiefs. Bouquets were also thrown to
them & every one seemed to think they could not do enough to make up
for the insult that had been put upon them. It was indeed scandalous to
drive strangers off the stage that way after they had been asked to sing &
when every one wished to hear them except the offending parties.

1. George Didlake, a Lexington attorney, boarded at the Broadway Hotel. See *Williams' Lexington City Guide*, 53.

SATURDAY MAY 10TH [1862]

It seems that Mrs. Monmollin[1] was the one that made George
Didlake tell the soldiers to stop singing, because forsooth she did not wish
to offend some few secesh who had been induced to come, though she is
herself a union lady. Today she & Mr. Didlake were forced to apologize &
when they found how indignant everyone was at their behavior they rode
about town together nearly the whole day trying to make it up & were in
the greatest anxiety lest the battery should refuse to come tonight to the
concert. They came however & were greeted with shouts of applause &
received a quantity of bouquets. . . .

1. Mrs. Montmollin was an officer in the Soldiers Aid Society. See Perrin, *History of Fayette County, Kentucky*, 455.

TUESDAY MAY 13TH [1862]

. . . The college has been taken for a hospital & Pa has moved his men from the Short street hospital up there. Mr. Patterson has been allowed the use of the Medical Hall[1] for his school. . . .

1.This building, located on the northwest corner of Second and Broadway, once housed the medical department of Transylvania University, but had been abandoned for several years. In late 1861, when Union authorities seized Morrison College and dormitories for use as military prisons and hospitals, the Medical Hall reopened to house Transylvania's literary and classical departments. In May 1863 it was taken by Federal authorities for use as a general hospital, but was destroyed by fire on May 22, 1863. See J. Winston Coleman Jr., *Lexington During the Civil War* (Lexington: Commerical Printing Company, 1938), 23, 39, 41.

JUNE 5TH 1862

. . . The ladies gave a strawberry party to Warners' men today at their camp.

JUNE 21ST [1862]

A body of soldiers left here today for Owen Co. to put down some outbreak of the secesh.[1]

1. On June 20, 1862, between thirty and forty Confederate sympathizers attacked a party of Kentucky Home Guard near Lusby's Mill. Federal forces retaliated by arresting some three to four hundered Owen County "secessionists." See *OR*, ser. 1, vol. 16, pt. 1, 726–28.

MONDAY JUNE 23RD [1862]

Sent for more men to go to Sweet Owen. Tonight some 13 prisoners arrived.

TUESDAY JULY 1 [1862]

Orders received at the hospital here from Gen. Morgan for all the men to come to Cumberland Gap.[1] About 120 volunteered from hospital no. 2.[2]

1. General George Washington Morgan commanded Federal forces in the vicinity of Cumberland Gap. Morgan was preparing the Gap for an expected assault by ten to twelve thousand Confederates. See Warner, *Generals in Blue*, 334; and *OR*, ser. 1, vol. 16, pt. 1, 58–59.
2. Located in Morrison College, Transylvania University.

THURSDAY JULY 3D [1862]

Pa received an official letter this evening giving him his dismissal from the hospital from the 13th of this month. The hospitals here are to be discontinued.

(Above) An 1860 view of Transylvania University. Morrison Hall, the columned building, was designed by Gideon Shryock, who rented the Stark house on the corner of Market and Mechanic Streets during the hall's construction (1831–33). The Stark house later became the longtime home of the Peter family. (Transylvania University Photographic Archives) *(Below)* Completed in 1840 with funds from the Lexington City Council, this building served the medical department until its demise ca. 1856. Transylvania High School was housed here in 1862 until it became a Union hospital following the battle of Perryville. The structure burned in May 1863 (see diary entry for May 22, 1863). (J. Winston Coleman Photographic Collection, Transylvania University Library)

TRANSYLVANIA UNIVERSITY—MEDICAL HALL.

Built in 1839—Burned in 1863.

TUESDAY JULY 8 [1862]

... A man named Curley, one of Col. Metcalf's Cavalry[1] was shot
today by G.B. Thomas, Freight agent of the Louisville & Lex. railroad.
The shooting took place at the Depot on Water st. The man was wounded
in four places. Thomas attempted to escape, but was arrested & put in jail.
They are moving the men from Hospital no. 1[2] to no. 2 there being so few
at present that one hospital is sufficient. ...

1. Colonel Leonidas Metcalfe's 7th Kentucky Cavalry (U.S.) contained two men,
William Curl, and Absalom Craily, each of whom might have been "Curley." See
Speed, *The Union Regiments of Kentucky*, 151, 189.
2. Located in the Masonic Hall, on the northeast corner of Walnut and Short Streets.
The site is now occupied by the Central Christian Church.

THURSDAY JULY 10TH [1862]

Three companies of the 3rd Ky. arrived today bringing some prisoners.
They are to serve as escort to a battery that will pass through here on the
way to the Gap.

SATURDAY JULY 12TH [1862][1]

John Morgan with a large body of cavalry said to be at Glasgow &
marching on Lex[ington] expected tonight. The whole town is in a stir in
consequence. Gen Boyle[2] sent a dispatch that men should be sent out to
meet Morgan. The Home Guards, Provost Guard & volunteers from the
hospital with a battery that arrived the other day went out on duty. A
company came to night from Cynthiana.[3] A dispatch was sent this evening
to Cincinatti for troops. For several days the atmosphere has presented a
very hazy, smoky appearance & at times a slight smell as of burning was
perceptible. We heard this evening that Lebanon had been burnt by
Morgan.

1. This and the following entries refer to Morgan's First Kentucky Raid, July 4–28,
1862, in which Morgan's cavalry rode north from Tennessee into Kentucky and around
Lexington. See Ramage, *Rebel Raider*, 91–106.
2. A Whig slaveholder and resolute Unionist from Boyle County, Kentucky, Jeremiah
Tilford Boyle (1818–1871) had studied law at Transylvania. His controversial administration as commander of the District of Kentucky was ineffectual against count-
less Confederate and guerrilla raids. See Kleber, ed., *The Kentucky Encyclopedia*, 109.
3. Cynthiana is the county seat of Harrison County, north of Fayette County, and
bordered in the south by Scott and Bourbon Counties.

SUNDAY [JULY] 13TH [1862]

Two of Morgan's scouts taken up this morning. Morgan is said to be

at Danville & has issued a proclamation calling on the secesh to rise.[1]
Martial law has been declared here, soldiers have been arriving all morning. Gen. Boyle is said to be in Morgan's rear.

1. A copy of this proclamation can be found in James Street Jr., *The Struggle for
Tennessee* (Alexandria: Time-Life, 1985), 26.

MONDAY JULY 14TH [1862]

The excitement increases. Gen Ward[1] has command here & martial
law is stricter than ever. Mrs Morgan and Mrs Curd[2] were sent out of
town as the people threatened to level their houses with the ground, &
Major Bracht[3] said he could protect them no longer. A regiment arrived
this morning from Camp Chase. Stayed here about an hour & hearing
Morgan was within 12 miles of Frankfort left for that place. The police
force from Cincinnatti is here.[4]

1. William Thomas Ward (1808–1878) was born in Virginia, but lived most of his
life in Kentucky. He served in the state legislature and represented Kentucky in the
U.S. Congress, 1851 to 1853. General Ward was the Union commander at Lexington at the time of Morgan's first raid into the state in July 1862. See Duke, *History of
Morgan's Cavalry*, 193.
2. Mrs. Richard A. (Eleanor) Curd was a sister of Mrs. Henrietta Morgan. See James
A. Ramage, *John Wesley Hunt* (Lexington: Univ. Press of Kentucky, 1974), 94. Also
see Mrs. James B. Clay to James B. Clay, July 9, 1863, Hunt-Morgan Papers, Division of Special Collections and Archives, University of Kentucky Library.
3. Major F.G. Bracht was provost marshal of Lexington in July 1862. An officer in
the 18th Kentucky Infantry (U.S.), he led a remnant of that regiment in retreat to
Louisville in September 1862, after the battle of Richmond, Kentucky. See Speed,
The Union Cause in Kentucky, 464, and Richard H. Collins, *History of Kentucky* (1882;
reprint, Frankfort: Kentucky Historical Society, 1966), 1:104.
4. All able-bodied men were ordered to report to the courthouse to be armed. Sa-
loons were closed and rebel sympathizers were ordered not to leave their homes. C.T.
Worley, mayor of Lexington in 1862, issued a proclamation urging loyal citizens to
join a Home Guard company and drill daily at 4 P.M. On July 13, President Lincoln
wired General Henry W. Halleck, the Union commander: "They are having a stam-
pede in Kentucky. Please look to it." About one hundred members of the Cincinnati
police force were dispatched to Lexington. See Perrin, *History of Fayette County, Kentucky*, 456; Ranck, *History of Lexington*, 332; and Roy P. Basler, ed., *The Collected
Works of Abraham Lincoln* (New Brunswick, N.J.: Rutgers Univ. Press, 1953), 5:322.

TUESDAY JULY 15 [1862]

The houses of the secesh are being pressed into the service of our
soldiers. The secesh have had to stay at home for the last two days but
today thinking martial law was over (Major Brachts proclamation had only
declared it for 48 hours) they ventured out & about 50 were imprisoned in

the court house yard, under another proclamation which declared that all persons that were not union, did not belong to any volunteer company or were not willing to enlist in one were to be arrested. . . .

A man was taken up last night for carrying the secesh mail. He inquired for Mrs. Morgan & thus betrayed himself. His name is Foley, the same who was taken at Mrs. Morgans before. The secesh on the borders of Scott & Fayette have risen, taken Pa's mill & done other damage. One of our men was killed by some of our pickets. He rode up to the lines at a gallop & refused to halt when told to do so & our soldiers thinking it might be one of Morgan's men (who are said to wear the Federal uniforms very often) shot him. The last news from Morgan is that he is at Georgetown. The wires to Covington are cut & the Cincinnati train was ordered back this evening as the secesh had put things in readiness to blow up the track. The Louisville railroad was also torn up at one place.

WENSDAY JULY 16TH [1862]

Morgan is said to be only 3 or 4 miles off on the Georgetown road, we expect a fight. Mr. Wm. Warfield[1] came in from Dr. R. Breckinridge's to tell that the rebels intend to make a feint at one point while they attacked at another. A regiment came today (I don't know which one unless De Courcy's, his was expected). Took up a spy in the dress of a federal officer. About dinnertime a man was sent to the hospital who had been wounded by some of Morgan's men.

1. Thirty-five-year-old William Warfield. See Eighth Census of the United States for Fayette County, 1860, Schedule 1, 419.

THURSDAY JULY 17 [1862]

. . . Had a skirmish with rebels on Newtown pike threw a shell among them & took two or three prisoners. Major Bracht has issued an order that all houses shall be closed & lights extinguished at 9 P.M. while martial law lasts. Everybody very much dissatisfied with Gen. Ward, say he is drunken & unable to attend to his affairs half the time.

FRIDAY JULY 18TH [1862]

The 9th Pennsylvania Cavalry & Gen G. Clay Smith arrived this morning from Henderson.[1] Marched all the way from Frankfort this morning. Gen Smith it is said will take command here. Morgan sent a summons the other day for Lex. to surrender.

1. General Green Clay Smith (1826–1895) organized an impromptu brigade for the defense of Lexington that included a portion of the 9th Pennsylvania Cavalry, two companies of the 18th Kentucky Infantry, and one hundred Cincinnati police. See John W. Rowell, *Yankee Cavalrymen: Through the Civil War with the Ninth Pennsylvania Cavalry* (Knoxville: Univ. of Tennessee Press, 1971), 62–72.

SATURDAY JULY 19TH [1862]

The rebels have taken Cynthiana. The 9th Penn. Cavalry left last night about 9½. It is thought they are going to Paris. Warner's regiment camped this morning on Winchester road & left this evening for that city. Had a fight at Paris. Rebels skedaddled as usual. Took four of Morgan's Texan rangers at Georgetown. Brought them to the hospital as they said they were just recovering from measles. But they were so unruly that the doctors had them marched off to jail to await further orders. Mean, dirty looking fellows they were. . . .

SUNDAY JULY 20TH [1862]

Captain Louis Postlethwaites' company of citizen guards encamped in the College lot[1] opposite our house. A part of the 54th Indiana arrived this evening.[2] In the fight at Paris 17 rebels wounded & good many killed.[3] On our side the only man hurt was one who had his finger cut off by the wheel of the cannon on which he was riding getting loose & rubbing

At the north end of Little College Lot is Transylvania University's main building. Designed by Matthew Kennedy, it burned in 1829.(Courtesy of Clay Lancaster)

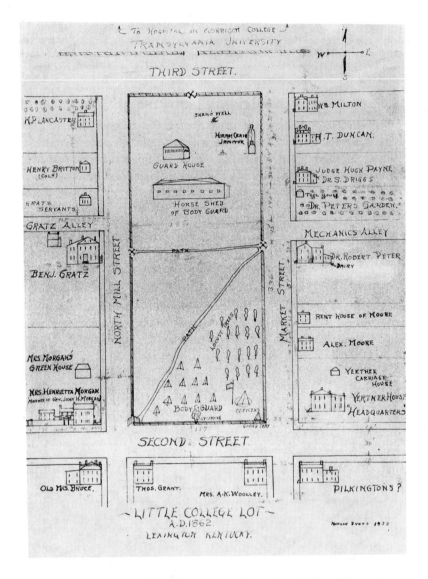

Map showing many of the sites mentioned in Frances Peter's diary. The area is now known as Gratz Park. (Evans Collection, Special Collections and Archives, University of Kentucky Libraries)

against the railing by which he was holding. An Ambulance with two of Warners' men was fired into by some secesh, but fortunately missed them, a few of the buckshot lodging in the horse. Brought in 23 prisoners tonight.

1. The Little College Lot, now known as Gratz Park, in the rear of the old Lexington Public Library, was the first site of Transylvania University. Before the war it was the favorite drill ground for Morgan's Lexington Rifles. See Coleman, *Lexington During the Civil War*, 11.
2. The 54th Indiana, a three-month regiment raised in June 1862, initially guarded prisoners in Indiana. A portion of the regiment was ordered south to defend against Morgan's raid followed by the remainder of the regiment when General Edmund Kirby Smith entered Kentucky. See Dyer, *A Compendium of the War of the Rebellion*, 3:1140.
3. On July 19, General Green Clay Smith's brigade drove Morgan from Paris, Kentucky, with no losses. Interestingly, Morgan suggested in his report that he had intimidated the Federals at Paris, and he mentioned no loss of any kind. See *OR*, ser. 1, vol. 16, pt. 1, 756–59, 769–70.

MONDAY JULY 21ST [1862]

. . . The 54th Indiana left this morning. An order issued today for all the secesh here to be forced to bear arms in the defense of the city.[1] Several were taken up & put some in jail & some with the guards in the College lot. . . .

1. The order Miss Peter reported was contradictory to others issued by the city council before and after this day that compelled southern sympathizers to remain in their homes. See Perrin, *History of Fayette County, Kentucky*, 456.

TUESDAY JULY 22ND [1862]

It seems that the order for the secesh to bear arms was only done to scare them a little; the reason for it was this. Some secesh meeting some of the home guards, made insulting remarks on their having to take up arms for the defense of the city & the soldiers took their revenge by that order. The companies were all dismissed today & business resumed, as all danger from Morgan is over for the present. The secesh are furious because he didn't come to Lexington.

WEDNESDAY JULY 30TH [1862]

Yesterday a body of rebels from Owen Co. went to Mount Sterling & summoned it to surrender. The people replied "if they wanted the town they might come & take it." A fight ensued & the rebels were driven from the town by the home guards, and had retreated but a short distance when they were met by a portion of Warner's reg. from Lex. who killed, wounded, & captured nearly the whole party, taking all their horses.

SATURDAY AUGUST 2ND [1862]

About 114 prisoners were brought from Mt. Sterling & lodged in the county jail. . . .

SATURDAY AUG 9TH [1862]

. . . Several young men left here today to escape enlisting but were arrested at Covington. The secesh comply very readily with the order requiring them to pay for the damage done by Morgan's guerrillas. They evidently expect that "*gentleman*" back in full force soon. The hospital has been ordered to be prepared for 1000 more men & it is thought hospital no. 1 will be opened again as no 2 can hardly accomodate so many.[1]

1. General Lew Wallace was preparing the city for an expected fight against General Kirby Smith's advancing Confederate army. See Perrin, *History of Fayette County, Kentucky*, 456–57.

SUNDAY AUG 17TH [1862]

One of last evening's trains was stopped by a messenger & returned to Lex. Pa came home this evening & told Ben he would have to leave town this evening if he didn't wish to be detained for an indefinite time as martial law would be declared tomorrow. The people of Richmond Ky are leaving that place & something is evidently in the wind. The Governor & Lieut-governor will resign at 10 o'clock tomorrow. Mr. James F. Robinson will be governor & Mr. D.C. Wickliffe Secretary of State. . . .[1]

1. Unionists in Kentucky's legislature attempting to lead the state toward the Union were hampered by Governor Beriah Magoffin's conservatism, especially his insistence on the state's "neutrality." After abandoning that policy, Magoffin agreed to resign. With the lieutenant governorship vacant, and after Speaker of the Senate John F. Fisk stepped down, Magoffin's hand-picked successor, Senator James F. Robinson, was inserted in Fisk's place. Magoffin resigned and, in a perfectly orchestrated scenario, Robinson assumed the governorship on August 18, 1862. See John David Smith, "James F. Robinson," in *Kentucky's Governors, 1792–1985*, ed. Lowell H. Harrison (Lexington: Univ. Press of Kentucky, 1985), 74.

TUESDAY [AUGUST] 19TH [1862]

The city council has issued a resolution that all able bodied citizens shall attach themselves to some company & drill every evening at 4 o'clock at which time all shops shall be closed[1] and Warner issued an order to enforce the resolution & that all disloyal citizens should not be permitted on the streets after 4 PM. News from Richmond today is that there were 3000 rebels there & the 400 home guards retreated in direction of Lex. The stage from there this evening brings news that there hasn't been a rebel soldier there. I imagine that dispatch was got up to make a sensation in Ohio & Indiana & hurry up troops.

1. Mayor Worley issued this order on August 18. See Perrin, *History of Fayette County, Kentucky,* 456.

WENSDAY [AUGUST] 20TH [1862]

A very bad accident occurd today. About three o'clock this morning a freight train of about 8 car was thrown off the track down a steep declivity about six miles this side of Cynthiana. It is thought the secesh of the neighborhood knowing troops were expected that way tore up the track in two places, to be sure of destroying them. All on the freight train were killed but the conductor. It is said a messenger was sent to warn the train but he was shot by the guerillas. A few days ago a squad of 70 men from the hospitals on their way to their regiments were attacked & taken by 1000 guerillas. But not without resistance for though not half of the brave fellows were armed they defended themselves as long as possible killing 9 of the secesh while they only killed 8 of ours. Cap Cochran[1] of Lex it is said when he found they were about to be surrounded tore off his shoulder straps & hid in the bushes till the rebels were gone when he came post haste to Lex. to give the news. . . .

1. Miss Peter may be referring to John C. Cochran of the 14th Kentucky (U.S.), formerly an officer in the Lexington Chasseurs. See Perrin, *History of Fayette County, Kentucky,* 449.

SATURDAY AUG 23D [1862]

An order issued last night that all able bodied hands belonging to secesh should be taken to work on the roads. Between 100 & 200 were obtained today.

MONDAY AUG 25TH [1862]

A skirmish took place Saturday between Metcalf's men & a body of rebels near Big Hill 18 miles beyond Richmond.[1] The greater part ran shamefully at the first shot, but the rest stood by their Col in a most gallant manner. The rebels were defeated in the end but Col Metcalf said if it hadn't been for a Tennessee regiment which came to the rescue in the nick of time he would have been cut to pieces. There are six generals in town today. Nelson, Lew Wallace, Jackson, Hanson, Craft & Cassius Clay.[2]

1. On August 23, Confederate cavalry under Colonel John Scott clashed with Colonel Metcalfe's brigade at Big Hill. The 7th Kentucky Cavalry (U.S.) fled the field in disorder while a portion of the 3rd Tennessee Cavalry (U.S.) remained with Metcalfe to delay the Confederates. This skirmish represented General Braxton Bragg's initial steps in the invasion of Kentucky. See *OR*, ser. 1, vol. 16, pt. 1, 884–86, and Connelly, *Army of the Heartland*, 213–14.
2. The concentration of troops in Lexington included Generals William Nelson, Lew Wallace, James S. Jackson, Cassius Marcellus Clay, and Mahlon Manson (*not* Hanson). See Warner, *Generals in Blue*, 26, 344, 536, 248, 84, 117.

FRIDAY AUG 29TH [1862]

Nelson was furious at the way Metcalf's men behaved & had the straglers arrested wherever found. They were taken to Col. McCook's camp near Lex. & every one made to run round a stump for 24 hours without stopping. A company of the 93d Ohio[1] has been encamped in the college lawn near our house as provost guard but left today & another company (from the 52 Ohio[2] I believe) has taken their place. A right funny story is told of Gen Nelson. When he was in Nashville or Danville, I forget which, he was one day passing a house at the door of which stood a very fine lady who spit on him when he was opposite to her. "Madame" said he "I don't allow anyone to treat me in that manner so you must apologize. I've been looking around for a house that will do for a hospital & I have 50 smallpox patients in my regiment. If you don't make me your best curtsey and apologize in the words I dictate, I shall quarter them on you." The lady obeyed at once & never gave him any more trouble. (He didn't really have any smallpox cases among his men, just said it to scare her).

1. Mustered just three days prior, the 93rd Ohio Infantry arrived in Lexington on August 23. The regiment marched to the aid of General William Nelson, contesting General Kirby Smith near Richmond, Kentucky, later that day. See Dyer, *A Compendium of the War of the Rebellion*, 3:1537.
2. Also mustered in August 1862, the 52nd Ohio was rushed to the aid of Nelson on August 29. See Dyer, *A Compendium of the War of the Rebellion*, 3:1521.

SUNDAY AUG 31ST [1862]

Fighting been going on at Richmond for the last few days[1] & there has been no end to the false reports & rumors. This morning they said Washington, Cumberland Gap & Glasgow all taken by the rebels.

Richmond surrendered, Col Warner killed etc. Last night a regiment (or it might have been two) arrived about 11 P.M. & stayed all night in the college lot. Hospital no 1 has been opened & about 200 sick & wounded there under Pa's charge, as Dr. Eversman has hospital no 2. Sunday as it was we ladies went to work making bandages & tearing up old linen as there was not much at the hospital & we didn't know how much might be wanted nor how soon. Gen Wright & staff arrived this morning & took command. Nelson came from Richmond wounded & went on to Cincinnati. Major Bracht came back with the remnant of Warner's regiment. I can learn nothing certain about Col. Warner. Jackson's cavalry arrived tonight, is going right on to Richmond. The news tonight was that the rebels had crossed the river & our troops were retreating, but that dispatch is by the grapevine telegraph.

1. On August 30, 1862, Confederates under General Kirby Smith fought and defeated General William Nelson's Federals at Richmond, Kentucky. The Federals retreated to the Ohio River, leaving Lexington and the rest of Kentucky open to advancing Confederates. See Connelly, *Army of the Heartland*, 215–16.

MONDAY SEPT. 1ST [1862]

The rebels have crossed the river so they say all the troops have left here. Gen Wright gone to Cincinnati. Every man sent from the hospitals that was able to go & Lexington surrendered for the time. . . .

[THURSDAY] SEPT 18TH 1862

Late Monday evening so I am told some of the union troops drew themselves up in battle array near the Fairgrounds[1] & begged their officers to let them make a stand & strike one more blow for Lexington. But knowing it to be useless to attempt to resist 30,000 desperate men the offer was refused & the command given for retreat. Meanwhile the citizens were in the greatest excitement. Rumors were heard throughout the day that our army was defeated & that the mayor had sent to surrender the city; but as no council had been called & the government officers seemed to know nothing about it, it was not generally known to be true, until too late to do much in the way of destroying stores etc. It was not until 6 PM that the fact was known at the hospitals when the doctors set to work to send off as many men both by the evening train & on foot & destroy as many stores as possible.

Still even though the next day some of the ladies took away a good many things that had belonged to the Aid society there were any quantity of stores fell into the hands of the rebels, which might have been destroyed if we had only been told sooner how matters stood. About 2 AM the rebels took possession of the depot & government storehouses at the edge of town but found no rolling stock (except I believe a small engine & car that had been used on the switches and abandoned as of no use) as it had all been sent away & next day Kirby Smith's[2] command entered the city. Very little demonstration was made over them & they went to work to parole prisoners. Young Randall (who is in one of their regiments) went to hospital no. 1 & ordered our sick to the provost office but when there the provost marshall ordered them to be marched back until an officer could be sent to parole them. When they went to put the secesh flag on the court house, they tried to make one of our men do it & when he refused they shot him but they forced a soldier to do it at last.

Wednesday night John Morgan & some one else (I suppose Basil Duke[3]) came to Mrs Morgan's; the next morning about 6 oclock while looking at a body of rebels who were marching out the Winchester pike I overheard one of our servants say to a colored man (who I know) 'Did John Morgan come in last night sure enough' 'No' said he 'and he ain't goin to.' 'Well' said the other 'I hear everyone say so.' 'Well,' said the man 'if he did they had mighty poor joy over it for they were crying over there for to break their hearts.' I am certain Morgan brought some bad news, for when he entered Lexington the next day his mothers house was shut up & they didnt come to the front door all that day. Morgan'[s] command came in about 11 AM Thursday Sept 4th A nasty, dirty looking set they were; wore no uniform but were dressed in grey & butternut[4] jeans or anything else they could pick up, but were not quite so dirty and mean looking as Kirby Smith's. They looked like the tag, rag & bobtail of the earth & as if they hadnt been near water since Fort Sumter fell. The secesh had said that when John Morgan came he would have such a welcome as had never been seen before I confess I was disappointed.

When he did come they did indeed ring the church bells in a doleful way & the secesh ladies paraded about with the stars and bars in their hands & streamers of red white & red on their dresses or bonnets. But so far from Lexington being thrown open to them, it looked liked it was deserted, the stores were shut, houses closed & the only hurraing was made by themselves & a few rowdies. They passed along the side street by Mrs Morgan's the officers dressed in grey or black & wearing different kinds of flat hats & feathers with cockades or streamers, the men in clothes of various colors only being uniform in respect to dirt, none or very few having haversacks or blankets (indeed of both infantry and cavalry very few had knapsacks, blankets or overcoats) & armed with different kinds of guns, but decorated like their officers with cockades, streamers, or little flags in their hats. The horses of both officers & men were very fine & were adorned like their riders. They camped in the court house yard (if we can say that of men who have no tents) & one company came & fastened their horses in the college lot, opposite our house. My brother who came in that day hearing that they were going to draft (as recruits didnt come fast enough) rode straight home & started on foot to join the Union forces. (as did also a good many young men) We heard from him several day[s] after that he was at Louisville How mad we were to see those rascals! We could hardly keep within bounds. I heard say that a young lady who lives on the hill while Morgans cavalry was passing her house, said to her sister 'Well I cant stand this any longer, I must say what I think.' & 'Look here' said she to one of the fellows, 'I say Hurra for Lincoln. (I mean the President of the United States if you dont know) and hurra for the Union and the union soldiers.' 'You do' said the man getting very angry. 'Yes, & hurra for Hell and Damnation.'

The secesh ladies didnt seem to like their looks much more than we did. Some of them went & sat with Morgan's men in the courtyard, & all went about waving flags at the men & in the officers faces but when any common men came to their houses to ask for something to eat they had them taken in at the back gate to the kitchen and let the negroes wait on them. For several days after [Kirby] Smith came in troops were sent out generally about 6 AM on the Winchester pike & once or twice they had 4 or 5 small cannon with them. Their regiments are most of them not much larger than a company of one of our regiments. But each had two flags the stars and bars (some had 'Shiloh' on them) & small blue flag with a crescent. & companies kept coming in & going out so that it was hard to tell how many men were here or whether the ones that came in were new, or just the same ones came back. & when they marched they straggled along so that it was almost impossible to count them.

Meantime the secesh forced the union men to open their stores or broke into them especially clothing boot & grocery stores sometimes paying in script & sometimes not paying at all Some of the union men had hid a good many of their stores. Mr Lancaster[5] among the rest had hid a good many boxes of boots in a house back of his store, but some of the neighbors knew of it & told. Mr Lancaster offered to give them two boxes if they would leave him the rest but they refused and took the whole with out offering the least compensation. They went to Mr Shaw's[6] and Mr Wirts[7] & to the Wheeler & Wilson rooms where the Aid Society used to meet, & helped themselves to hats & clothes a[nd] took everything belonging to the Society. Saxton[8] had concealed the instruments belonging to his band in some house on Main Street, as he said he would rather break them than let the rebels get them, but as they were worth about 400 dollars he thought he might perhaps save them. But a Mrs. Wood who lived opposite, found it out & told the rebels who got them & litterally forced Saxton & his band to play for them.

They took Hospital No 1 & sent some of our men to the Medical Hall until they could get passes & we could hear them in the evenings while they sat on the hall steps singing 'Star Spangled Banner' and 'Red, White and Blue,' never minding the guards in the least They took Mr. Montells Iron Foundry,[9] to make shot & sent a company to Estill Furnace[10] to get iron. There was for 4 or 5 days a company of Buford's[11] men in the college lot opposite us, who went out every day either during the day or late at night on picket or scouting duty & once they were relieved by another company (whose I don't know) but they had with them a blue flag with a red cross surrounded by stars on one side & 'on to victory' on the other. They didnt trouble anyone except by their noise & there being so many horses near us, but we kept our house shut & doors locked, from the day Morgan came in, as also did other union people & even the secesh for a while for fear that some fellow might take it into his head to pay us a visit & because we were afraid of the house being searched

One evening after this company left the lot, for good, Pa asked my sister for some music for we hadnt had any for fear of attracting the rebels & while she was playing somebody knocked on the front door with their fist. Lettie jumped up & ran to the door, thinking nothing but that she might prevent them from entering & found two rough dirty fellows who told her they would like to come in & hear her play & tried to do so, but Lettie pushed them out & told them if they wanted to hear her play they could stand by the window & listen. But they couldnt come in. & then went back to the piano. The night after John Morgan came in we were woke up by whooping in the streets. We naturally supposed it to be fire and so it proved to be, two stables out Broadway. Mr. Lawless[12] and some one else, I forget who. And all the while this horrid whooping continued and at the same time the rebels at the college were singing and laughing and talking. It sounded exactly as if Indians had set the town on fire and were dancing and whooping and singing around the flames. It proved to be Indians that made the whooping, there are one or two with Morgan's guerillas and several others in one of the Florida regiments; horrid fellows they are.

The first day the rebels came in Miss Carrie Preston[13] went down to Main Street & amused herself by tearing up & trampling on a union flag which had been taken from one of the buildings there.[14] They got hold of the Union flag belonging to the hospital & fastened it to one of their horses and the man he belonged to rode him down the street dragging the flag in the dust. Once the horse hitched his foot in the flag & nearly threw the scamp off. When hospital No 1 was full the rebels took half the Dormitory and supplied themselves with beds from the college & put the men under charge of Dr Jim Keiser of this city. They sent off our men from hospital No 2 (all that could or would go for some of the nurses & the steward and Dr Evermann[15] would not leave the sick) & when all were gone but a few, they took the college & put our men in the empty half of the Dormitory leaving them to depend to the care of the ladies for stores. & appropriated all the clothes knapsacks & stores in the college for their own use.

When our men were being sent off we couldnt help comparing *them*, so clean & gentlemanly looking & looking so well fed & the half starved, half clothed, dirty wretches who guarded them. Our men all seemed in good spirits when starting & told us they were coming back as soon as they could. It looks so strange to see some of the dirty rebels dressed in our soldiers uniforms & they seem to be ashamed of it too, for if any one remarks upon it, they hang their heads & hurry by pretending not to hear A good many arrests have been made, some for refusing to obey Gen [Kirby] Smiths order to take script[16] (nobody will take it if they can help it & some of the country people stopped coming to town or only went to private houses where they could get good money in order to avoid taking script. One man in market on[e] day having a large jar of butter finding they wouldnt let him sell for anything but that gave it all away rather than take it.) & some at the instigation of resident secesh.

Pa has been arrested three times the first time Col Gracie[17] sent for him & wanted him to take the oath to the confederacy; of course Pa refused, the Col then wanted him to leave the state. Pa represented to him that his family & business were here & he preferred to stay. The Col then made him give parole not to give information to the union party & said he might stay here while any of our soldiers were here. The next time the Col had him arrested (upon what charge I dont remember) he ordered him not to leave his house except to go to the hospital. & the last time he was arrested by Capt Haws orders but the Capt not being found he was allowed to go. . . .

We have had the exquisite pleasure of reading once more the Kentucky Statesman which was begun shortly after their arrival. By whom edited it not stated. . . . It is the only paper allowed to the citizens of Lexington. Among other things is issued an order from headquarters (which are at Mrs. Vertners house on the corner below us) that all free negroes should come before a certain time & deliver up all government stores in their possession (for before Quartermaster Brown left, a good many stores were given away to anyone that wanted them) on pain of having their houses searched & of being arrested.[18] Which order was carried into effect & a good many houses searched & from one colored man named Laurence Hawkins[19] they took lately on pretence of this order some 400 dollars he had saved.

One day of the second week after their arrival John Mc——— who drives our wagon said when he was coming in from [the] mill he met about 400 cavalry going out the Newtown road & soon after met the halfbreed Wash. Morgan[20] (who is some kin, I don't know what, to John Morgan) who asked him if he had seen any cavalry pass. "Yes" said John "they are just ahead.["] "Well" said the half breed, "I wish you would give me some tobacca for my nigger has all of mine & he has gone on with the rest.["] John gave him some & asked where he was going. "To Cynthiana" said Morgan . . . our men are fighting there & we are going to reinforce them.[21]

One night last week John came to tell Pa that the rebels were going to send stores to Harrodsburg & that Rogers who lives near Pa's place on the hill where he keeps his wagon & horses wanted them to press them into the service. John was very much disturbed about it but finally concluded it would be better to go with them quietly. When he represented to the officer however that to take away the wagon was to take from him the means of supporting his family, the officer ordered it not to be touched & said John was a fine fellow.

Last Saturday a train of 41 or 42 ambulances came from Cincinnati under a flag of truce to get such sick and wounded from Richmond & Lexington as could be moved. They went on to Richmond & returned

Monday night. It was a very dark windy evening but nevertheless the ladies got supper and took to the men. They stayed one day and then left taking all of our men but about 27. The hospital steward went with them & said he was coming back as soon as exchanged to get the rest. Mr. Elrod[22] of this city also went with them in a wagon borrowed from a friend, but his wife told that he had gone & as he had no pass, they sent & arrested him and sentenced him to solitary confinement.

One of the doctors who came with the ambulances brought Pa a *Cincinnati Gazette* the first we had seen since the rebels came here (for they have possession of the post office & don't allow any papers or letters to pass without being sent first to headquarters, & anyone writing from here has to show the letter to the General). It [*Cincinnati Gazette*] told us that McClelland had whipped Jackson in Maryland,[23] which was some compensation for the news that Bragg had Munfordville. An extra Statesman was issued stating that Bragg had won a bloodless victory there on Monday 15th & Buell had no longer a chance left. We have seen two Louisville Journals during these three weeks both brought good news from Maryland & said the rebels have been driven out of Agusta & Maysville by the gunboats.[24] The last time any papers were brought here the man who had them was imprisoned & Kirby Smith issued a order that anyone who should be found reading northern papers should be arrested.

We saw a proclamation of Gen Braggs Wednesday I think[25] (though I am not sure for everything has gone on in such a disorderly manner & time has hung so heavy on our hands that one day seems like two or three) addressing the people of Kentucky in the usual style & telling the women to buckle on the armor of their fathers & give free vent to their enthusiasm, which we did accordingly by saying every thing we pleased. A poor sickly looking fellow stopped at the door the same day & had a talk with Ma. He was dressed in an old suit of the Lex. Chasseurs that he said a young man (a neighbor of ours) whose cousin left them with him, had given to him. He said he was from Florida, that he & a good many others had been "poked" into the army at the point of the bayonet,[26] but he said "don't say anything about it for I only tell it to you as between friends for they would poke a bayonet through any of us that said so". . . . He said he had had the measles when they first started & had never been well since, that he had never fought a stroke against the union troops and didn't intend to. That he never expected to come this far & that all he care for now was to see home once more. Ma asked him what he got to eat at the hospital & if he was taking any thing for that dreadful cough he had. No, he said, he wasnt & that they had plenty of bread & mutton up there.

Ma said he ought to be taking something else than that & asked if the secesh ladies didn't bring things up there for the sick. "Yes" he said "but they leave them with the steward (Ma told him that was because his doctor had ordered the ladies not to distribute things to the men) & sometimes he will give me things & sometimes he won't. He says they are for the sickest and men like me can eat meat & bread." That they had milk up there every day but not enough & he had only been able once to [get] any & then it was buttermilk. That he thought if he could get milk or chicken soup he would get well. Ma told him she would very willingly have given him some milk but that the evening before some of the secesh who are quartered in or near our lot milked & maltreated not only our cow but several others & so she had none. But some union ladies coming by just then from our hospital she told them what he wanted & they got it for him the next day. He appeared to be very thankful & said the union ladies here had always spoken kindly to him. Once when Ma said something very strong against the Confederacy he said I don't say it to threaten you, but as a friend, that I heard there was an order out that any one who spoke against the Confederacy was to be arrested & I wouldn't like to see that happen to you after you have been kind to me.

Thursday was appointed as a day of thanksgiving for Braggs victory & all the churches were ordered to be opened but the Episcopal minister Mr. Shipman[27] pleaded illness & at Mr. Branks? (the 2nd Presbyterian) there were only one or 2 people present. Mr. Mathews[28] of the 1st Presbyterian didn't come & when they sent for him he said he couldn't come & when they sent a second time he said he neither could nor would come. So as their own chaplain had been ordered to preach at camp Kirby Smith read the service himself which gave rise to a good deal of fun among the union people. That same evening they had a concert at Odd Fellows hall but the only performers were Saxtons Contra bands & the music was miserable. . . .

1. The old Lexington Fair Grounds, owned by the Agricultural and Mechanical Association, were located near the south edge of town, where the University of Kentucky Administration Building now stands. The site served as a camp and drill grounds for Union troops for several months early in the war. See Coleman, *Lexington During the Civil War*, 25.
2. A Floridian, Edmund Kirby Smith (1824–1893) is best known for his command of Confederate forces in the Trans-Mississippi Department, 1862–1865. He took part in Bragg's invasion of Kentucky and led the victorious Confederate troops at

ODD-FELLOWS' HALL

THE

SECOND SOIREE

OF THE

UNION MUSICAL ASSOCIATION,

WILL TAKE PLACE

THIS EVENING,

Monday, Nov. 24th, 1862,

AT ODD-FELLOWS' HALL,

Corner Main St. & Broadway, Lexington, Ky.,

FOR THE

BENEFIT

OF THE

SUFFERING SOLDIERS

IN HOSPITAL.

On which occasion will be presented the following Programme of Select, New & Popular

Vocal and Instrumental Music!

PROGRAMME.

1. Melody of Airs, (for Violins, Flutes, Horns, &c.,)
   Messrs. BOYD, DOZIER, and others.
2. "Brave Boys are They," (Duett and Chorus,)
   Miss PETER and Lieut. BURGEN.
3. Solo, ("Tempest "—Bass Song)..............Mr. M. S. DOWDEN.
4. "Cottage by the Sea," and "Brightest Eyes," (Cornettino,)
   WILL. A. STIVERS.
5. "Gently Sighs the Breeze," (Vocal Duett.)
   Misses BRIGHT and SKILLMAN.
6. Serenade by Kreuzer, (Vocal Quartette,)
   Messrs. KRAUSS, LANGE, SEEP and KROESING.
7. "O, Dolce Concento," (Solo and Variations for Flute,)
   S. D. McCULLOUGH.
8. "The Ould Irish Gintleman,".............Mr. CHRYSTAL.
9. Annie of the Vale," (Solo and Chorus,)..........Lieut. BURGEN.

INTERMISSION.

SCENE FROM SHAKSPEARE'S "WINTER'S TALE."

PROGRAMME RESUMED.

1. Pacific Polka, (Orchestral,)..............DOZIER, BOYD, and others.
2. "The Indian Drum," (Vocal Trio,)
   BURGEN, DAVIDSON, and STILSON.
3. "The Union Forever."................Miss E. LETCHER.
4. Transcription—"Her bright smile haunts me still. (Cornettino.)
   WILL. A. STIVERS.
5. "Man the Life Boat,"—(Descriptive Song.)....Mr. M. S. DOWDEN.
6. "O, Give me back my Arab Steed."............Miss B. BRIGHT.
7. "The Umbrella Courtship,".................Mr. CHRYSTAL.
8. "The Irish Volunteer," (Song and Chorus,)......Mr. DAVIDSON.

MUSICAL DIRECTOR, ... PROF. SCHULTZE.
SECRETARY,......................................J. T. DAVIDSON.
TREASURER,...................................H. SHAW, JR.
COMMITTEE OF ARRANGEMENTS, Messrs. BOYD, CHRYSTAL, KROESING
AND STIVERS.

ADMISSION:

Chairs, - - 50 | Children, - - 25
Gallery, - - 25 | Servants, - - 25

Doors open at 6.30.   Commence 7.30.

Tickets may be had at DeRoode's Music Store, Bodley's Book
Store, J. S. Wilson's Drug Store, Fitch's Drug Store, Col. Goodloe's
China Store, Phoenix Hotel, Broadway Hotel, at the Door, and of Mr.
Jas. Chrystal, Mill Street.
SEATS RESERVED, may be secured on application to Hiram
Shaw, Jr., Treasurer of the Association, Main Street.

J. Dunlop, Job Printer, opposite the Post Office, Lexington.

A flyer announcing one of many benefits staged during the war for Union soldiers in Lexington hospitals. The Miss Peter listed in the show's second song is probably Lettie, Frances's older sister. (Evans Collection, Special Collections and Archives, University of Kentucky Libraries)

Richmond on August 30, 1862. See Robert L. Kerby, *Kirby Smith's Confederacy* (New York: Columbia Univ. Press, 1972), and Joseph H. Parks, *General Edmund Kirby Smith, C.S.A.* (Baton Rouge: Louisiana State Univ. Press, 1954).

3. Basil Wilson Duke (1838–1916), a native of Scott County, Kentucky, was educated at Centre College and Transylvania University. Early in the war he enlisted as a private in the Lexington Rifles, the company commanded by his brother-in-law, John Hunt Morgan. Duke was captured during Morgan's raid into Ohio and Indiana, but was exchanged and later held commands in eastern Kentucky and western Virginia. At the close of the war his brigade served as escort to Jefferson Davis and the fugitive Confederate government. See Michael B. Ballard, *A Long Shadow: Jefferson Davis and the Final Days of the Confederacy* (Jackson: Univ. Press of Mississippi, 1986), 122–27.

4. Late in the war many Confederate soldiers wore uniforms colored by a yellowish-brown dye made of copperas and walnut hulls. See Faust, ed., *Historical Times Illustrated Encyclopedia of the Civil War*, 101.

5. Owner of a dry goods business, George Lancaster was a member of Captain S.D. Bruce's Lexington Chasseurs. John Ennis, one of Lancaster's clerks, was a member of the rival Lexington Rifles. Perrin, *History of Fayette County, Kentucky*, 646.

6. Hiram Shaw, a Unionist, was a partner in the hat firm of H. and J.P. Shaw and Co., located on the south side of Main Street, between Mill and Upper. The store was raided again in June 1864 by Morgan's men, who exchanged their battered headgear for stylish new beaver hats. See Perrin, *History of Fayette County, Kentucky*, 466, and *Williams' Lexington City Directory*, 83.

7. John H. Werts operated a clothing store on the south side of Main Street, opposite the Court House. See *Williams' Lexington City Directory*, 101.

8. Born in Boston, Henry A. Saxton arrived in Lexington in 1838. His trade was ornamental painting, but he loved and taught music. In June 1861 Saxton organized a "Cornet and Orchestral Band," later led by his son, Henry Jr. See Perrin, *History of Fayette County, Kentucky*, 714.

9. Probably the Lanckhart and Mentelle Iron Foundry, located on the southeast corner of Spring and Short Streets. During their brief occupation of Lexington in September and October 1862, the Confederates prepared to use this facility to produce armaments. See *Williams' Lexington City Directory*, 105, and Coleman, *Lexington During the Civil War*, 36.

10. Iron first was produced in Estill County around 1810. The Estill steam furnace operated from 1830 to 1874. The county's iron industry declined after the Civil War. See Kleber, ed., *The Kentucky Encyclopedia*, 298.

11. A native of Woodford County, Kentucky, Abraham Buford (1820–1884) attended Centre College and graduated from West Point in 1841. When General Braxton Bragg invaded Kentucky in 1862, Buford cast his lot with the South and was appointed a brigadier general.

12. R.C. Lawless lived on the west side of Broadway opposite the Lexington Brewery. See *Williams' Lexington City Directory*, 65.

13. Caroline H. Preston was daughter of Confederate General William Preston. Her mother, Margaret, was the daughter of Robert Wickliffe of Lexington. See Preston-Johnston Papers, Division of Special Collections and Archives, University of Kentucky Library.

14. The preceding seven sentences, missing from the original manuscript in the Evans Papers, are derived from a partial transcript of the Peter diary.

15. Dr. D.H. Eversman was in charge of Hospital No. 2 at this time.

16. The order requiring Lexington citizens to accept Confederate script, issued September 4, 1862, was intended to allow poorly clad Confederate soldiers to supply themselves from abundantly stocked stores. See Perrin, *History of Fayette County, Kentucky*, 460–61.

17. A native of New York City and a graduate of West Point, Archibald Gracie Jr. (1832–1864) recruited and commanded the 43rd Alabama Regiment. After serving in East Tennessee and in the Kentucky campaign, Gracie was killed at Petersburg, Virginia, on December 2, 1864.

18. In addition to free Negroes, the order compelled citizens and slaves to surrender any Federal property to Confederate quartermasters at two locations on Main Street. Home Guard companies turned in their arms and equipment as well. See Perrin, *History of Fayette County, Kentucky*, 461.

19. A free black, Lawson Hawkins, was a grocer on the west side of Broadway near Main Street. See *Williams' Lexington City Directory*, 58.

20. A second cousin of John Hunt Morgan, George Washington ("Wash") Morgan's mother was part Cherokee. George openly identified himself as a Native American by wearing traditional Indian clothing. He served as an aide, with the rank of major, on General Morgan's staff. See Ramage, *Rebel Raider*, 8, 89, and 274 n.

21. Morgan's cavalry attacked and captured Cynthiana on September 18, 1862. See Duke, *History of Morgan's Cavalry*, 199–202.

22. Perhaps Miss Peter referred to T.B.E. or E.W. Elrod, brothers in the photography business. See *Williams' Lexington City Directory*, 47.

23. Simultaneous to Bragg's and Smith's invasion of Kentucky, Confederate General Robert E. Lee led the Army of Northern Virginia into Maryland. He was pursued and stopped at the battle of Antietam by General George B. McClellan's Army of the Potomac on September 17, 1862. General Thomas J. ("Stonewall") Jackson earned notoriety as a threat to Washington during his Shenandoah Valley Campaign of May 1862, and was part of the Confederate army at Antietam.

24. Miss Peter was ill-informed. On September 27, 1862, Basil Duke's cavalry attacked Augusta, Kentucky, on the Ohio River. Gunboats near the fighting left the scene without firing a shot, compelling the Federals under Colonel Buford to surrender. See *OR*, ser. 1, vol. 16, pt. 1, 1013–15.

25. General Bragg issued his proclamation on September 14, 1862. See *OR*, ser. 1, vol. 16, pt. 2, 822.

26. After four months of conscription, Florida had enlisted fewer than two hundred men in the Confederate army. See John E. Johns, *Florida During the Civil War* (Gainesville: Univ. of Florida Press, 1963), 116–18.

27. The Reverend Jacob S. Shipman, a New York native and Yale graduate, became the minister of Christ Church in October 1861. See Ranck, *History of Lexington, Kentucky*, 201.

28. The Reverend J.D. Mathews had served Lexington as the Superintendent of Public Instruction. Despite his unwillingness to preach for Confederates, the Reverend represented the Southern Assembly in a sectional rift of the church during and after the war. See Ranck, *History of Lexington, Kentucky*, 112–13.

FRIDAY 19TH SEPT [1862]

John told Pa last evening that the secesh troops from Georgetown had taken possession of his mill. Pa went down today to see the general about it & told him he thought he had said private property should be respected. Kirby Smith said he had & Pa should be paid for the use of the mill & for whatever was in it. Pa replied, yes, they would pay him in Confederate notes, which would be of no use at all to him as there was 1200 bushels of wheat at the mill unpaid for & the person of whom he bought it wouldn't take "script." Smith then promised to send an officer to see about it, & said Pa might supply himself as usual with what was wanted for the use of his family & gave him the liberty of the city again. About a week ago they took Montmullins mill in the same way.

The company that went to Estill came back the other day with several wagons of iron & they are working as hard as they can making shot & shell. We asked Mr. Montell if he couldn't manage to spoil them in some way but he said they had their own workmen & he had no chance to do anything. Anyhow they cant make many shell for they havnt the ammunition & they say the shot is not larger than 6 pound.[1] The last Statesman advertised for 100 girls to make cartridges. . . .

1. Artillery ammunition was often designated by its weight. Six-pound shot, abundant early in the war, was phased out by Union and Confederate armies because of insufficient range and power. See *Echoes of Glory: Arms and Equipment of the Confederacy* (Alexandria, Virginia: Time-Life Books, 1991), 289.

SATURDAY [SEPT.] 20TH [1862]

This morning several soldiers passed going to the hospital & Ma asked one "where he was from." "Texas" he said gruffly. Ma told him she meant where he was from last. "Covington" he said. "You've had a fight there haven't you" said Pa. Yes, he said surlily. "And have had to retreat?" No, he replied angrily, "we didn't retreat we only came back to get water.["][1]

A short time after one of our neighbors came in & said she had just been to Mrs. Woolleys[2] & heard good news. She said she went there to see Mrs. John Payne & she hadnt been there but a few minutes when Nannie Bain[3] came in. "Well Nannie" said Mrs. Payne "whats the news!" "Oh nothing" she said "only I have spent the morning at Mrs. Curds & had such a splendid time. All the officers were there to breakfast and Theo & I had just as many beaux as we wanted." Then she asked Mrs. Payne why she hadnt come to help make cartridge bags & Mrs. Payne said she had a boil on her arm & wasnt able to do anything or she would have come. Oh she said (Nannie Bain) Mrs. Duke & Lu Robb[4] & Theo Curd & I have been making them as fast as we can. After a while Mrs. Payne said "Nannie did you hear that our men have had to retreat from Covington?" "Oh no!" said Nannie Bain & all the time she kept looking first at Mrs. ——— & then at Mrs. Payne & winking to the latter to hush, "no, they didn't retreat. They only fell back for want of water. I saw a letter this morning from one of the officers & he says he breakfasted within four miles of the Ohio." "If he did" said Mrs. Payne "why did the[y] come back to Lexington for water instead of going on to the Ohio? Nannie, you know that is not true & it is no use telling a story about it; *our men have retreated*" . . . .

1. General Smith ordered General Henry Heth's Division to fall back from Covington toward Lexington on September 11, 1862. See Connelly, *Army of the Heartland*, 220.
2. Perhaps Miss Peter refers to the wife of the woolen manufacturer George Wolley, who lived at the southeast corner of High and Mulberry Streets. See *Williams' Lexington City Directory*, 93.
3. Twenty-three-year-old Nannie Bain lived in the Robb household with another member of the Bain family. See Eighth Census of the United States for Fayette County, 1860; Schedule 1, 606.
4. Lu Robb, twenty-one years old, lived with her family and members of the Bain family in Lexington. See Eighth Census of the United States for Fayette County, 1860, Schedule 1, 606.

SUNDAY 21ST [SEPT.] 1862

Last night about 11 wagons came in the Georgetown road to the hospitals & we heard that some of them had wounded in them but we cannot learn anything certain for the rebels are always very quiet about such things & keep them as secret as possible. Pa went to the mill today & found a Captain that [Kirby] Smith had sent overlooking things.

This morning another rebel soldier stopped at the door & had a long talk. He said he had been at Sumter & Fort Pickens & several other battles. He appeared to be a good natured fellow & took all that was said in good sport. He admitted he thought they were in a bad fix here. He didnt see how they would get out & when he went away he told Ma if the Union troops got Lexington he was going to come to her house, & he was going to come back some time & have a long talk with my sister Jo, whom he seemed to be very much pleased with, because she wasnt afraid to say what she thought of the rebels.

Last evening some of the girls said they would like to know when Gen. Smith was going to preach again & where, as they wanted to hear him. So they sent down to ask at headquarters. The guard said he didnt know indeed. So they sent again to ask the general & they replied that Gen. Smith didn't preach. Those officers seem to have a dull time & it looks very dreary to see the bare, carpetless rooms all lighted up & the windows thrown open & the officers lolling about on the chairs or yawning over poor old Mr. Vertners books. It is a good thing he didn't live to see it. It would have broken his heart to see the secesh in his house.

Last night while Pa was at Mr. Gratz's[1] two fellows stopped & asked Mr Gratz if they could get supper there & stay all night. Mr. Gratz told them they had better go to the hospital or the tavern on Water Street. They said they had been to the last. Pa then asked whose men they were & they said they belonged to Churchills regiment[2] that had just come in from Georgetown.

1. Benjamin Gratz was born in Philadelphia but in 1819 moved to Lexington, where he engaged in the manufacture of hemp until his retirement in 1861. An ardent Unionist, Gratz made his house, adjacent to Mrs. Morgan's, available as a commissariat depot and cookhouse for Federal soldiers. See Perrin, *History of Fayette County, Kentucky*, 612–14.
2. This may be the 1st Arkansas Mounted Rifles, a regiment raised by Kentucky native Thomas James Churchill. See Ezra Warner, *Generals in Gray* (Baton Rouge: Louisiana State Univ. Press, 1959), 49–50.

MONDAY [SEPT.] 22ND [1862]

Last night there was a very large fire. It broke out about 3 oclock in the morning & was not entirely out at 8 oclock. Parker Craigs livery stable & dwelling house, Dr. Majors house & office & Mr McGowans & Mrs. Cochrans were destroyed. The last name is union & is not in Lexington at present. The other I believe are all secesh. They say the livery stable was full of the horses & accoutrements of the secesh & that there were some kegs of ammunition & some arms at Craigs. We heard several explosions like muskets being fired when the fire had burned a short while, but they must have save the greater part. Nearly the whole square was burnt. A good many horses were injured. All that could be done was to prevent the fire from crossing the street. The engines were out of order & no use. By the time they found that out the fire was too far advanced to put it out by hand. This morning about 8 oclock about 11 wagons passed here going out, one man told Ma to the country for corn. . . .

TUESDAY SEPT 23D [1862]

We heard this morning that cannon had been sent back here from Georgetown & that some of our forces are at Mt. Sterling. Some one told us this evening that a flag of truce had been sent to Kirby Smith today giving him 5 hours to surrender the city. . . . A squad of about 30 rebs came in the Georgetown road this evening & put up in the college lot opposite us. The rebel officers seem to be in a very bad humor today. As one of their niggers said, "Dey's heard de news & dey looks mighty oneasy."

WEDNESDAY [SEPT.] 24TH 1862

The men in the college lot left about 10' o clock this morning. A short while before they left however Dr. Eversmann was here & when he left Ma came to the door with him to open it (for we had all the doors locked & windows closed since the time those fellows came in last evening) and my little sister wanted Ma to stay at the door. Ma was afraid some of the fellows might come over if they saw her there but the Dr. said, "Oh let her stay, I dont reckon they will come." But they hadnt been at the door but a few minutes when one came over & ask Ma to lend him a bucket to water the horses. Ma told him she had very few in the house & that the last time she lent one the young man didn't bring it back though he promised to do so. The man said he would be certain to bring it back. "No" said Ma "I'd rather not lend any. Why dont you go to one of those secesh houses (pointing to Mrs. Woolley's & Mrs Morgans) and get some of your friends to lend you one?" "Why," said he "are you an inimy?" Ma told him she was union if that was what he called "an inimy." Then he went back to the lot & Ma heard him say pointing to our house "Why if that there isnt a damned union house." The rebels have found a good many more union houses here than they looked for. For John Morgan made them believe that they had driven all the union people away.

Mr Hulett told Pa that Humphrey Marshal[l][1] was certainly coming here today from some where in the direction of Mount Sterling, & that he (Hulett) had been told by the toll gate keeper between here & Georgetown that bodies of men were passing the gate all night not in companies but stragglers who came by different roads from the direction of Georgetown going in this direction. But whether they were retreating or what he couldn't tell.

3½ PM. Pa has just come home the mill & says a man named Coyle who had just come from Georgetown said that the rebels had all left that place & gone to Paris. That the commander of the rebel force at Paris had sent to Gen Smith begging him "for God's sake to send reinforcements," that there were 80,000 Yankees there. Pa said the rebels hadnt been at the mill since Sunday and had used only about $340 worth of wheat. He went down to see Kirby Smith to get paid for it as he was promised but the Gen was not there & hasnt been there all day.[2]

Mr. Montelle says he saw 4 or 5 wagons of sick and wounded brought in today & that the rebels here are casting about 150 shell a day besides shot. They appear to be getting very strict about liberty of speech. They wont allow us to say anything presently. . . .

Pa went to the commissary about the mill business. When he told his errand to that individual he was very much surprised & said that there was not the least necessity for taking the mill as they had plenty of supplys & that it was the first he had heard of it. So it must have been the doing of the neighborhood secesh. Pa didnt get paid & I dont suppose he will.

Humphrey Marshall hasnt come that I can learn but his quartermaster was here today & took 2 wagon loads of goods from Allen's. Besides paying Mr. Lancaster's store a visit & helping himself there & at Mr. Shaws. They went to Cochrans carpet store[3] & took nearly all his finer carpets to cut up for saddle blankets, & said if they couldnt get enough blankets they would go to private houses & get them.

1. Humphrey Marshall (1812–1872) was born in Frankfort, Kentucky, and graduated from West Point in 1832. Giving up his commission to practice law and enter politics, Marshall served four terms in Congress. He became a brigadier general in the Confederate army in October 1861 and participated in Bragg's invasion of Kentucky in 1862, but his war record was not outstanding. After resigning his commission Marshall represented Kentucky in the Confederate Congress. In addition to Warner, *Generals in Gray*, 212-13, see Thomas B. Alexander and Richard E. Beringer, *The Anatomy of the Confederate Congress* (Nashville: Vanderbilt Univ. Press, 1972), 298.
2. General Kirby Smith moved his army away from Lexington to Mt. Sterling on September 24 in an attempt to block the retreat of Federal General George W. Morgan's force from Cumberland Gap. See Connelly, *Army of the Heartland*, 237.
3. Fifty-year-old James W. Cochran owned the Campbell & Cochran carpet store. See Perrin, *History of Fayette County, Kentucky*, 584–85.

THURSDAY 25TH [SEPT.] 1862

Dr. H——said he saw a poor fellow sitting by the side of the street as he came by looking utterly worn out & he stopped & said, "my poor boy you oughtnt to be here. You ought to be with your mother." The poor fellow looked up & clapped his hands. "Oh," he said, "I do wish I was home. I don't know who or what you are sir, but I am a union man & I was forced into the army else I wouldnt have been here.["] I saw a wagon load of sick pass here up towards the hospital no 2. Kirby Smith packed up & went off about noon today to Mt Sterling, leaving Col Gracie in command. . . . About 6 ambulances passed this evening & one of the drivers said they were going to Mount Sterling. About 400 men with 4 or 5 cannon & several wagons went out the Winchester pike about 3 PM. Marshall's quartermaster took $700 worth of goods from Shropshires[1] today paying double price in script.

1. James H. Shropshire and John L. Cassell sold staples, dry goods, and cloth in their store on Main Street between Mill and Upper Streets. See *Williams' Lexington City Guide*, 99.

FRIDAY SEPT 26 [1862]

About 3 dray loads of the tents used at the fire were brought to the College lot to dry. We heard that the Louisville Democrat says . . . that Humphrey Marshall is "gobbled up." Whoever did it had a mouthful. . . . John says the secesh have taken possession of the mill again & they say Marshall is cut to pieces.

John Morgan is in town today & they say he admits he lost 150 men. One of the Cincinnati papers says that Bragg is marching towards Lexington. We heard too that our forces from Cynthiana were on the way to Winchester. Gen Smith said that he would be back in 4 days so they say. But of all the news we hear how much is true. Heaven only knows!

SATURDAY SEPT 27TH 1862

Pa received pay today for the wheat the rebels used at the mill. 8 wagon loads of sick & wounded came in the Georgetown road. One man died at Hospital No 2 today. They have been dying lately nearly every day. . . . Some of John Morgans men came in today. They had been stationed near Richmond. But the loyal men of the neighborhood "bushwhacked" & made the place too hot for them. They dont like that way of proceeding at all. An Alabama fellow who belonged to some guerilla company (Stonebys I think he said) or as he called them "Partisan Rangers," who had a long talk with Pa at the door about three weeks ago said that coming through the mountains they had been "bushwhacked" by the union people & once when five or six of their men had been killed in this way his company caught some of the offending parties. Pa asked what he did to them. "Why,["] said he, "we didn't go & shoot at them from behind a fence & murder them like they did our own men. We tied them to stakes and shot them like honorable men."

SUNDAY SEPT 28TH [1862]

Report says this morning that Kirby Smith has been whipped.[1] His body servant came back the same day they started because his horse gave out & told the person who told us that the general said to him "if I'm not back in a week, you had better get back to Virginia the best way you can." One or two of Bragg's officers were in town yesterday & Bragg himself is said to be at Bardstown.

A few days before Gen Smith left a deputation of secesh ladies, Mrs. Parker Craig, Mrs. Mitchell, the Misses Jackson & others, went to him & told him that "his lenient conduct to the union people was ruining them." We heard that the rebels had treated Mr. Isaac Scott[2] very badly. That they took some $1200 worth of jeans from him, besides refusing to let him sell any coal or even to fulfil engagements already made with his customers, but appropriated the whole.

We heard again this evening (& it generally believed) that Smith is retreating before Morgan & is expected here Tuesday. And some one sent word to Wm. Warfield to save his horses as they expected the rebels would take all they could get. . . . 8 PM Gen Smith has returned & headquarters is lighted up as if for a victory.

1. No engagement took place and General Kirby Smith failed in his attempt to block General George Morgan's retreat. See Connelly, *Army of the Heartland*, 237.
2. Forty-eight-year-old Isaac Scott was a prominent Lexington dry goods merchant. See Perrin, *History of Fayette County, Kentucky*, 712–13.

MONDAY SEPT 29TH [1862]

They say the alarm of fire the other night was at Fisher's Dye shop.[1] He had the overcoats the secesh took from our men to dye & I suppose on that account some one tried to set the place on fire. Bragg is at Perryville & S.B. Buckner is at Harrodsburg & Stevenson at Nicholasville.[2] They say Gen. Smith is going to move his headquarters to the last place & they were sending arms away from here as fast as they could yesterday. They pressed all the black men they could get, as teamsters & levied on Allen's[3] & on White[4] for about $10,000 worth of goods each. . . . Mr. Montell said that the rebel Gen Hunter was at his foundry this morning & heard some of the men complaining that they had got no wages. The Gen ordered them to hush instantly & that if at the end of the week he should hear anyone complain of not being paid or even say they were union, they would be bound hand & foot and sent south. . . . I hope it will not be long before the union troops whip these scamps here, for at the rate they are proceeding now they will strip us of every thing we have. Lexington is almost ruined now. . . . The secesh robbed a good many free Negroes today of blankets, etc. . . . There is a concert at Odd Fellows Hall tonight for the benefit the bills say of the "sick & wounded" & they say there was a guard put round the hall to prevent attempts to set it on fire. That looks like the Lexingtonians were glad to see the rebels, dont it!

The secesh have got a new dodge lately. Today when Buckner came, Bufords *brigade* (I should say not a 1000 men by far) escorted him in & nearly every man led a riderless horse & sometime three or four to make the people think there were more than there really was. Our ambulances returned from Richmond this evening & go tomorrow at 8 AM. They expect to return again a third time in about a week as some of our men at Richmond is not able to be moved yet.

1. The J. Fisher Dyeing and Tailoring Establishment stood on the east side of Broadway near Short Street. See *Williams' Lexington City Directory*, 49.
2. Simon Bolivar Buckner (1823–1914), a Kentucky native and West Point graduate, supported Kentucky's neutrality as commander of the State Guard before siding with the Confederacy. He commanded a division in Bragg's army. A Virginian and a West Point graduate, Carter L. Stevenson led a brigade in Kirby Smith's force. See Faust, ed., *Historical Times Illustrated Encyclopedia of the Civil War*, 88, 719.
3. The firm of Allen & Boyd sold dry goods and ready made clothing on the south side of Main Street and between Mill and Upper. See *Williams' Lexington City Directory*, 25.
4. Thomas W. White and Brother sold foreign and domestic dry goods. *See Williams' Lexington City Directory*, 91.

Tuesday Sept 30th [1862]

Our ambulances were detained this morning by Mr Buck Allen[1] having the wagon master Jackson arrested on charge of being a spy. They detained him at the provost office a long time & when Mr. Jamison (the late hospital steward) went down to see about his release they arrested him too, questioned him about the hospital stores & searched his pockets. When they found they couldnt get anything out of him they let him go. When he returned to the ambulance he was standing talking to a lady, when Dr Fox came up & said to Jamison "report yourself to headquarters immediately sir." Mr. Jamison replied "I have already do so sir & have been released." "Oh," replied Fox, "I beg your pardon ten thousand times. Is there anything I can do for you or the men?" & slunk away. . . . Someone who was at the concert last night told us it was the most shamefully low affair they had ever seen & they didn't see how ladies could have the face to listen to such obscenities ... The[y] arrested Mr Geo Hale[2] this evening & forced him to take an oath not to bear arms against the Confed & not to give information to the union forces & not to be exchanged or break his parole on pain of being shot. The charges against him were I believe that he had belonged to the home guards & wasnt willing to take script. . . .

1. Perhaps Miss Peter refers to B.E. Allen, a member of the Baptist clergy. See Eighth Census of the United States for Fayette County, 1860, Schedule 1, 476.
2. George B. Hale, a salesman, lived on the northwest corner of Main and Walnut Streets. See *Williams' Lexington City Directory*, 56.

WEDNESDAY OCT 1ST [1862]

About 11 AM a salute of 17 guns was fired to honor so they said the arrival of Gen Bragg. He didn't bring his army with him. They say his men are half naked & would have to be clothed before they could enter any city. . . . Gens Preston[1], Buckner & Bragg made speeches saying among other things to the farmers that they wouldnt be bothered with them long. That they were going to the lakes to feed their armies off of the Yankees, and praised the Kentuckians very much. . . . They had appointed 6 PM this day to shoot some 60 of the prisoners but did not for some cause or other carry out their intention. One of their men was shot today from some house on Water St. by whom could not be ascertained. . . . The Statesman suggests that an order be issued to search all kitchens, storerooms, & negro houses for government arms & stores. . . .

1. General William Preston (1816–1887) was born near Louisville and studied literature at Yale and law at Harvard. After service as lieutenant colonel with the 4th Kentucky Volunteers in the Mexican War, he embarked on a successful political career, first as a Whig and later as a proslavery Democrat. In 1858 Preston was appointed U.S. minister to Spain. In April 1862, he was appointed brigadier general and commanded troops in the Western theatre. Early in 1864 Confederate President Jefferson Davis named Preston Confederate diplomatic representative to Maximilian, emperor of Mexico. Preston later served under General Kirby Smith in the Trans-Mississippi Department. See Kleber, ed., *The Kentucky Encyclopedia*, 738–39; Peter J. Sehlinger, "William Preston, Kentucky's Diplomat of Lost Causes," in *Kentucky Profiles: Biographical Essays in Honor of Holman Hamilton*, eds. James C. Klotter and Sehlinger (Frankfort: Kentucky Historical Society, 1982), 73–98, and idem, "General William Preston: Kentucky's Last Cavalier Fights for Southern Independence," *Register of the Kentucky Historical Society* 93 (summer 1995): 257–85.

THURSDAY OCT 2ND [1862]

Last night Mrs. Castleman had all her out buildings, negro cabins, most of the farm implements & $1000 worth of lumber destroyed by fire. She is a secesh & that is the 5th fire since the rebels came. . . .

Bragg issued a proclamation giving the Kentuckians 4 or 5 days to rally to his standard & said that after that if he didnt have enough recruits the Conscript law should be enforced. . . .[1]

The rebels say they are going to take the capital, call a legislature & vote the state out of the Union. The provisional governor Rich. Hawes[2] left here for Frankfort yesterday. . . . John heard from his brother in law, who says he thinks we may expect Buell[3] Saturday night (he is with Buell) I hope he will come soon for we are all very tired of the southern Confederacy, and as the darkies say "we'd be monstrous glad to see Massa Buell," or Massa anybody else that would get us out of this fix. Fuel is very scarce, at least for the Union people. Coal sells for 75 ct the bushel & hardly to be got for love or money. The secesh are keeping it all for themselves. They say that for the last week 400 bush[els] have been delivered daily at Mrs. Morgans. . . .

1. General Braxton Bragg had expected thousands of Kentuckians to flock to his banner upon his entry into the state. When the recruits failed to appear, he suspected that loyal southerners feared the loss of their property to Kentucky Unionists. To protect them, Bragg sought to compel them, or rather to give them, an excuse to join the army by instituting a draft. See Connelly, *Army of the Heartland*, 241–45. See also Grady McWhiney, *Braxton Bragg and Confederate Defeat, Volume 1: Field Command* (New York: Columbia Univ. Press, 1969), 295–97.
2. The Provisional Government of Kentucky, which had its genesis in the Frankfort Peace Convention of September 1861, and "secession" meetings in October of that year, appointed George W. Johnston governor and Richard Hawes lieutenant governor. Hawes succeeded Johnston upon the governor's death at the battle of Shiloh. See E. Merton Coulter, *The Civil War and Readjustment in Kentucky* (Chapel Hill: Univ. of North Carolina Press, 1926), 137–38, and McWhiney, *Braxton Bragg and Confederate Defeat, Volume 1*, 297.
3. Buell's arrival at the battle of Shiloh, April 6–7, 1862, helped stave off Union defeat. His cautious response to the Confederate invasion of Kentucky and his failure to pursue the enemy after the battle of Perryville led to his removal from command. See Faust, ed., *Historical Times Illustrated Encyclopedia of the Civil War*, 88, and James Lee McDonough, *War in Kentucky: From Shiloh to Perryville* (Knoxville: Univ. of Tennessee Press, 1994), 223–226.

FRIDAY OCT 3RD [1862]

. . . A Mr Harcourt[1] [?] was imprisoned the other day an kept in that dirty jail two days & nights. They told him that he had been arrested because they heard his daughter had waved a flag at the union ambulances. That is only one out of a great many arrests that have been made lately. An order was issued to the shopkeepers not to sell anything until the rebels had got what they wanted. So all today they were going the rounds of the stores helping themselves.

Humphrey Marshall was in town today & I suppose that order was partly for his benefit. . . .

Gen Smith has always seemed to be a peaceable person who wouldnt take the trouble to annoy other people, so long as they didnt interfere with him. And most of the things he has done to the Union people have been at the instigation of resident secesh who are much more bitter than the rebel soldiers. . . . A man was drummed out of one of the regiments this evening for what I don't know. They say 500 have deserted since they came here. The troops at Georgetown received marching orders today for Frankfort. The Governor is to be inaugurated tomorrow & the rebels say they are going to have 30,000 men there to witness it.

50 sick came from Frankfort today. As they were on their way to hospital no 2, one of them dropped down on the steps of one of our neighbors. The lady of the house seeing him drop down as if about to faint came to the door with some water and had a long talk with him. Among other things he said they were from Frankfort. That the people there were all union. They wouldnt give them (the rebels) anything to eat if they could possibly avoid it. . . .

The secesh released the prisoners at the jail today on parole. They say they had been paroled before, but were stopped by the secesh & brought back. All the time they were in jail the rebels never pretended to give them anything to eat & if it hadn't been for some of the union ladies sending them things they most likely would have starved.

A guard was posted all over town tonight . . . this is the first night there has been a sentinel on our corner. They say they are going to send away the women who have been staying with our sick as nurses & washer-women. When the secesh came these women would not leave the men, but stayed & worked for them just the same as if they still got wages & when the rebels took hospital no 2 & our men had no one to cook for them these women did that too. If the rebels send them away the poor fellows will be left entirely dependant on the ladies of the town & the one or two regimental nurses who still remain. . . .

1. R. Harcourt, a Lexington grocer, had two daughters, M.L., twenty-two, and S.W., twenty. See Eighth Census of the United States for Fayette County, 1860, Schedule 1, 564.

SATURDAY OCT 4TH [1862]

Some of the union ladies who were at the hospital no 2 today as usual taking things to our sick said the secesh begged them to give them some too. The ladies asked if the secesh ladies didnt send things up there. "No" they said "they have stopped sending." So the ladies gave them what was left after the union soldiers were fed. The secesh ladies like very well to flirt with the officers but they dont take any notice of the common men. Poor wretches! The Confederacy hasn't done much for them! A great many of the secesh soldiers . . . wear the clothes that were found at the quartermasters & the hospitals when our own men left. The union ladies teased them every where they went, about the "Lincoln breeches" & wearing the "livery of Lincoln's hirelings" (as the secesh used to call our soldiers uniforms) and would pretend sometimes to think they were our men and ask them if they had been paroled & when they were going to be exchanged. One day when a lady had teased one in this way he turned to her & said, Ma'am if you knew how much these pants cost us you wouldnt call them "Lincoln breeches" for we didnt get them for nothing. We had to pay $5 a pair to the quartermaster & so we have a good right to them. A good many of them have had black stripes put down the sides.

We heard that Crittenden[1] had said he would be at Frankfort with 40,000 men today to witness the inauguration of the provisional governor. About 5 o'clock Mrs. Curds servant told us that a messenger brought a letter to headquarters saying Kirby Smith had been whipped at Frankfort. I hope it is true. . . . Pa also heard it downtown. We heard that an order had been sent to the secesh ladies to be ready for first they said 200 & then 1000 wounded, and that R. Scott had sent to Mrs. Morgan not to come to Frankfort as she had intended. . . .

John Morgan came in about 5 or 6 oclock this evening with about 60 of his advance guard & put up in the College lot. They seemed to be mostly the raw recruits that have joined since he came here. About the same time John came up to see Pa with a wagon load of oats. The guerillas saw it & came over to get it for their horses. John wasnt very willing to give it up as he had had some trouble getting it and wanted it for his own horses. But the officer who came over said he must have it and offered to pay $5 in "Lincoln money" double price. He did so & also let John take enough of it to feed his horse. . . .

1. George Bibb Crittenden (1812–1880) graduated from the U.S. Military Academy (1832) and fought in the Mexican War. Appointed a brigadier general in the Con-

federate army in 1861, he lost the battle of Mill Spring in January 1862. Though exonerated for his part in the defeat, Crittenden resigned his commission in October 1862 and served the rest of the war as a colonel. See Kleber, ed., *The Kentucky Encyclopedia*, 240.

SUNDAY OCT 5TH 1862

The guerillas left this morning about 4 oclock, all but about a dozen. The secesh are packing up at their camp & about 40 were sent from Hospital No 2 to their regiments. They say our men have Frankfort & the rebels are going to make a stand at Laurenceburg. . . .

At 10 AM Humphrey Marshalls army came in the Paris road & passed right through to join Bragg & Smith. There were only about 2000 men, 8 or 10 cannon with caisons, 150 wagons with 2 U.S. ambulances, & 3 old fashioned Virginia stages full of men. A good many of the wagons had men in them too. Falstaffs "ragged regiment" was nothing in comparison with these, and they marched very slowly as if they had come some distance. It took more than an hour for them to pass a given place. They had also a large drove of horses & mules with them. The union people are afraid the secesh will run a good many negroes off when they go.

They say that while the rebels were inaugurating the governor a shell came & cut the rebel flag all to pieces. . . .

2 PM The secesh are packing up as hard as they can. Good many of the rebel citizens too, getting ready to skedaddle . . . All day they have been sending away every man from the hospital that could possibly go & taking away or destroying stores. Wagons & carriages have been driving about. All the baggage remaining at headquarters sent off & officers getting ready to go as soon as they can. They say they are going to send the sick & all the stores they can carry off to Harrodsburg. 18 horses, two wagons & 2 servants were stolen from Mr Aleck Brand. The rebels tried to set the depot on fire, but did not succeed. . . . Mrs. Morgan & various others are getting ready to leave. The secesh are taking up negroes tonight & putting them in jail, to be ready to take with them tomorrow when they leave. They arrest all the negro men they meet in the streets & even go to private houses & take them . . . mostly from the secesh as they would be confiscated when the union troops come in, and they think to save them by running them off south where their masters can join them. . . .

[THE FOLLOWING ACCOUNT IN FRANCES PETER'S
HANDWRITING WAS NOT INCLUDED AS PART OF HER DIARY.
IT WAS WRITTEN AFTER OCTOBER 5, 1862, THE DATE
INDICATED IN HER DIARY THAT HUMPHREY MARSHALL'S
TROOPS ENTERED LEXINGTON.]

The entrance of Humphrey Marshall's "brigade" as the secesh grandly styled it, or regiment as we would say (for it consisted altogether of about as many men as would form a regiment or two of ours. And the portion of it that entered the city could not have been one thousand men. I say portion because the whole brigade did not come in on the day of which I speak.) This entrie of Marshall's men in to Lexington was a spectacle such as the Lexingtonians had never seen before and would not care to see again. One could hardly say whether it was most ludicrous or pitiful. The long train of ricketty wagons, the antiquated, yellow Richmond Va. stage coaches which had been dragged from their shelves where they had been laid up, certainly not in lavender, for length of years and brought out once more into the light of day much against their will to judge from the creaking and groaning of their rusty wheels, to deck the baggage train of the fat General in his weary march through Kentucky and serve as ambulances for his sick and wounded. The poor, dirty, ragged, barefooted, or almost barefooted men (for very few could boast a decent pair of shoes, though these were the best dressed of his brigade) with their downcast looks and shuffling gait, straggling along like a flock of sheep, and every now and then raising not a good hearty hurrah, but a yelp like that of a pack of whipped hounds.

One could hardly help laughing and yet it was a pitiful sight in one point of view, for what true American with that pride of country and countrymen which is inborn in Americans could not feel sad and ashamed to see Americans in such a state of wretchedness and degradation even though brought to it by their own folly and ignorance. By ignorance, for the slaves who worked the plantations of Dixie could not be more ignorant of the most common learning, than were the greater part of the common soldiers of the rebel army that occupied Lexington (which was no doubt only a sample of all the rest of the confederate armies) every one of whom considered himself as fitted to be a dictator to the rest of mankind. We had heard much before of the ignorance of the Southern people but never believed until we saw for ourselves that it could be so great, but we no longer wondered that a few designing men could gain such influence over the South and be able to array so many thousands against the Union of their fathers. How could unlettered men judge of the right or wrong of such a question as was put to them by these politicians? How could men who had never read the Constitution or heard it read by a faithful interpreter know whether what they did was constitutional or not?

Accustomed to place implicit confidence in their politicians and statesmen and to depend on them in all political matters, how could they tell if what they represented to them as constitutional was not true? And what would be easier than to deceive such a people? It was too tempting a bait for politicians to withstand and as soon as possible they tried to turn it to their selfish interests. And yet so artfully did they go to work and so speciously did they talk that they, poor deluded people, believed it was all their own action and rubbed their hands joyously over the great plan they thought they had hit upon for restoring the constitution which had never been so nearly destroyed, or so terribly violated as by this very act of secession they were so jubilant over, as being such a great stroke of policy.

And these people willingly arrayed themselves against their own fellow countrymen, and shed their own blood in an unjust cause, and all because they had been led by bad men to believe they were fighting to prevent usurpation and tyranny.

And then to think of the long march of Marshall's men over the mountains to get into Ky. How, barefooted and ragged they scrambled through the rocks and brambles, with no food but the green corn standing in the fields, "mutton corn" as they called it. And no resting place at night but the bare ground. No shelter from the frost and cold air of the nights which have lately been chilly, but a scanty blanket or an old overcoat that they had taken from some of our soldiers, and often not even that, and that when they arrived here, a greater part of them had not even rags enough to be able to enter the town but had to remain without the city until clothes could be procured for them.

If these sufferings had been endured in a good cause they would have been worthy of unbounded praise and commiseration but when we think that they were endured only to bring misery and death to the homes of citizens loyal to the Union, one can only feel indignation and horror for the vile men who could so delude a people as to make them think that they were thereby releasing Ky from bondage, and pity for the deplorable ignorance of a people that could be so deluded. For these poor common soldiers firmly believed they were conferring a great favor in driving the Federal troops from among us and were no doubt both surprised and disappointed that we did not treat them with more consideration and attention.

MONDAY OCT 6TH [1862]

. . . John Morgan has command here now. He made the people open the shops again today but we heard they were not taking script. There has been a great bustle and a great deal of galloping about & traveling of wagons, etc. About 250 head of cattle were brought in today. We have heard random musket shots all day today. They say the report of the union forces coming here was merely a feint on the part of Buell to capture the whole of Braggs army.

TUESDAY OCT 7TH 1862

. . . This evening several guerillas went to Mr Gratz's & asked for hay to feed their horses. There was no one at home but Miriam (Mr G.s oldest daughter) & the servants. She told them that they had an order from J. Morgan for the protection of their property; but the fellows said their horses were famishing & as they were already in the stable proceeding to help themselves, Miss Gratz had to surrender with the best grace she could.

Some three or four others came a short while afterward and made the servant tell them when supper would be ready. And at Mr. Gratz's supper hour they came stalking in & Mr. G had to take them into the dining room & sit them down to his table. The guerillas & southern chivalry in general are very different from the Union soldiers. The latter will sit down anywhere you tell them, & are not affronted if you bring them something to the door, but always seem thankful & say it is too good for them. But the chivalry expect to be taken into the best parlor & have everybody in the house waiting on them no matter how dirty & slovenly they may be and even then will hardly think you did enough for them. For our part we never would let one put his foot inside the house & tell them if they come & take away every thing we have they oughtnt to expect us to feed them. . . . There is another point of difference between the north & south. The northern men if they can't get anyone to wash for them will do it them-selves. But the chivalry expect to have a 'nigger' to do everything & if they can't get one will do without washing & every thing else rather than help themselves. . . .

. . . we saw a light on the lower end of town towards Main St. which we thought must be the rebels burning the stores which they had taken out of the depot & piled in the Branch.[1] . . . A large wagon load of things was sent from Mrs. Morgans about 8 or 9 P.M. I think the whole family will go soon. About the same time a few of Morgans men from the College lot set off, I suppose on scouting duty on some of the roads; for I heard the officer say "fall·in scouts, we rendezvous at the Phoenix hotel". . . .

1. Lexington was settled on the Town Fork of the Elkhorn River. See Perrin, *History of Fayette County, Kentucky*, 219.

WEDNESDAY OCT 8TH 1862

A few days ago the ceiling of Mrs Morgan's parlor fell down breaking the mirrors, picture frames, etc. The ladies were much alarmed & thought it a very bad omen, as there was apparently no cause for it, as the plaster was not cracking. . . . The fire we thought was stores, was only a barn on the edge of town. . . . A great many secesh left today taking their negroes. Reported fighting at Perryville yesterday & last night. . . .[1]

1. Converging Federal and Confederate armies met at Perryville, southwest of Lexington, and fought to a draw. Bragg withdrew his troops during the night. See McDonough, *War in Kentucky*, 297–325.

THURSDAY OCT 9TH [1862]

. . . The rebels were scouring the country yesterday taking all the two horse wagons & negroes they could lay hands on. We heard they went to Mr Tom Clay's[1] & demanded his wagon & horses & a man to drive. There was no one at home but Mrs. Clay & the servants. The rebels were told they should have what they wanted. The man servant was sent to harness the horses but when all was ready he jumped into the wagon & drove off as fast as he could. The rebels fired at him, but missed & the man made his escape. . . .

We got the Cincinnati papers of Monday. . . . Mr. Jamison told Pa it was true about Crittenden throwing the shell during the inauguration of the rebel governor.[2] And that our troops did drive the rebels out of Frankfort & march into the town; but they only did this to deceive them & make them think they were coming right on to Lexington, when in fact they turned round & marched toward Harrodsburg. They succeeded pretty well in their designs for the rebels have actually thought they were coming here by way of Versailles (& so did the union people for a while) & got ready to leave. The rebels were pretty well scared for a little while. . . .

If the rebels knew we had had northern papers today wouldnt we pay for it!

They sent Mr. Patterson word again today to move out of his house.

Mr. P. went down to see the officer about it. Told him he was a British subject & would complain to the consul. But the officer persisted & told him if he wasnt out in three hours he would have him put out at the point of a bayonet. That was extremely short notice. Mr. Isaac Scott gave Mr. P a place to put his furniture but the difficulty was to get it moved as every dray & wagon in town was in the service of the rebels.

I saw a stage & spring wagon full of sick taken to hospital No 2 this morning. They say the rebels at the hospital are very badly attended to, though hundreds of dollars worth of provisions are stolen every day. Yet the poor fellows are some times nearly starved. They say men desert all the time.

Pa was telling us today a funny story of Mr. Davy Sayre.[3] Before the secesh came he was a very strong union man (and is now at heart I have no doubt) but when they took possession here he got so scared or was so afraid of losing his property that he declared himself a secesh. He used to pay a visit to headquarters nearly every day & always took the newspaper there when he had any. One day Col. Gracie was talking to him about Pa & remarked he thought him a dangerous man. "No, no,["] lisped Uncle Davy. "Heth not at all dantherous. Heth very quiet, very quiet. Heth the moth quiet and inefficienth man in town." I suppose he meant to say innocent. . . .

The rebel officers at the Phoenix when packing up told their wives not to stop to pack large trunks as they couldnt wait for much baggage. So Col. Worley told Pa this evening . . .

Mrs Martin told us the secesh had come after their two horse wagon when there was such a push for wagons a few days ago. Her husband had disabled it & they told the secesh that it couldnt be used & would take a good while to repair it. They not being inclined to wait for repairs went off & a few days after Mr. Martin mended the wagon & went into the country after wood. While it was gone a secesh officer came and asked Mrs Martin for the wagon. She told him it was in the country & he went away. Emboldened by their success they sent the wagon out the next day also & again the officer came after it just as it had turned the corner. Mrs Martin told him it was in the country & fortunately the rebel did not ask the road, being perhaps in too great a hurry. But next evening just as the wagon stopped at the door several rebels came up & seized on it & wanted to take it away. Mrs Martin told them her husband was a cripple & the wagon was his only way of making a living but they wouldnt listen to her. So pulling out a small pistol which she had got from her husband, she got into the wagon by the secesh & determined to make one attempt to keep it. "I can only shoot once" said she, "but I intend to do it & you can kill me afterward if you like. I will try on one of you first." She pointed the pistol at one of them & they seeing she was in earnest, jumped out of the wagon & skedaddled. But when they got to the next corner stopped & cursed & swore at her for everything they could think of. Of course she cared very little for that as they had left her the wagon & never came back for it again.

1. Thomas Clay was a fifty-six-year-old Fayette County farmer. See Eighth Census of the United States for Fayette County, 1860, Schedule 1, 506.
2. Actually, General Joshua Sill's division of Buell's army crossed the Kentucky River and bombarded Frankfort during the inauguration. Crittenden's division was on the road to Danville. See Connelly, *Army of the Heartland*, 251–52.
3. Penniless when he arrived in Lexington from New Jersey in 1811, David A. Sayre amassed a fortune in banking. The land and buildings for the Sayre Female Institute were donated by Mr. Sayre in 1854. See Ranck, *History of Lexington*, 405, and Kleber, ed., *The Kentucky Encyclopedia*, 799.

FRIDAY OCT 10TH 1862

. . . Mrs Curds servant said that the rebel officer who has been staying at their house got an order from Kirby Smith to come away from here as the place would be evacuated, but the poor fellow was too sick to go, I believe, & Mrs. Griggs[1] & my Sister Lettie sent him word to stay. That our men wouldnt trouble him in the least. I dont know whether he will stay or not. The secesh took possession of the Sayre Institute[2] this morning. I think they might have left it alone now after waiting all this time. It look[s] rather spiteful to take it just when they dont expect to stay here long & dont know whether they will have any use for it.

They say there is not much more than a corporals guard of rebel soldiers in town this morning. The secesh wear very long faces. The soldiers told the secesh ladies they were only going a little way to whip a few yankees & would be back soon. They hadnt the least idea of evacuating the town, not they! We will see . . .

Mr. J. Elliott dismissed his clerks this evening & wants to get union ones. When the secesh came he had mostly, if not all Union, but he sent them away & got secesh. And now that he hears the Union troops are coming he wants to change again.

About 6 PM we heard that the secesh major Thomas went in great haste to Mr. Watson[3] (one of the clerks in Shropshires store) about some business or other & told Watson that he (Thomas) would have to be off. That our men were at Versailles & that our cavalry would be here tonight. . . . Thomas is quartermaster. Watson said it was amusing to see the way the secesh were skedaddling this evening, catching up any old horse or mule or seizing on any conveyance that was convenient. . . .

1. She may be referring to Mrs. Margaret Griggs, twenty-eight, wife of John Griggs. See Eighth Census of the United States for Fayette County, 1860, Schedule 1, 319.
2. Sayre Institute was founded in 1854 as a private school for females. See Kleber, ed., *The Kentucky Encyclopedia*, 799.
3. William Watson, twenty-six, appeared in the 1860 Census as a laborer. See Eighth Census of the United States for Fayette County, 1860, Schedule 1, 302.

SATURDAY OCT 11TH [1862]

. . . The hospitals are pretty full. There dont seem to have been any arrangements made for removing the sick. It seems they want all their wagons to put their stolen goods in, for even as late as yesterday evening

Shown here as it appeared in April 1866, the Sayre Female Institute was founded in 1854. (Transylvania University Library)

the Provost Marshall made them keep the stores open. . . . The secesh say they are going to Knoxville to try to get out of the state that way.

Pa sent to the mill for Mr. Hoover to set to work & grind night & day. That he thought as he had done it for the secesh he could do it for him. For the neighbors threatened to mob the mill because Pa had stopped it. The secesh when they had possession used up all the wood & Pa wouldnt buy any more for fear they would come back & so he would lose it. . . .

4 PM Pa came from down town & says the secesh sent the Mayor word that they were certainly all going tonight & wanted him to have out a citizen police to guard the town from stragglers. I believe there will be a meeting held for the purpose at 7 o clock. . . . About 6 PM some 400 prisoners were brought in & lodged in the court house. They were mostly or all stragglers taken on the different roads & teamsters of a wagon train which the secesh captured. They were paroled & I suppose will start tomorrow for Cincinnati. They say the guard treated them very well until near the place when they took away all their blankets & every cent of pocket money they happened to have. Three wounded men were also brought in at the same time to the hospital no 2 (or rather to the part of the Dormitory that our men occupy). . . .

The citizens went at 7 oclock to the meeting at the Phoenix hotel[1] (as the secesh hold the court house) but the secesh sent them word "that a sufficient military force had arrived tonight to guard the town & the citizens neednt trouble themselves."

1. A Lexington landmark, the Phoenix Hotel stood at the corner of Main and Limestone Streets. See Kleber, ed., *The Kentucky Encyclopedia*, 719–20.

SUNDAY OCT 12 [1862]

. . . The reason the secesh asked for a citizen guard last night was that some of them were afraid the negroes would set the town on fire. I don't believe the rebs had any force here last night, or if they did they went away before morning, for this morning there were only 10 or 12 at the courthouse & they had their horses ready saddled as if about to go. . . .

I saw one of the waiters from Phoenix hotel this evening. He says that when the rebels first came they wanted Col Worley to take down the union flag that was on the hotel. The Col told them they had the power. They could go & take it down themselves if they wanted to, but nothing could make him do it. That he would "die in torments" before he would lower that flag. So they got some one else to take it down & even then the Col threatened them so that they did not destroy the flag, but allowed him to keep it. (Only tell this, as Col Worley has always been thought to be rather "weak kneed" & though it is from a black man, I want to see if it will prove correct that the Col is strong union). He also said that last night . . . After supper the secesh called for whiskey. The Col refused at first telling them he had been ordered not to sell any to secesh soldiers. But they would have it & more than that it must be bottled, & they wouldnt pay near the value even in script. & as soon as they had emptied the bottles threw them out of the windows. In short they went on in such a manner that the Col did not know what they might do next & ordered all the servants except a few who had to wait on them, to keep out of their way. . . . John Dudley was riding about today with a sword in one hand & a pistol in the other followed by some others, stealing all the wagons & horses they could find. . . .

Monday Oct 13th [1862]

. . . Our neighbor Mr Hardesty[1] (secesh) sent off some of his family this morning. Miss Hardesty on a horse & Mrs. Hardesty with the baby & another of the young ladies riding in a cart . . . The secesh are driving their sick out of the hospitals today telling them to "make their way to Knoxville the best way they can". . . .

. . . I heard a little incident to day that shows very plainly the cowardice of the rebels. A small party of them went to a place a few miles from town, for the purpose of horse stealing & told the overseer to show them where the horses were. This the man agreed to do if they would let him take his rifle with him. When they came to the lot the horses were in 'There they are' said the overseer, 'you can help yourselves, but the first man that gets down from his saddle will have a hole made through him' and although there were four or five to one they turned tail and galloped off, without making the least attempt to get any of the horses. . . .

1. Forty-two-year-old Henry Hardesty, a soap and candle manufacurer, lived with his wife and seven children near the Peter family. See Eighth Census of the United States for Fayette County, 1860, Schedule 1, 599.

Tuesday Oct 14th 1862

The rebels took down all their flags about 9 last night.[1] 8 AM the rebels are all gone they say & several union flags raised. Before they went Mr Charley Polk[2] & several other young men went to the Phoenix hotel to look around. While they were walking about there looking at the register & amusing themselves a party of rebels came up & ordered them to leave the hotel. Mr P. told them he would when he was ready & not until & didnt go till he was ready. Then he went to Beards stable where a number of union men were assembled. In [the] meantime this same party of rebels went to Mr. McCrackens stable[3] & began stealing horses. Their Captain found them out & called out for some one to arrest them. The Union men came & took two or three of them & found among the stolen horses, the rebel captains horse, which his own men had stolen. The rest of the gang ran down a back street where they had two or three horses ready saddled & bridled but the Union men took two of the horses. The rebel captain was so angry at their stealing his horse that he gave the men entirely into the power of the Union men to be punished for the theft. & so they were put in jail till they could be sent to Frankfort to the penitentiary. . . . They are going to put our sick in the session room near the Episcopal church.[4] Mr. Jameson has taken possession of the hospitals & is preparing to have them cleaned. . . .

The standing joke of the day is this. "Beau" Barkley as he is called, who within the last two years married to one of Mr. Alex Brands daughters, the other day took a notion to visit Camp Dick.[5] So he borrowed a horse & two servants from his father-in-law & set off. Every thing went well & he made his journey in safety but when about starting to return, his horse & servants were not to be found. Accordingly he bought a fine horse from one of the rebels & came home. On his arrival he found that the servants had come back before him with the horses. The fun of the thing was that the horse he had bought turned out to be the very one that had been stolen from Mr. Dudley Craig a few weeks ago, & that gentleman saw it & claimed it, & it had to be returned to him.

We heard that one or two rebels took down one of the Union flags (belonged to a Mr. Harris, I think) & dragged it about at the horses tails. Nothing was done by the Union men for they say that there was a company of Bufords men who had stopped just outside town & it was thought they only wanted some pretext to do mischief. . . .

A woman told us she had seen some of our men in town today & they said some of our cavalry would be in tonight. I will believe that when I see it. We hear reports like that every day. Mrs. Morgan said "the Union people had better not be putting up flags so soon. John Morgan will be in tonight with 1500 men." Mrs. Duke wanted her to go away from here with her but she refused & said (so they say) that the Union people might take every brick in the house away but she wouldnt leave. About 20 stragglers (rebels) came in tonight & made them get supper for them at the Phoenix.

The secesh told Messr. Fitch, Harrison & John Wilson[6] to go to the hospital & take medical stores enough to pay them for what had been bought of them by the rebel doctors as they reckoned they hadnt been payed & wouldnt be. So they might take the things back. It is likely the secesh dont intend to return the same things taken from the druggists but to pass on them the stores left by our men at the hospitals. Our sick were all moved to the session rooms this evening. The women nurses (some of them) are still allowed to wait on them.

1. Following the battle of Perryville, Federal troops reoccupied Lexington on October 16, 1862. See Perrin, *History of Fayette County, Kentucky*, 462.
2. Charles E. Polk made watches and jewelry in Lexington. See *Williams' Lexington City Guide*, 91, and *Williams' Lexington City Directory*, 78.
3. William McCracken's stable was on the north side of Short between Walnut and Mulberry Streets. See *Williams' Lexington City Directory*, 68.
4. Commonly referred to as Christ Church, located in the northeast corner of Church and Market Streets. See *Williams' Lexington City Directory*, 16.
5. During Kentucky's neutrality crisis, Unionists began to organize troops in camps of instruction. Camp Dick Robinson, twenty-six miles south of Lexington, was the largest. See Kleber, ed., *The Kentucky Encyclopedia*, 157–58.
6. Frank and Fred Fitch, T.J. Harrison, and John S. Wilson operated drug and apothecary shops in Lexington. See *Williams' Lexington City Directory*, 49, 57, 92.

WEDNESDAY OCT 15TH [1862]

. . . Mrs. Williams[1] related an incident to us which shows the state in which the rebels were sent from the hospital a few days ago when they were hurr[y]ing them off so. Mr. Vorhees saw one of the poor fellows stop & sit down at his door & he came out & asked him what was the matter. "I'm sick" said the man. "Where are you from?" "The hospital." Why you are certainly not discharged. It is not customary to discharge men until they are cured. I'm not cured, thats certain, but they told me to go. "Go, go where." "I dont know" said the poor fellow sadly, "they told me to go to the devil." We heard that a good many of the poor fellows who were sent out so weak they could hardly stand, died in the streets. . . . A good many of the sick didn't want to leave at all & some of them shut themselves up in a room & refused to let any one come in. A squad of men were sent to force them, but they wouldnt be forced & persisted until they carried their point & were allowed to stay. They broke up the guns at hospital no 1 today & also the new stoves which our doctors had had to send to Cincinnati to get. . . .

We heard that John Morgan & Bragg had quarreled. Bragg wanted to dismount Morgans men for 60 days & let them serve as infantry. Morgan refused & withdrew his command from the army & is now acting "on his own hook."[2] John Morgan it seems isn't fond of putting himself in the post of danger. A lady stopped a rebel & pretending to be a secesh made a good many inquiries of him. Among other things she remarked that J. Morgan was a brave man. "A brave man" said the rebel "he's the greatest coward I know. When his division is on a march he doesnt lead his men like other officers do. He rides behind in an ambulance." I have heard some ladies say they had seen him do it. That he rode in one the last time his men left here.

There is a story afloat that for the last few weeks back a wounded man has been staying at Mrs. Morgans about whom there was a great deal of mystery. That when even the doctor came to dress his wound the patients face was always covered & he never spoke, which made people think it must be some great man. Monday night when Mrs. Duke left an ambulance followed her from Mrs. Morgans which was supposed to contain this person. But all this may be "much ado about nothing" for anything I know. . . .

1. Possibly Mrs. S.R. Williams, principal of the Sayre Female Institute, which was used as a hospital. See *Williams' Lexington City Directory*, 92.
2. Basil W. Duke, Thomas Connelly, and Grady McWhiney mention such a dispute. Morgan began his Second Kentucky Raid on October 17. See Duke, *History of Morgan's Cavalry*, 280–81.

THURSDAY OCT 16 [1862]

. . . I heard a very rich story on Col. Wm Hart this evening. When the rebels were all through the country some of them went to his house in Woodford Co. & asked for something to eat. "Havent got a thing in the house. I'm as poor as Jobs turkey, havent got a thing to give you," said the Col. So the men went on to the house of a poor widow who lived near & she gave them something. While there they saw two large wagon loads of bacon pass & asked the driver who they belonged to. "To Col. Hart." "Then" said the secesh "we'll have to confiscate them for the use of the confederate government." Again not long ago a body of federals went to his house & asked if he had any government property on his place. "No indeed" he said "he hadnt a single thing." (Now when the rebels took possession of Lex. he had come up here & taken off a good many things). The soldiers said they would have to search & in the garret they found 1000 pounds of bacon, several hundred barrels of flour, tents, clothing & 6000 rounds of ammunition. "Well" said they "you deceived us about the stores now we will have to look if you havent got some government stock." And sure enough they found several mules marked U.S.. So Col Hart was sent to Frankfort to be tried, but Gen. Dumont[1] thought it was more a civil than a military affair & gave him over to the authorities who made him give bail to a large amount. . . .

It seems that there is a body of our cavalry camped on Suttons farm. . . . Some gentlemen rode out to see them. We heard Col. Worley went & came back perfectly intoxicated with delight & perhaps with something else, for he treated the ladies & gentlemen at his hotel all round & then brought his horse (which is a beautiful creature & a great pet of his) into the barroom & treated it also. . . .

1. General Ebenezer Dumont (1814–1871), a lawyer, politician, and Mexican War veteran from Indiana, commanded the 12th Division in the Army of the Ohio. See Warner, *Generals in Blue*, 132–33.

FRIDAY OCT 17TH [1862]

. . . Davy Sayre said that while Col Gracie was here he saw a black book that he (Col Gracie) kept in which were marked down the names of everybody, whether they were union or secesh, & what they had been doing for the last 9 months back against the Confederacy & even the division in families.

We all were saying one day that the meanest man in town ought to take down the rebel flags when they went away & all of us decided that Jack Keiser was the man. And sure enough the other night when the secesh left they paid Keiser to take their flags down for them. . . .

12 AM some cavalry came in, some of our men . . . Mr. Henry Duncans[1] black boy went by late this evening grinning from ear to ear & told us his "master" had come home.

1. Mr. Henry Duncan Sr. lived at the northeast corner of Mulberry and Winchester Streets. His son, Henry Jr., was a neighbor of the Peter family on Market Street. See *Williams' Lexington City Directory*, 45.

SATURDAY OCT 18TH 1862

About daybreak some 1500 of Morgans guerilla came galloping in & they surprised our men who were camped at James Clays,[1] & a fight took place in which we had six wounded & two killed as far as I can learn. Our men then fell back to the Courthouse intending to make a stand there & shut themselves up in it, but Col. Worley sent them word the rebels were going to shell the place . . . and at last our men surrendered, for what could 400 do against 1500 with artillery as they thought they had. If our men hadnt been surprised they might perhaps have done better but they had been in the saddle 50 days & were worn out. They placed pickets on all the roads & even sat up all night, but towards morning everything being quiet & no enemy in sight, they went to sleep, still leaving pickets out. The rebels didnt come by the roads but sneaked in across fields & by paths around the pickets & so surprised them. It was foolish to send such a small force here. A good many people think it was Worleys fault. That night he was drunk & took his horse in the barroom he sent a courier with dispatches to Louisville saying Kirby Smith had surrendered & that Lexington was in the possession of the Federals when there were no federal soldiers here outside the hospital & then fined himself $10 & paid it. The rebels took down the fine flags belonging to Col. Worley & Mr. Fitch. I don't know what they did with Worleys, but Fitch's was saved in this way. Miss Ella Bishop was standing by when they took it down & she asked them to give it to her. They thought she was a secesh & did so & she started to go home. Some one called to the rebels & told them she was Union so they sent a squad of men to her house to get the flag but she wouldnt give it up.

A great many citizens who came home yesterday had to go again today. Mr. H. Duncan escaped in safety. The secesh were hunting everywhere for Capts. Postlethwaite & Wilgus threatening to hang them if they caught them.

I don't know how many of the rebels were killed or wounded. Nash Morgan and another were brought to Mrs. Morgans. The other was moved somewhere else but Nash Morgan was so badly wounded in the neck that he couldn't be moved & Dr Bush says he cant live. I think the rebels lost more than they gained for Nash Morgan is one of their best officers & always takes the lead & is not a coward like John.

Two of our soldiers came here about 12 AM. They had their side arms & wanted Pa to take them, but he told them he couldnt as he was under parole himself. So Ma took them & concealed them. The men came back afterward to get them among others. . . . They said the rebels hardly took time to parole them right & treated them just like dogs. Took all their things away from them & even struck & shot at some after they had surrendered. . . .

Old Jack Keiser was boasting today that he knew last evening the rebels were coming, & no doubt a good many secesh knew it. They say some of Morgans men were in town yesterday disguised & with federal uniforms on. . . . Tom Major was in town when our men came in yesterday & shortly after left & was back again today. It is thought he was acting as a spy. The secesh ladies are in high glee but the gentlemen dont seem to be much more delighted to see Morgan than the Union people. . . .

Col. Worleys brother who is one of Morgans men[2] was at the hotel yesterday sick they say. Worley made a speech yesterday when his flag was put up & said "he had no words to express his gratitude at seeing that flag up again & that if a shred of it should be hurt he hoped his life might lay low." And today he was over at Mrs. Morgans as large as life, talking away. I dont know how people can be such double dealers. Mr. Davy Sayre too stopped John Morgan on the street & shook hands as if he was delighted to see him. Rebels didn't stay long. They were all gone at 4½ PM. We also heard that when the rebels passed along Broadway they were fired upon from the houses.

1. Colonel Basil Duke's 2nd Kentucky Cavalry attacked the 4th Ohio Cavalry, encamped at Ashland (the Clay estate). Morgan remained in Lexington for the day before leaving for Versailles to the south. See Duke, *History of Morgan's Cavalry*, 283–87.
2. Colonel Worley's brother may have been either James W. Worley of the 2nd Kentucky Cavalry, or J.T. Worley of the 7th Kentucky Cavalry. See Janet B. Hewett, ed., *The Roster of Confederate Soldiers: 1861–1865* (Wilmington, North Carolina: Broadfoot Publishing Company, 1996), 16:502.

Sunday Oct 19th [1862]

. . . Capt Ferrie was taken prisoner. The story goes that when he reported himself to Mrs Morgans they were all at breakfast & John . . . told him he didn't intend to parole him, but to take him south with him.

Capt Ferrie replied he might do what he liked; kill him if he chose, but for every drop of his blood there would be a thousand shed in Lexington. Mrs Morgan became alarmed & begged John to let him go, which he did at last.

The guerillas left by the Versailles road, & there is a report today that Morgan was met by 1800 of our men from Frankfort & cut to pieces. The fight took place between Versailles & the [Kentucky] river. Our infantry were in wagons & Morgan mistaking them most likely for a baggage train attacked them, when our cavalry came up & charged him & the fight became general. The rebels lost 180 killed & 300 paroled. . . .[1]

They say that yesterday Mrs. J Wilgus[2] had a fight with three guerillas. It was very early in the morning & none of the family were up when three guerillas came to see if the Capt was at home. When Mrs Wilgus heard it was guerillas she guessing what they wanted wouldnt let the Capt go down but slipping on a wrapper went to the door herself. The men asked if the Capt was at home. She told them "no." They replied that they knew he was & tried to get in. She pushed them back & struggled with them till she got his gun away from one of them. He took it away from her; again she got possession of it & said if she only knew how to use it she would blow his brains out & tried to pull the trigger but couldnt. He got it from her again & started round to the stable to look at the horses. She followed them talking to them all the time & kept them there until Capt Wilgus had had time to make his escape. . . .

1. Morgan camped on the Kentucky River the night of his pass through Lexington. His troops, however, were driven away at 1 A.M. by pursuing Federal cavalry and infantry. They were surprised, but not cut to pieces. See Duke, *History of Morgan's Cavalry*, 287–88.
2. Mrs. J. Wilgus, wife of a Lexington grocer and commission agent, lived on the north side of Short Street between Broadway and Jefferson Streets. See *Williams' Lexington City Directory*, 92.

TUESDAY OCT 21ST [1862]

. . . I forgot to mention the other day in telling about Mrs. Wilgus, that while she was contending with the rebels one of their capts passed by & swore at them and asked why the devil they didnt let the woman alone & look for Capt Wilgus & one of them replied, that he'd better come & try it himself. That it was easier said than done. . . .

My brother came home today from Louisville where he has been during the last 6 or 7 weeks . . . said Col Davis hadn't had any thing done to him for killing Nelson;[1] that Davis & Nelson hadn't been on good terms for a long time. That Davis had the command of the provost guard under Nelson & when he went to report to Nelson the latter found fault with him for not having more men & said he didnt make arrest fast enough & he deserved to be kicked out of town by his own provost guard. Davis demanded an explanation & Nelson slapped him on the face. Again Davis came & asked for an apology & again Nelson slapped him & Davis not being able to stand it any longer went out & got a pistol from a soldier & came back & shot Nelson.

Jack and Jim Keiser were both arrested today. Jim on charge of stealing Uncle Sams blankets & Jack for what I didn't hear. The soldiers also took a quantity of stolen groceries, etc. from their house & John Dudleys.

Mr. Shaw they said didnt lose all his stock. That he hid a good many of the newest. There is a story which is a standing joke about town, of a good bargain he made off a secesh during the "invasion." One day a rebel came in his store to buy a hat. Mr. Shaw brought out one that had been on hand for several years & was entirely out of fashion & told him that there was a hat that would suit him exactly, a beautiful hat, latest fashion, just come out from Paris & worth $10 at least (it was in fact worth only $2 or 3 when it was in fashion). Well said secesh, thats rather high but if its the latest fashion I suppose I must get it. Mr. Shaw protested it was extremely fashionable & that he was selling it at a losing price, etc. Secesh asked if he had any sort of a cord & tassel or feather to put in it. Mr. Shaw didnt have any but showed him a small brass ornament such as some of our soldiers loop their hats up with & told him that was all the rage now & it would never do to be without one. Secesh wanted to know the price. "Let me see" said Mr Shaw "I think it $3, isn't it George["] (to his clerk). "Oh yes" he replied "certainly it worth 3 dollars at least (it was only worth 10 cents). Well said secesh, I'll take it too but I havent got any kind of money but "greenbacks." Would you take them. Oh, said Shaw, as you are a soldier I suppose I'll have to accommodate you. . . .

Gen Wright is in no very good order with the Kentucky people at present. They are dreadfully impatient at his tardiness. After the battle of Richmond 7 or 8 weeks ago, & the report we heard of his wanting to evacuate Kentucky entirely a good many persons have doubted his loyalty. In fact since the rebels have been here, I have heard no one speak in his favor & nothing but a splendid victory over the rebels will restore confidence in him. . . .

1. After a dispute between General William Nelson and General Jefferson C. Davis, the latter was relieved of command following the battle of Richmond. When Davis encountered Nelson at the Galt House in Louisville on September 29, 1862, an argument ensued, and Davis shot and mortally wounded Nelson. Though Davis was imprisoned, he was released without trial and joined Buell's army during Bragg's invasion of Kentucky. Davis never faced charges and became a respected Federal corps commander. See Faust, ed., *Historical Times Illustrated Encyclopedia of the Civil War*, 201–8, 523.

WEDNESDAY OCT 22ND [1862]

. . . Mrs. Curd . . . thinks the Union ladies ought to have been drummed over the lines. Mrs. John Dudley also expressed a similar charitable feeling. . . . The secesh had one of the city schools for a hospital & left it in such a condition that there isnt a nigger in town who has up to this time been found bold enough to undertake the job of cleaning it. The bed clothes, etc. used by the rebels (which by the way belonged to the Aid Society) will never again be fit for any thing but the flames. . . .

FRIDAY OCT 24TH [1862]

. . . Speaking of secesh two were buried today from hospital No 2. They die off very fast & no wonder, they keep themselves & everything about them so dirty. I wonder any get well. Cart loads of dirt were taken out of the court yard & the cellars at hospital No 2 are so dirty that it be almost impossible to get them cleaned. Not quite as bad however, as hospital No 1. The filth up there is beyond mention. . . .

Last Saturday we heard when Morgan was here there were a good many of the union prisoners he had taken in the jail & he threatened to hang a good many. Mr. Madison C Johnson[1] went down to the jail so they say & made a speech there to the secesh in favor of the prisoners & among other things said the secesh could hang them, most certainly they could if they felt inclined. They had the power & we were not strong enough to prevent them, but if they did it would be a most woeful day for them (the secesh) a day they would regret to their dying day, and made them some dreadful threats. The secesh didnt hang any one. . . .

When the rebels were here they all declared they would rather to a man leave their dead bodies here than endure again the hardship they suffered in crossing the mountain country to get into the state & said they would object very much if they were forced to leave this state to return by the same way they came. . . .[2]

... "rumor with her hundred tongues" is very busy with Gen. Buells fame. People are much dissatisfied & one says this & another that. Some say Buell is Braggs brother-in-law & for that reason he allowed him to escape & many other things of the same sort. I dont like to think ill of any of our officers. I would like them all to prove heroes of the first class & I dont intend to believe anything against Buell until I have proof positive & I hope he will by his deeds give the lie direct to all such scandals & show himself to be "all our fancy painted him."

1. Madison C. Johnson, lawyer, professor of law at Transylvania University, and president of the Northern Bank of Kentucky, later was elected to the presidency of the Law College of the Agricultural and Mechanical College. See Ranck, *History of Lexington*, 60.
2. Confederate armies in Kentucky withdrew through London and the Cumberland Gap, the same route Kirby Smith had taken upon entering the state. See Connelly, *Army of the Heartland*, 212–80.

SATURDAY OCT 25 [1862]

We had today the pleasure of reading once more the Observer and Reporter[1] which has resumed circulation. The schools will be resumed next week and Lexington is generally returning to her former state Of course until the full communication with Louisville & Cincinnati is restored (which will be in a few days nothing preventing) every thing is very scarce & there is little or no silver in circulation I am sorry it is such a bad, cold, sleety day, on account of our soldiers.

1. During the Confederate occupation of Lexington in September and early October 1862, General Morgan made the *Observer and Reporter* office his headquarters. Printers under his command operated the presses and turned out handbills, pamphlets, and military forms for the army. See Coulter, *The Civil War and Readjustment in Kentucky*, 452; *Williams' Lexington City Directory*, 18; and Perrin, *History of Fayette County, Kentucky*, 460–62.

SUNDAY OCT 26TH [1862]

There were about 75 of our sick taken to Hospital No 2 the other evening. The hospital is not all cleaned yet but there were one or two rooms in the third story ready for them. . . . Mr. Wickliffe said he would have issued his paper two weeks ago but Morgan had used his office for his headquarters & printing office . . . and left the rooms & types in such a state of dirt & confusion that it took two weeks to put them in any sort of order.

The secesh citizens who went with the rebel army & the recruits that they got from around here seem to be returning.[1] One was arrested today & we hear of the return of other through the country.

Some one told me today the following account of the way Mr. Davy Coleman[2] had his horses stolen & got them again. It was on a market day & before day the black man who was going in to market, came to Mrs. Coleman & told her that the horse she had ordered him to drive in the cart that morning couldnt be found. Mr. Coleman got up & dressed & went to the pasture & found his two Carriage horses were gone also. He told the servant to drive one of the work horses to market that morning & suspecting who had a hand in the business, had a horse saddled & rode over to Mrs Castlemans. When he got there it was just beginning to be light & fastened before the front door what should he see but his two carriage horses, saddled & bridled & with halters round their necks, like Morgans men always do their horses so that in case they should have to skedaddle & the horse should not have a bridle on they could use the halter. Mr. Coleman did not disturb any one but quietly took off the saddles & bridles & taking hold of the halters rode off home. On the way he saw one of the guerillas come up the road who walked away very quickly when he saw him. On reaching home it being then broad daylight, he found his other horse in the pasture, he having managed to elude the pursuit of the horse thieves. Mr. Coleman strongly suspected Capt John Castleman[3] either stole the horses or sent some of his men to do it.

1. The period following Bragg's return to Tennessee was marked by widespread desertion due to extreme shortages in food and equipment within the Confederate army. See Thomas Lawrence Connelly, *Autumn of Glory: The Army of Tennessee, 1862–1865* (Baton Rouge: Louisiana State Univ. Press, 1971), 15–18.
2. David S. Coleman, a graduate of Transylvania, farmed in Fayette County. See Perrin, *History of Fayette County, Kentucky*, 801–2.
3. Twenty-one-year-old John B. Castleman, a former member of the Lexington Chasseurs, joined Morgan's 2nd Kentucky Cavalry in October 1861. He returned to Lexington to recruit a new company. He lived with his mother on the Newtown Pike. See Dee Alexander Brown, *The Bold Cavaliers: Morgan's 2nd Kentucky Cavalry Raiders* (Philadelphia: J.B. Lippincott Company, 1959), 67–68, and John B. Castleman, *Active Service* (Louisville: Courier-Journal Job Print. Co., 1917).

MONDAY OCT 27 [1862]

. . . The soldiers have commenced searching secessionists houses. The house of Mr Young[1] was searched & they were about to give up the search, having found nothing, when some of them observed that the wall paper of a recess by the fireplace of one of the rooms appeared to be loose & coming off. They tore off the paper & found a kind of closet full of government stores. Gen Gilmore does not allow his soldiers to gad about like the secesh or to interfere in any way with private property or citizens without orders & the guards & sentinels are not allowed to ask citizens for food. Some of the guard stopped here the other morning & asked Ma for something to eat, as they had been on guard all night & had had no supper. But I expect they didnt know of the order. We wont hear now like we did while the rebels were here, "Is there any chance of our getting something to eat about here."

We heard Mr David McCullough[2] said he had a piece of the flag that the secesh destroyed & he was going to have it framed & write a list of the names of all the persons that had any hand in the deed & was going to hang them up in some public place where everybody could see them. . . .

1. Perhaps this is E. Young, an Englishman who worked as a cabinetmaker and grocer in Lexington. See Perrin, *History of Fayette County, Kentucky*, 754.
2. Davis McCullough, a mustard manufacturer, lived on the north side of High Street between Mill and Upper Streets. See *Williams' Lexington City Guide*, 79.

TUESDAY OCT 28TH [1862]

. . . 5 regiments came in between 12 & 2 this morning. . . . They came in the Paris road and seemed to be in high spirits & sang & cheered as they marched along. It was very different cheering from that of the secesh. Sounded full & hearty & not like the yelping of a pack of curs. A squad came over into the College lot & after they had had their dinner two came over & had a long talk with Ma at the door. They said they had seen more union flags today than they had seen for some time & thought if there were so many union people in Lex we must have had a disagreeable time while the rebels were here. . . .

Dr Major (secesh) who has been occupying Mrs. Vertners house since Kirby Smith left it, received an order today to move as Maj General Granger[1] intended to take it for his headquarters.

1. An 1838 West Point graduate, Robert Seamen Granger (1816–1894) was an Ohio native. During the war Granger's activities were limited mainly to camp and garrison duty in Kentucky, Tennessee, and northern Alabama. In September 1862, he assumed command of Kentucky State Troops and on October 20, 1862, took over the Federal garrison at Bowling Green. See Boatner, *The Civil War Dictionary*, 352.

FRIDAY OCT 31 [1862]

Company F 1st Mo. Cavalry camped in the college lot today. We had a talk with the ensign of the company. His flag was torn and Lettie offered to mend it for him. It was a small blue regulation flag, which he said a lady had given them in Missouri. The silk was worn threadbare in many places, but it was not soiled, not much faded and considering the time it had been used, was well preserved. He said he had had it sixteen months and had carried it in the battle of Pea Ridge. . . .[1] They had a drill in sword exercise this evening. It is very pretty. I wish they had been here to exercise on John Morgans gang. One of the guards was a Frenchman, who said he was from New York. He asked my little brothers to come over & see him & when he was relieved from guard, took them over the camp to a kind of little tent, which he called the music tent, where the musical talent of the company was assembled. One played the flute, another one the violin & another the accordion. . . . They saw Lieut Davis too, who asked Arthur (who is about 11) if he wouldnt join & be his orderly. . . .

1. Battle fought on March 7–8 in Arkansas. See Faust, ed., *Historical Times Encyclopedia of the Civil War*, 566–67.

Saturday Nov 1st [1862]

. . . No one can leave town without a pass & there are schools of instruction at all the camps & the orders about guards are very strict. There was some talk lately of having a concert soon for the benefit of the Aid Society. One of the regiments (I believe the 22nd Wisconsin[1]) has a very fine brass band which we were anxious to engage, but are afraid it will not be here, if indeed it hasnt left already.

Three ambulances of sick went to Hospital No 2 this evening. It is pretty full, but the doctors who have the direction of it at present (some Drs Root & Fox, who I hope wont stay long & I suppose they wont after Dr E—— comes back) dont give satisfaction & have very bad management. They do just like the secesh doctors did. Wont let the ladies take things to the men themselves like they have been used to do, but want them to leave what they bring with two sisters from the Nunnery at Bardstown[2] who stay there who put the things in a cupboard & no one knows whether the men ever get them or not. The nuns never went to the hospital until the secesh came & then the secesh ladies furnished a room for them at hospital No 2 & I suppose they dont want to leave it. The nuns have always been looked upon as secesh. The men complain very much & say they are not well attended to & sometimes are almost starved. Two died yesterday. I cant tell how many secesh have died at Hospital No 1. The secesh ladies say it was shameful the way our doctors treated the secesh sick, When they were moved from hospital No 2. That they were put into the wagons any way, some with their legs hanging over the sides & no blankets nor bedclothes of any kind, and that was the reason so many died. But if that was true it was the fault of their own doctors for they had the care of moving them. Our doctors had nothing to do with it.

The Frenchman brought a pony over & got Ma to let Arthur ride with him when they went to take their horses to water this evening. There is an Indian with the campany. A guide or scout. They say he is a real Indian of some Mexican tribe. He is good looking for an Indian and appears to be civilized and can speak English very well. . . .

1. Mustered in September 1862, the 22nd Wisconsin participated in the defense of Cincinnati and Covington during Kirby Smith's invasion of Kentucky. The regiment quartered in Lexington in late October awaiting assignment to the 1st Brigade, 1st Division, Army of Kentucky. See Edwin Bentley Quiner, *The Military History of Wisconsin* (Chicago: Clarke & Company, 1886), 697–98.
2. Thirty-seven members of the Sisters of Charity of Nazareth, whose motherhouse was three miles north of Bardstown, served in Union and Confederate hospitals as nurses. See Kleber, ed., *The Kentucky Encyclopedia*, 824.

Sunday Nov 2nd [1862]

. . . There is an order out that those secesh who have been active in assisting the rebellion & aiding the rebels while they were here shall be arrested & sent to Vicksburg.

Monday Nov. 3 [1862]

A salute of 13 guns was fired this morning in honor of the arrival of Maj Gen Wright. The cannon . . . was brought first into the little college lot. But finding they would break the windows of the houses round they went further out. The men were all fine looking & some of the officers handsome.

Wednesday Nov 5th [1862]

. . . An order has been issued that passes will not be required from persons within a circuit of 10 miles which will be a good thing as the market people had nearly stopped coming in on account of the trouble of getting passes. Gen. Boyle has ordered that all rebel prisoners at the hospitals in Ky will report at once to Louisville for removal to Vicksburg. . . .

Thursday Nov 6th [1862]

... The secesh storekeepers are not allowed to import any stores. So they will not be able to carry on any business this winter.

Mrs. Miller the housekeeper at the Masonic lodge[1] was here the other day & told us an anecdote which shows that the rebel ladies had better be careful what place they choose to insult our guards in. Mrs Miller was engaged by the Masons to live at the Lodge & take care of it. And when it was taken by our doctors for a hospital she stayed and kept house for our soldiers. When the rebels took possession she kept her place, both because they threatened her if she left and because the Masons thought it best she should stay & do what she could to prevent injury to the building. She said that after our troops returned & had put guards up there, a secesh lady one day as she was passing through the gate, turned and made a mouth at the guard in an insulting manner. Now the Lodge is built on an elevation and the yard slopes down from the building to the gate which is several feet above the level of the street and has a flight of seven or eight steps leading down to the pavement. The gate opens in the middle and there is an iron bar or spike in the center on which the leaves of the gate rest when it is shut. Now coming through the gate the ladys hoops caught upon this spike while she was sneering at the guard and jerked her down the stone steps bruising her badly. The guard had to go and unhitch her hoops & lift her up and she limped off....

Lieut ——— of Shoeffs staff was here today.... He was here on the 1st of Sept & left about 9 oclock that night. Not being able to find his horse or to procure another, he (the Lieut) walked to Versailles where he bought a suit of common clothes (which may be judged of by the fact that the whole suit including shoes and a broad brimmed palmetto cost only $8). Thus equipped and carrying his uniform, and saddle etc, in a bag, he set out on foot to join Buells army at Nashville. About 23 miles from that place he was stopped by a party of rebels, who put the usual question. He told them he was a shoemaker and was going through the country buying leather. They asked where he got that uniform & saddle he had in his bag, and wanted him to take the oath to the Confederacy. This he refused and said he couldn't tell who the uniform etc. belonged to. He had picked them up on the way. He didnt take any part in politics and didnt care for either side except so far as the price of leather was concerned. That he went with the ones that could sell it to him cheapest. Then they wanted him to take a parole, but he wouldnt, so they asked him to promise not to give aid or comfort to the enemy, or reveal what he saw that night, which he agreed to.

After he got to Nashville he saw among the prisoners one of the very rebels who had stopped him. The man knew him directly, and said he had played a very good trick on them, for they hadnt the least suspicion that he was deceiving them.

He said that march through the Green River country, following Bragg to Perryville was terrible.[2] The dust lay on the roads a foot thick and filled their eyes and mouths, blinding and almost suffocating them, and with all this dreadful dust no water to be met with for miles, but stagnant pools and slimy ponds redolent of the odor of the cattle of the neighborhood. There was water at Perryville but the rebels held that place & our men had to do the best they could. He blames Buell very much for letting Bragg escape. Says he had him completely surrounded at one time, and Crittenden was in the rear, only waiting for the order to close up & effectually cut off the retreat of the rebels. But that order never came. That when Buell was pursuing Bragg they marched two miles & camped and next day three miles and camped and so on. But when Bragg was out of reach they marched about 20 miles a day. That he would not allow the heads of divisions wagons enough to carry the baggage and so they couldnt carry tents enough and during all that snow and bad weather we had not long ago, they slept on the bare ground with nothing but their blankets to cover them and that a good many of the men and officers think Buell is a traitor. His Conduct certainly looks very suspicious.[3]

1. The Grand Hall of the Masonic lodge was located on the northeast corner of Short and Walnut Streets. See *Williams' Lexington City Directory*, 18.
2. Area of south central Kentucky through which the Green River flows. Buell had gone from Bowling Green through Monfordville to Louisville in pursuit of Bragg. See Connelly, *Army of the Heartland*, 226–32.
3. Federal authorities relieved General Don Carlos Buell of his command on October 24, 1862, following his slow pursuit of Bragg after the battle of Perryville. Buell's actions were investigated by a military commission but no charges were made. He never regained his former position. See Warner, *Generals in Blue*, 51–52.

FRIDAY NOV 7TH [1862]

Two rebel ladies went to Shropshires yesterday (so some one who knew told us) and when one of the clerks, Mr. Watson, went to wait on them, instead of telling what they wished to look at one of them said "Oh, we cant look at anything! We feel so indignant we cant possibly look at any goods. When I think of the shameful way in which that estimable young Southern man, who died at Mrs Prestons the other day (some rebel soldiers Mrs Preston had taken to her house) was treated by the Lincolnites, I am perfectly shocked. There were so many interesting incidents connected with his illness. And to think that at his funeral, there were only five carriages, and not men enough allowed us, to shovel the earth into the grave, so that he had to be put in the vault! And that was not enough, but the Lincoln soldiers must come and break open the coffin, and search the body for a Confederate flag! If we had known they were going to do it we would have made a handsome flag, and envelloped his body."

They also said that when the rebels were moved from the college, the Union ladies stood on the lawn and saw them pitched into the wagons "with no covering to protect their limbs from the winds" and clapped their hands and cried "Good, good, we hope you will all die." That the Union ladies had been the cause of so many of their sick dying, because they wouldnt let them (the secesh ladies) bring things to them. That Bragg, Kirby Smith and all the rest would be back in three weeks and then they hoped there wouldnt be a single Lincolnite, man, woman or child left in Lex. . . .

And now there are one or two things I would like to ask of these charitable personages. What would have become of the secesh citizens if all their wishes had been granted; the secesh army quartered here for the winter, and all the Union people driven beyond the lines and Ky made one of the Confederacy pro tem. What would have become of the secesh and what would they have done in that case. They would most likely die by hundreds of cold and starvation. Dont they remember the miserable condition things were in when the rebel army left! How there was not a bit of coal or wood to be had for love or money, no coal oil or candles in town, dry goods and groceries (what there was of them) selling at ruinous prices, and the country people refusing to come to market! If such was the state of things when the rebels hadnt been here two months what would they have been if they had remained all winter. Do they suppose the rebels would take the trouble to cut wood, grind flour and steal clothes for the citizens when they had their own dear selves to attend to? I saw enough of them while they were here to make me very doubtful that they would . . . the resident secesh should be thankful the Union army has come back to restore plenty, and that they are kind enough not to drive them at once from their homes. As for our not allowing men enough to bury that rebel, and the soldiers searching the coffin and the Union ladies killing the secesh sick, etc. Those are lies too palpable to need refutation. The secesh ladies Consciences (if they have any) doubtless reproach them for their own neglect and inattention. Do they remember how their sick scoffed and jeered at six ladies coming to bring them a teacup full of something? How they begged the Union ladies when they went to take things to our sick, just please to give them some for they were half starved? How one poor fellow would everyday about the time the Union ladies visited the hospital, take his cup and plate and hide behind some barrels near the path to watch for them to come to give him something? How some of the sick in the dormitory begged some of the Union ladies with tears in their eyes "for God's sake to ask Dr. Bush to watch over them and not let Drs. Jim Keiser and Bob Johnson[1] kill them." And how Dr. Bush who wouldnt see a cur suffer when he could help it, did what they asked?

But you might do everything in your power for these resident secesh (I dont include the soldiers for most of them are grateful for kindness) and they wouldnt give you a "thank you" for it.

One of the Mo. cavalry was wounded this evening. Two of the men got to fighting and one fired his pistol at the other wounding him badly but not dangerously in the side. We heard the shot fired and the man cry out and when we found one of them was wounded Pa went over to see if his help was wanted. The wounded man was taken to the hospital and the other was put under guard. Capt Clifford said they were both bad fellows.

1. Perhaps twenty-four-year-old Robert F. Johnson, who later became a prominent Lexington real estate investor and stock raiser. See Perrin, *History of Fayette County, Kentucky*, 638–39.

SATURDAY NOV 8TH [1862]

They say seven men have died at hospital No 2 within the last few days. I wish Dr Eversman would make haste and come here. If he was here things would go on better than that. He understands his business, and I am afraid the doctors now at our hospital do not. Gen Granger seems to know how to deal with the secesh: finding that hospital No 1 where the rebels are was out of fuel he ordered Mrs Hart Gibson[1] to supply that place with wood until she received orders to quit. She is a daughter of Mr Duncan and has a farm in Woodford Co.

. . . Lexington it seems is the headquarters of the army of Ky at least that is what is on the door of headquarters.[2] Mrs Morgan and some other secesh ladies, went to headquarters this morning, looking very angry about something. We learnt this evening that it was because an order had been issued to remove the secesh sick from the hospital and quarter them on the secessionists. Some of the rebels who have been arrested and allowed to go at large again to attend to their affairs have to report daily at headquarters.

1. Mrs. M.D. Gibson lived in Fayette County with her husband, a lawyer, next door to her parents, F.S. and Eliza Duncan. See Eighth Census of the United States for Fayette County, 1860, Schedule 1, 506.
2. The handsome Bodley house on the northeast corner of Second and Market Streets served, at various times, as the headquarters of Union Generals Granger, Willcox, and Burbridge. It is located directly across the Little College Lot from Mrs. Morgan's residence, and down the street from Miss Peter's home at Market Street and Mechanics Alley. See Perrin, *History of Fayette County, Kentucky*, 463.

MONDAY NOV 10 [1862]

Mrs Preston went to Gen Gilmore the other day to ask him to protect her property. The Gen told her that so far as pilfering was concerned he would attend to it, not because *she* asked it, but to keep discipline in his army but that if any of his men ever wanted forage or supplies he should certainly send them to Mrs Wm Preston in such case he would give her a reciept for what they took, to be payable after the war, or at such time as she should declare herself loyal to the Union, or should bring her husband back and make him a union man. Mrs Preston said that was a perfect farce. "I am perfectly aware of it madam" replied Gilmore. She then said he had used insulting language to her and took her leave. She afterward went to Gen Granger, and Gen Gilmore said if she called his language insulting he didnt know what she would call Grangers, for what he said wouldnt "hold a candle" to what Gen Granger told her, that he gave her a complete setting down.

The Grand Jury is sitting now, and they say they intend to be very strict in inforcing the law against the secesh.[1] Gen McClellan has been relieved from his command. . . . We were somewhat surprised at the news but did not object. McClellan was too slow to suit Kentuckians, who always prefer a "go ahead" policy in everything. There was County Court held today for the first time since the rebels came here. . . . Pa resumed command at Hospital No 1. . . . Pa said that when he went to hospital No 1 today, Drs Root & Fox were there, and the provost Marshall came to see about moving the rebels. The doctors didnt seem to wish to have them moved until after Dr Fox (who is going back to his regiment and who has had command of that hospital) should have left. But Pa go[t] introduced to the Provost Marshall, and urged their immediate removal. During the conversation the two Drs congratulated themselves that there had been no death within the last 36 hours, when Pa said that there were as he found afterwards four corpses lying in the house two of whom had died last night.

1. This Grand Jury indicted 208 persons for "treason." See Perrin, *History of Fayette County, Kentucky*, 463.

TUESDAY NOV 11TH [1862]

The concert of the musical association of the Aid Society came off last night. There was a full house and everything went off well. Mrs Col Doolittle[1] & Mrs Capt Parsons took part in the performance. Mrs Doolittle is wife to the Col of one of the Michigan regiments (the 18th I think) & Mrs Capt Parsons is his sister. Her husband is at Washington. She says she hasnt seen him for nine months. His regiment was ordered off the day they were married. . . . Gen Gilmore was present with a good many other officers. Gen Granger couldnt come but promised to send $5 instead. When the Star Spangled Banner was sung, a very pretty tableaux representing the Goddess of Liberty was exhibited. . . .

1. Miss Peter refers to the wife of Colonel Charles C. Doolittle of the 18th Michigan Infantry. See Michigan Adjutant General's Department, *Report of Service of Michigan Volunteers in the Civil War* (Kalamazoo, Michigan: Ihling Brothers & Everard, n. d.), 32.

FRIDAY NOV 14TH [1862]

There was a large flag suspended over the street by headquarters this morning. One end of the ropes fastened to the roof of headquarters and the other to one of the trees in the college lot, so that now all secesh in driving up our street will have to pass under it, and I dont think they will be so fond now of troubling the Generals with visits. This street is now called "Union Row" by those living on it, for there are no secesh living on it from headquarters to the corner next [to] the big college lot.

Mrs JB Coleman's house was searched soon after the union troops came (she lives about 8 miles in the country on the Newtown pike & is a secesh) and a wagon load of tents and other government property found which had been taken by them from the Fair Grounds. They tried to get off by saying they took them to take care of, and wanted to be paid for keeping them! . . . The rebels are all out of the Hospitals, some to private homes and others put in a large framed house on Broadway. . . .

SATURDAY NOV 15 [1862]

Keisers Boarding house and Patterson's Furniture warehouse adjoining
have been taken for a hospital as when Gen Grangers division leaves there
will be a great many sick left, who are now attended to at the camps by
their own surgeons, and there was talk of taking McGowans hotel[1] also, as
the damages done by the fire have been repaired. . . . Jim Keiser says (as
[do] also all the rebels) that the rebel army will soon be back here.

The other day two officers of I think the 15th Illinois[2] . . . went to
Mrs Wm Preston's, but just as supper was announced a messenger from
Gen Gilmore informed them that their presence was required at headquarters. I don't know whether the Gen did it on purpose or not, but I
think it serves them right. Union officers have no business keeping
company with the secesh. If we fight them on the field we should keep
them down at home too. Secesh ladies can do a great deal in the way of
giving information. It is known pretty certainly by the officers here that a
southern mail leaves nearly or every night, but they have not as yet been
able to find who takes it or from what house it is sent. It is thought
however that it is not carried by men but by boys or ladies. And indeed it
would be very easy to send a messenger out of the town through the fields,
for it would be almost impossible to surround Lex with guards. . . . The
men belonging to the Michigan regiment are not near as nice as the Ohio
and Indiana boys. There are so many mean fellows among them and more
Abolitionists than in all the Ohio & Indiana regiments put together. In
fact I have never seen an Ohio Abolitionist yet. The servants as usual
would sometimes run off to the camps. One lady's servant ran off & stayed
at the camp a day or two (though it is against orders I think to let negroes
in) with one of the Michigan regiments. His mistress went out and
demanded him of one of the officers. He asked her how long she had had
the negro. She told him, & then he said "well now I think that nigger has
served you long enough," and wouldnt let her have him so she had to go to
one of the Generals. . . .

1. Owned by T.B. Megowan, Megowan's Hotel was located on the north side of
Short Street, between Upper and Mulberry Streets. *Williams' Lexington City Guide*,
34.
2. While the 15th Illinois Cavalry was not yet organized, the 15th Illinois Infantry
served in Mississippi at this time. See Dyer, *A Compendium of the War of the Rebellion*,
3:1030–51.

SUNDAY NOV 16TH [1862]

Another fine day, and with the exception of a slight accident that occured this evening, everything quiet. About 3 PM when the cavalry in the lot were starting to take their horses to water (for we have had so little rain for the last three months that water is scarce and they have to go out of town) two shots were heard, and we saw the soldiers who had been walking about the lawn at the hospital [Hospital No. 2—Morrison College] run down to the fence & some of the cavalry rode up to the by street or road [Third Street] that separates the two lots. They found that their captain's servant had been fired at and slightly wounded by the son of Mr E. Morgan the blacksmith.[1] The negro was sent to the hospital but soon returned to camp, and several men went in pursuit of Morgan who had 'skeedaddled' after firing. I dont think they caught him. Why the negro happened to be there or why Morgan fired at him I did not learn. One man died last night at Hospital No 2.

1. Lexington had two blacksmiths by the name of Morgan: George W. Morgan and N. Morgan. See *Williams' Lexington City Directory*, 73.

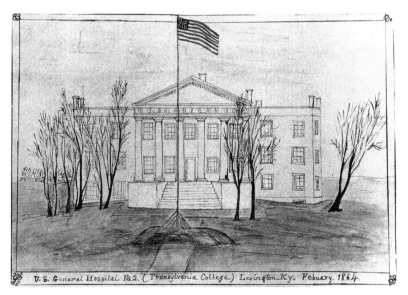

Frances Peter's contemporary sketch of Morrison Hall. Prior to becoming a Union hospital in May 1862, it housed Transylvania High School (see diary entry for February 19, 1862). (Evans Collection, Special Collections and Archives, University of Kentucky Libraries)

MONDAY NOV 17 [1862]

Today is the day the Mo. Cavalry expected to receive their pay and they said their Captain always let them have a "spree" on that day. . . . They seem to think a great deal of their Captain. Say he is kind to them & is brave, always keeping his place in the front and they have great confidence in him as a leader.

The ladies are practicing for another concert (at the last they made $166 after expenses were paid) & this evening Lieut Burgan came home with Lettie (He is to sing with her in a quartette called "Brave Boys." He belongs to the 10th New York and is one of the signal corps.[1] There is only two of that body here Lieut Hopkins and himself. They came out to organize a signal comp[any] here. Their signals are very different from those used at sea. They make use of only three flags, only one of which is used at a time. They have a flag staff 12 feet high, and another the same h[e]ight at the top of which is fastened a torch made of copper in which caseine or pin[e] knots are used. . . . The signals are made by the motions of the flag, a different motion for every letter of the alphabet and for numerals. He says a practiced eye can see and read the motions at 16 miles with a telescope. He says the inventor of this method, a Mr Alexander, went over to the rebels,[2] and of course imparted his knowledge to them, but we have made changes in our signals . . . so the rebels cannot read them. . . .

1. A branch of the U.S. Army, the Signal Corps was responsible for communication using flags, pistols, rockets, and torches. See Faust, ed., *Historical Times Illustrated Encyclopedia of the Civil War*, 688–89.
2. Prior to the war, Edward Porter Alexander worked as a regular army officer with Alfred Meyers to develop a system of signals using flags. Alexander resigned his commission and served the Confederacy as a talented engineer, ordnance, and artillery officer. See Gary W. Gallagher, ed., *Fighting for the Confederacy: The Personal Recollections of General Edward Porter Alexander* (Chapel Hill: Univ. of North Carolina Press, 1989).

TUESDAY NOV 18TH [1862]

. . . The papers say that several days ago some of our troops <u>hung</u> nine rebels, stragglers they had taken, in retaliation for the murder of Capt King and the 16 others whom Bragg hung near Crab Orchard on his way out of the state. They would have hung more than nine if they had had them.

THURSDAY NOV 20TH [1862]

. . . When Pa resumed command at Hospital No 1 there were four nuns attending there. Two were secesh and soon left, but the others said they were union and were allowed to remain and have a room there. Today Pa heard two more sisters had been sent for, and as he had not given any such order he went to one of the sisters and told her he had heard two more were coming, and asked who had sent for them. She said yes two more had been sent for by Mr Currie (who was steward there before Pa came) Pa told her it had been done without his orders & that he couldnt accommodate any more there, he was very well satisfied to have two, but not more for he couldnt spare another room & the one they occupied at present was too small to hold four without running the risk of their getting sick. The sister said Pa insulted her. Pa went and talked to Currie about it, who got angry but didnt say anything until he got downstairs, when he cursed and swore about it and very likely made mischief with the nuns, for the Superior took the two sisters away and told Pa that she couldnt allow less than four to stay there. . . .

The draft has put so many Abolitionists and mean men in the Regiments that the Generals have almost if not more trouble with them than with the secesh. One of the city schools has or will be taken as an addition to Hospital No 1. . . .

Saturday Nov 22 [1862]

The Observer this morning contains extracts from a paper called the "Vidette" said to be edited by John Morgan[1] which praise[s] Buell very much and says he is a "perfect gentleman" and regrets he is engaged in such a "vile cause." But of Halleck and McClellan it says "their lying dispatches have sunk them beneath the contempt of the southern people." I'd much rather Morgan would say that of our Generals than to call them "perfect gentlemen." The last would be the same to me, coming from him, as if he called them secessionists.

A man was brought to Pa's hospital today from the camp. He was sick of measles and was so low when he reached the hospital that he died while they were taking him in.

1. While encamped at Hartsville, Tennessee, Morgan's men found a press and type. They used the contraband to publish *Vidette*, which included general orders, promotions, accounts of maneuvers, and political commentary, as well as humor, sarcasm, and exaggeration. See Duke, *History of Morgan's Cavalry*, 226–27.

Sunday Nov 23 [1862]

The man who was sent to Pa's hospital yesterday was under Dr Roots charge at the camp and Dr Root came today and apologized to Pa for sending him. Said he had no idea he was so ill. The idea of a doctor not knowing how his patients are when he has them moved!

Several officers were arrested today for running off negroes from their owners.[1] There are a good many negroes in jail here who have followed the soldiers here from Tennessee and Alabama.

1. Federal policy returning slaves to their owners broke down in the summer of 1862 as Union soldiers in Kentucky began to disregard it. Tension created between the army and citizens caused a reinforcement of the order in October 1862. Federal authorities arrested several officers, including the Colonel of the 18th Michigan, for failing to return fugitives to their owners. See Howard, *Black Liberation in Kentucky*, 12–28.

MONDAY DEC 1ST 1862

A government agent was here today inquiring for information against Mrs Morgan. He said she had been in the habit lately of taking things to the rebel prisoners and using very abusive language to the guards and in speaking of the Federals. He also said he thought James B Clay[1] should and would be made a public example when in our power.

1. The son of Henry Clay, James B. Clay, served in the antebellum period as a congressman and diplomat. A Confederate sympathizer on his way to join the Confederacy, Clay was arrested and exiled to Canada, where he died in 1864. See Ranck, *History of Lexington*, 390.

WEDNESDAY DEC 3 [1862]

This mornings Observer had some extracts in it from a letter of Col Wm Preston to his wife, which somehow found its way into one of the New York papers. The Col writes in a very gloomy way. Tells Mrs Preston if she cant stay here, not to come south but go to Canada but to stay as long as she can get any protection and in such case she ought not by word or deed to insult the Federals.

FRIDAY DEC 5TH [1862]

I was disturbed about 10 or 11 oclock last night by the guard on this side of the lot, firing his pistol, and going to the window I saw a squad of the cavalry men rush, shouting down the side street and stop opposite my windows. They all talked at once, and cursed and swore so that I couldn't tell what was the matter but I afterward found that one of their company had been detected stealing from some of his comrades & on his attempting to escape had been fired at by the guard & pursued.

SATURDAY DEC 6TH 1862

. . . There is talk of taking the Methodist Church across the street from the Episcopal, the McGowan hotel and Keiser the Coach Makers for hospitals.

WEDNESDAY DEC 10TH [1862]

. . . No less than 17 negroes were arrested the other night at the house of Mr Wm Fleming.[1] They were drinking and playing cards in the kitchen. Mr F was from home. The negroes were punished with thirty lashes apiece. . . .

1. The home of William R. Fleming stood at the southwest corner of High and Rose Streets. See *Williams' Lexington City Guide*, 51.

THURSDAY DEC 18TH [1862]

Mr. Isaac Scott was arrested today. What the charges against him are we could not clearly learn, but a letter was intercepted address[ed] to him which contained a letter for Miss Anne Picket[1] (a rebel) who lives at Mr Scotts, which was thus intended to reach her under cover of Mr Scotts good name, for he is a union man. Mr. Scott was released on parole to report himself daily either to headquarters or the provost marshall. . . .

1. Thirty-nine-year-old Ann Pickett lived with her sixty-four-year-old mother at the home of manufacturer Isaac W. Scott. See Eighth Census of the United States for Fayette County, 1860, Schedule 1, 425.

SUNDAY DEC 21ST [1862]

We heard a good story of Mrs Morgan today. She went to headquarters, saying she had heard that several of the southern mails had been intercepted and requested Gen Granger if he had any letters from John Morgan in his possession to send them to her. Gen Granger immediately sent one of his aids Mr J Fullerton to Mrs Morgan's with one of John Morgans intercepted letters with directions to read to her a passage from said letter in which Morgan inquired about some clothes she had promised to send him and told where to send them. Mrs. Morgan of course was very angry. A good many mails and mail carriers have lately been intercepted passing between the rebels here and their friends in Dixie.

MONDAY DEC 22ND [1862]

Last night Mr Gratz's large bagging factory, hemp house, etc. on Short Street were burnt. They contained a large quantity of forage belonging to the troops here. There was a guard stationed there, but it is not known whether it [was] the work of some secesh or whether it was through carelessness of the teamsters. The guard was not allowed fire after dark. . . .

On account of some rumor about John Morgan that he was expected to come or send some one of his spies here or something of the kind Gen Granger surrounded the city with a perfect "cordon" of pickets not only guarding the roads but every lot or dwelling at the edge of town where it was possible for anyone to enter. They searched the houses of Mrs Morgan, Mrs Curd and old Mrs Bruce. Nothing came of it, but today three of Morgans men were caught and put in jail.

TUESDAY DEC 23RD [1862]

The doctors have decided to take the Camelite or Reform Church on upper of Main St as the next hospital. The congregation were mostly secesh.

MONDAY DEC 29TH [1862]

. . . Several ambulances of sick arrived at Hospital No 2, and 500 or 600 expected at Hospital No 1 from Richmond, Ky. The Camelite Church will be opened and the Baptist Church also taken [for hospitals]. . . .

Thursday Jan 1 1863

... A battery or part of one was brought into the College lot last night. One of the guards said it was from Nicholasville and had been left in Capt Cliffords charge "for" said he "we heard that when the rebels were here before you had no cannon and so couldnt help yourselves. So this time we thought we would be prepared". ... The small cannon that were brought into the lot today were taken out to some other place, perhaps one of the other camps.

Sunday Jan 4 1863

Col Basil Duke is said to be certainly dead. He died at Boston Ky. After John Morgan was whipped at Rolling Fork by Col Harlan of the 10th Ky[1] he (Morgan) sent a courier to Mrs Morgan here, to tell her Duke was only slightly wounded but we heard that the man told others that Duke couldnt live. That Morgan asked him if he would stay and be made prisoner or go with him and Duke could not answer. ... One of Morgans spies, a scoundrel named Bill Owens, was taken up today disguised in womans clothes. ... The aforesaid courier was named Coons or Coontz[2] and was taken at his own house. He was in bed when the house was surrounded & escape made impossible. A number of papers & letters were found on him.

1. The engagement at Rolling Fork occurred during John H. Morgan's "Christmas Raid." A portion of Morgan's command under Colonel Basil Duke was surprised by the advance of their Federal pursuers. After a sharp skirmish, the Federals withdrew, allowing the Confederates to escape to safety. Duke was wounded in the head by a shell fragment, but not killed. See Duke, *History of Morgan's Cavalry*, 336–40.
2. The courier might have been James J. Coons, a member of Cluke's Regiment and landowner in the Briar Hill precinct. See Perrin, *History of Fayette County, Kentucky*, 781.

Monday Jan 5th [1863]

About 53 rebel prisoners who had been captured at or near Danville were received here Saturday, and were sent off today to Louisville by Provost Marshall, Capt Hurlbard. 20 others came today and will probably be sent off in a day or two. Col Wisener of the 22nd Michigan died in this city today.[1] His remains were taken to the Covington depot to be sent home. The Generals & large body of troops attended.

1. Colonel Moses Wisener of Pontiac, former governor of Michigan, died of typhoid fever January 4, 1863, in Lexington. See John Robertson, comp., *Michigan in the War*, 420–21.

TUESDAY JAN 6 [1863]

Gen Granger has had a tent put up in his yard to be used as a telegraph office. About 300 more sick are expected here and it has been decided to take the Medical Hall. It will cost some trouble & money to fit it for the purpose, As new floors will have to be made for the present ones are fitted only for lectures or school rooms as they are made in steps to hold rows of benches and of course would not be of any use for a hospital. Pa was over there last night packing up his chemical apparatus to be brought over here and a great many other things will have to be moved from there.

WEDNESDAY JAN 7TH [1863]

Pa is very busy today packing up at the Hall. Gen Granger detailed 10 men to help in packing & moving the things. The Chemical & Philosophical apparatus belonging to the college & medical school will be taken to the Sayre Institute. A place has not yet been found for the library of the school but I suppose that is because Pa has been too busy to be able to look for one. The workmen have already commenced tearing up the floors which resulted in the destruction of all or nearly all the benches as they were nailed in such a way that they couldnt be unfastened from the flooring. . . .

THURSDAY JAN 8TH [1863]

Had a fine fall of snow last night but as is generally the case here, it commenced thawing towards the middle of the day. Some few sleighs were out but the snow was too wet to make good sleighing. The cavalry are just as merry as crickets this morning and go about singing & whistling and snow balling each other. It seems to me they are more merry in bad weather than good. . . . A few days ago they received their pay, which was the signal for a good many getting drunk. Even some of the guards managed to get liquor. Some black women were seen to carry them some whether of their own accord to sell to them or whether the men hired them to do it I dont know. Some of us thought the secesh might have sent it, for it is certain that they did at one time try to play that dodge on our soldiers. At any rate Capt Clifford had them tied up by the wrists to a tree, their arms being raised above their heads (his usual way of punishing unruly fellows) and when they had stayed in that position until they were tired, he set them to work by turns digging a large hole in the ground near the tree. Two would dig awhile and when they were tired (the ground was hard frozen) they were tied up again & two others untied & set to work. When the hole was tolerably deep he made them fill it up again.

FRIDAY JAN 9TH [1863]

. . . Capt Clifford sent over this morning to borrow our flag to use at the funeral of one of his men named Simms. Simms got wounded about a week ago. He had been down town and got drunk and attempted to go by one of the guards down town without showing his pass or halting. The guard fired his pistol (as was his duty) meaning only to "wing him" as the soldiers say but the ball passed through his arm making a very bad wound of which he died at Hospital No 1 yesterday. . . .

MONDAY JAN 12TH [1863]

. . . The Opera troupe from Pikes Opera House Cincinnatti[1] gave their first entertainment tonight. ('The Bride of Lammermore') They will stay two weeks.

1. The Opera House was built by Samuel N. Pike on 4th Street in Cincinnati. The Opera Troupe gave performances during the war to raise money for the Union cause. See Clara Longworth De Chambrun, *Cincinnati: Story of the Queen City* (New York: Charles Scribner's Sons, 1939), 193.

FRIDAY JAN 16TH [1863]

. . . Last night part of the stable of the cavalry fell down. Luckily they discovered yesterday morning that it was not safe and watched it, so they enabled to get the horses out before it fell. The scaffolding of the iron bridge now building over the river near Frankfort was washed away by the rise in the river.

WEDNESDAY JAN 21ST [1863]

. . . There has been a great deal of sore throat (Diptheria) lately both in the hospitals and in the city. A week or two ago two or three of the doctors took it but they are all well now. And Col Warner lost three or four of his little children I think he has only one left. My cousin Mrs. McCauly[1] died of it last Sunday, and her husband & her five children all have it. My brother Bob is just getting well of it, and several of our neighbors have it. In short it has been all over the city.

1. John McCauley and family resided on the south side of Maxwell Street, between Mulberry and Rose Streets. See *Williams' Lexington City Directory*, 68.

FRIDAY JAN 23 [1863]

I heard today another story of the rebels. One of the first days after the rebels entered Lexington a union officer went to Mrs Persicules Scott[1] and asked her if she could hide him, that the rebels were looking for him. She said no, she couldnt hide him, but if he would step into a back room he would find a suit of jeans that had just been sent home. If he put that on he could pass the rebels without attracting their notice. While the officer was engaged in putting on the suit, a party of rebels came in the front room & asked Mrs. Scott if this officer was hid in her house. She told them he was not, and said that if they choose they could search and see for themselves. They said no as she seemed so willing they should search they believed what she said. They then went round to the back of the house, when who should come out but this officer dressed in the jeans suit, and asked the rebels who they were looking for? They told him the name of the officer (his own of course) and described him. The officer then offered to help them search and went all round with them without being found out. A good many of the soldiers who were here then might have saved themselves in the same way if they had only been bold enough to play their part.

We heard that a gentleman in Louisville said he had for fifteen years been a member of a secret society for the purpose of destroying the union, some of whose members had belonged to it more than twenty five years. I have no doubt there have been such societies all over the country and that this secession has been the result of many years deliberations, and that they only waited till they were able to get a president whom they could control as they did Mr Buchanan. . . .

The Missouri Cavalry are going away. They received ammunition, and guns were given to those who had none [this] evening. They received orders to be ready to go at a moments notice. . . . We shall miss them very much. They say . . . there will probably be another company of cavalry in the lot, but I hardly expect to find it as well behaved a one as Capt Cliffords. . . . The soldiers in the hospitals dont like at all the new order forbidding the ladies from visiting & feeding the sick. One cavalry man said he "wished John Morgan was hanged and he wished the Medical director that wouldnt let the ladies come to see them was hanged too." Mr. Shipman (the Episcopal minister) proposed at the prayer meeting the other day that the gentlemen members of his congregation should join together and visit the sick in the hospitals one day in every week, and read and talk to them. They will meet for the purpose of arranging this matter next Wednesday at 4 PM at Mr. Shipman's. I think it will be an excellent plan.

1. The wife of a Lexington hemp manufacturer, Mrs. Scott lived on the west side of Broadway between Second and Third Streets. See *Williams' Lexington City Directory*, 83.

MONDAY JAN 26TH [1863]

The cavalry left about 10 oclock this morning. A good many of the men came over to tell us goodby. They said they felt almost as sorry to leave this city as if they were leaving home, that they had liked this place better than any they had been before . . .

. . . Mr Marshall[1] in the Legislature made a very sensible speech the other day about all this disputing over the Presidents Proclamation[2] He says he thinks it is enough for the Governor & Legislature to declare it unconstitutional and not meddle any further but leave the matter alone. . . .

1. "Mr Marshall" could refer to either Thornton F. Marshall, Unionist member of the state senate from Bourbon County, or to Martin P. Marshall of Fleming County, also a Unionist and member of the state legislature. See Speed, *The Union Cause in Kentucky*, 77, 80.
2. Lincoln's Emancipation Proclamation of January 1, 1863, declared all slaves then in areas still in a state of rebellion to be free. The Proclamation actually freed no slaves, because it applied only to those areas over which the Federal government lacked control. For the text of the Proclamation, see Basler, ed., *The Collected Works of Abraham Lincoln*, 6:28–30.

WEDNESDAY JAN 28 1863

. . . The Ladies Aid Society heard today from Capt James Dudley, of the 21st Ky V.I. who says his company is in a very destitute condition, nearly all the men being unable to go on parade on account of having no socks, nor good clothes, and the ladies are going to work directly to supply them. About dusk Gen. Gilmores body guard arrived in the college lot. Most of them fine looking men, mostly mounted on grey horses. One of the officers brought one of the men over here, and asked to let him come in and warm, as the poor fellow was almost frozen. Of course we complied and as it was supper time, gave him his supper. He said this company belonged to the 7th Ohio Cavalry.[1] That they had come all the way from

Danville (about 38 or 40 miles) since 8 AM and that he had had nothing to eat all day. As they were passing a large house on the road he said he stopped and asked a gentleman whom he met coming out, if he would give him a piece of bread (as he had had nothing that morning and was very hungry but didnt like to ask for anything else, but he thought from the looks of the house rich people must live in it.) The gentleman looked hard at him and then said very shortly "Ive got no bread," and went on. The man knew then he was secesh.

1. Organized in October 1862, the 7th Ohio Cavalry patrolled the District of Central Kentucky during the winter of 1862–1863. See Dyer, *A Compendium of the War of the Rebellion*, 3:1477.

SATURDAY 31ST JAN [1863]

. . . We heard that Lee Bradley (son of Wm Bradley of this city) who was in the rebel army, came & delivered himself up the other day, and was put in jail. He was taken prisoner before with young Tom McCaw[1] and they were both sent to Camp Chase Ohio from which place they succeeded in making their escape and went to Canada, but not being able (so Bradley said himself) to stay there he came on here and gave himself up. Bradley said Tom McCaw wouldnt come with him, and he didnt know where he was. Some people think that Bradley didnt come here as he said to give himself up to the authorities but because he expected to find the rebels here, & went too far before he found out his mistake. Tom McCaws family are very uneasy about him, not having heard from him since he left home last. There are several other young men of this city or neighborhood in jail here who have delivered themselves up. I suppose they were tired of the rebel service and thought that the best way of ridding themselves of it. For the secesh dont care whether a mans time of service has expired or not, he is made to stay, and fight, willing or not. Old Mrs. Beshears told Ma that her daughter Mrs Gibbons had two sons in John Morgan's division, who had enlisted for 12 months. Their time was already out, but they were forced to stay with their Company although they wished very much to come home.

1. Twenty-four-year-old Thomas D. McCaw, a lawyer, lived with his parents and siblings in Lexington. See Eighth Census of the United States for Fayette County, 1860, Schedule 1, 577.

MONDAY FEB 2ND 1863

Dr. Samuel M Letcher[1] of this city who has been for some time doctor at Hospital No 1 died last evening of this sore throat ("rebel sore throat" we call it because it originated among the rebels here). The doctors of the various Hospitals held a meeting & passed resolutions to attend the funeral & wear the mourning badge for 30 days etc.

The Medical Hall is complete now, but there is no use for it at present. For though a number of sick have been expected for some time they have not arrived & the Baptist Church is only half full.

Some snow last night, & weather very cold today. It will be very hard on the poor soldiers if it continues as it promises to do. If one feel[s] it so much in a warm house, how much worse it must be in a tent, even though it may have a stove in it! I dont see how any one could look on our camps & think how many thousands of men have been driven from their homes by this war, suffering cold & hardship, and yet have any sympathy for the rebels who have brought all this on the Country!

It seems secession is making another desperate attempt to get Ky out of the union. The other night several senators, members of the Kenton bar & others, met in secret caucus at the capitol in Frankfort to concert measures of secession. It was proposed to the Governor to send the military to break it up, but nothing was done. Most likely to give them an opportunity of proving their treason more fully, as yet they had done nothing decided. . . .

Basil Duke is not dead at least not by last account but the wound he received was a very dangerous one, the cannon ball taking off his ear & part of the skull with it. A wound which if it does not prove mortal, will at least, as all the doctors here think take a long time to heal. So he is out of the war for a time at least.

1. Dr. Letcher had served as a faculty member of the Transylvania University Medical School. His office stood on the north side of Short between Broadway and Mill Streets. See Ranck, *History of Lexington, Kentucky*, 55, and *Williams' Lexington City Guide*, 75.

TUESDAY FEB 3RD [1863]

Hard frost still continues. The streets & roads which a few days ago were like so many quagmires are now frozen so hard they are actually dusty. There is little news today except that Mr Speaker Buckner[1] says there is talk of removing the capitol from Frankfort, to Lexington and building the state Agricultural College here.

1. Born in Green County, Kentucky, Richard A. Buckner Jr. opened a law practice in Lexington after graduating from Transylvania University. Buckner served as circuit judge, 1842–1851, and was a member of the state legislature, 1859–1863, where he was elected speaker of the house. In 1863 Buckner ran for Congress, but was defeated by Brutus J. Clay. See *Biographical Encyclopedia of Kentucky Dead and Living Men of the Nineteenth Century* (Cincinnati: J.M. Armstrong and Company, 1878), 18.

WEDNESDAY FEB 4TH [1863]

The papers say that when Gen Grangers division got to Lousiville some of the regiments (Michigan & Illinois I have no doubt) tried to take with them on the boats a number of negroes whom they had carried off. They succeeded in getting some on board one boat, but the Capt of another boat on which they tried to bring negroes refused to allow them to do so, saying his orders would not allow him and when they insisted, he and the whole crew left the boat. . . . Gen Granger issued and order approved by Gen Wright that no negroes no matter who or what they were should be taken on the boats with the soldiers.

. . . The negro regiments that have been raised at Port Royal[1] and elsewhere have proved a failure, the negroes refusing to work and deserting on every occasion and of the celebrated Kansas regiment[2] only 148 are left and Gen Saxton[3] has petitioned to be removed to some other command as he is tired of [the] negro and every thing about him. So say some of the papers, and others make out that every thing is going well and the black soldiers, are so patriotic and etc. I doubt it. The first account is by far the most probable. From all I have observed of the negro he is much too averse to work, too timid to make a good soldier, and has got it into his head that liberty means doing nothing. I think it is acting against the Constitution to make soldiers of the blacks, and however much the abolitionists may say to the contrary, they will find in the end that this arming & equiping of negro regiments is a mere waste of time and money[4]. . .

Gen Gilmore has issued an order that no negroes are to be allowed to enter the camps and that any negro found in the United States uniform shall be arrested and punished, which I think is very right. . . .

1. In early 1862 General David Hunter began recruiting black troops for the Union army in this part of South Carolina. Historians dispute Miss Peter's contention that the experiment was a failure. See Willie Lee Rose, *Rehearsal for Reconstruction: The Royal Experiment* (Indianapolis: Bobbs-Merrill Company, 1964); Dudley Tay-\nrnish, *The Sable Arm: Negro Troops in the Union Army, 1861–1865* (New York:

Longmans, Green and Company, 1956); and Edward Miller, *Lincoln's Abolitionist General: The Biography of David Hunter* (Columbia: Univ. of South Carolina Press, 1997).
2. The first black regiment enrolled in a free state was the 1st Kansas Colored Volunteers, organized on January 4, 1863, at Fort Scott, Kansas, by Colonel James M. Williams. See George W. Williams, *A History of the Negro Troops in the War of the Rebellion, 1861–1865* (New York: Harper & Brothers, 1888), 101, and Cornish, *The Sable Arm*, 70–78.
3. Rufus Saxton (1824–1908) was a Massachusetts native and West Point graduate. Commanding at various times during the war, Saxton primarily enlisted blacks into the Union army and served as a Freedmen's Bureau assistant commissioner. See Paul A. Cimbala, *Under the Guardianship of the Nation: The Freedmen's Bureau and the Reconstruction of Georgia, 1865–1870* (Athens, Georgia: Univ. of Georgia Press, 1997).
4. It is interesting to note that in 1862 Dr. Peter, while serving as a Lexington councilman and mayor pro tem, sponsored various Negro petitions concerning church and school issues. In contrast to his daughter's explicit racism, Dr. Peter resigned from Lexington's City Council when it denied blacks proper educational facilities. See Evans Papers.

THURSDAY FEB 5TH [1863]

... The Cincinnati Gazette announced the people of Lexington as in great excitement at the news of Morgans approach but I have seen nothing of it myself and Gen Gilmores scouts could find no enemy.[1] John Mc——who drives our flour wagon says he heard from a friend at Nicholasville, who say the people there are moving their property from there, but as to the reports of Morgan being at Crab Orchard and Danville, I dont believe a word of it, indeed I know the last to be false for a friend of ours got a letter from her cousin there making no mention of there being any enemy in that vicinity. ...

1. Morgan's rumored approach was indeed just a rumor. See Christen Ashby Cheek, ed., "Memoirs of Mrs. E.B. Patterson: A Perspective on Danville During the War," *Register of the Kentucky Historical Society* 92 (autumn 1994): 390–91.

MONDAY FEB 9TH [1863]

... The local news is that the rebels think Kentucky in a fair way for joining the Confederacy and have sent John C Breckinridge[1] to assist in taking her out of the Union and that "honorable" or rather dishonorable gentleman is at present speechifying at Mill Springs. ...

1. John Cabell Breckinridge (1821–1875) was a Centre College graduate and Mexican War veteran. Vice president under James Buchanan, Breckinridge was a Democratic candidate for president in 1860. As a Confederate general he commanded a division at Chickamauga and Missionary Ridge, and later served as the Confederacy's

last secretary of war. See William C. Davis, *Breckinridge: Statesman, Soldier, Symbol* (Baton Rouge: Louisiana State Univ. Press, 1974).

WEDNESDAY FEB 11 [1863]

The Committee on Federal Relations has sent in an excellent report to the effect that if abolition is bad secession is still worse & Ky though she regrets the bad state of affairs is not in the least inclined to desert the stars & stripes and the union.[1] There was great rejoicing in the rebel senate a few days ago when some one announced the arrival of rebel commissioners from Ohio & Indiana and said that Kentucky was getting ready to join them and Gov Robinson was going to raise 60,000 men to drive the abolitionists out of the state and that Ohio & Indiana and other northern states were getting ready to come over to the Confederacy. All of which lies were founded I suppose on the proposal to raise a union State guard to defend Ky while the other regiments were away, and on a few secret meetings of secesh in some of the northern states which can not come to anything. . . .

1. The resolution by the Kentucky House of Representatives Committee on Federal Relations, passed on February 6, 1863, denounced the Lincoln administration and Congress for arbitrary and unconstitutional usurpation of power, particularly in their efforts to emancipate slaves. The committee condemned the Confederate government as well for its severe actions, the worst of which was its continued successes, which allowed the Federal administration to continue its own destructive course. See *Journal of the House of Representatives of the Commonwealth of Kentucky* (Frankfort: John B. Major, n.d.), 2:1346–55.

FRIDAY FEB 13TH [1863]

A "butternut" was taken up tonight at Mrs Morgans with letters & papers about him.

WEDNESDAY FEB 18 [1863]

Today was the day appointed by the rebels at Frankfort for their grand so called Democratic Peace meeting. They thought they would have it at the capitol but found themselves mistaken.[1]

1. The Kentucky State Rights Party, energized by Kentucky's vehement disapproval of the Emancipation Proclamation, changed its name to the Democratic Party and called a convention to nominate a candidate for governor. The legislature refused the party customary use of the legislative hall. See Coulter, *The Civil War and Readjustment in Kentucky*, 170–72.

Thursday Feb 19th [1863]

The rebel convention met at 11 AM yesterday but as soon as the Convention was called Col Gilbert of the 44th Ohio (acting Brigadier General) read them an order stating that reliable information having been received that a number of rebel emissarys were in the city it was ordered that all persons not residents, members of the Legislature or government officers should report their names to headquarters with satisfactory references as to their loyalty to the Union. Col Gilbert then took down all the names of the delegates none of whom dared to oppose the measure. The Colonel then addressed the convention expressing the "hope" that no one present would utter secession sentiments, for probably that would lead to the arrest of all. He then invited them to quietly disperse and depart for their homes assuring them that it was decidedly the wisest course for them to pursue, for the Ky Legislature had failed to endorse them by refusing the use of the capitol and their loyalty had not been satisfactorily vouched for he would not permit any assemblage of the kind within the limits of his command. He told them also it was useless to hold such conventions in Ky as none but men of undoubted loyalty would be permitted to run for office or if elected by disloyal votes would not be allowed to hold office. The secesh were much enraged but did not dare to say or do anything as they knew there was a strong Provost guard in the square.

Sunday Feb 22nd [1863]

Washingtons birthday, but no demonstrations were made most likely on account of the rebels being so near. . . . Capt Ashburys company 7th Ohio (the same that is camped in the lot opposite us) went out scouting about 4 oclock this evening.

Monday Feb 23rd [1863]

The cavalry came back about midnight bringing three rebel prisoners whom they had taken between here and the river. The also searched the houses of Frank Hunt[1] and Alex Morgan for Charlton Morgan[2] but found no one.

Ma saw old Mr Martin and his son at the door this morning, and had some conversation with them. The old man is strong union but his son is secesh. The young man tried to find out if Ma knew how many troops were here and told her that Saturday there was only half a regiment here. This goes to prove what we suspected that the secesh believed that all but a few of our troops had left here. The secesh have said for some time that the rebels would be back this spring and no doubt they think the secesh convention is ready to assist them and Ky is certainly going to be taken out of the Union this time. . . .

The town is full of refugees from Richmond and a good many persons have left for Cincinnati and other places of greater safety but not so many as went the last time Richmond was taken, for a good many of the union citizens have armed themselves and say that this time they are going to help defend the city.

There was no passenger train to Louisville & Frankfort this evening as the cars are being used to bring up troops. Which will be somewhat of a hindrance to persons going to the ball at Frankfort given to the union ladies of Ky. The rebels are at Winchester and Nicholasville and it is thought they will try to get to Midway and Paris and cut the railroads. John Morgan is said to be at Athens.[3] Last night three men dressed in full federal uniform went to the house of Mr Thos M Wallace, near Athens in this county and asked to see him. Mr Wallace came down and they told him they had been sent by Gen Gilmore to find out how many men he could send to help defend Lexington. Mr Wallace believed them and told them about twenty five with arms and plenty of ammunition. The three rebels then said he was their prisoner. Mr Wallace said he was not and ran through the passage to the back porch taking his gun from the closet as he passed. The men fired at him and he tried to return the fire but his gun missed and as the men had revolvers he did not try again but made his escape and came to Lexington. The rebels then made his eldest son prisoner telling him Capt R.S. Cluke wished to see him. It was feared here that the young man would be put to death as he had been very active against the secesh as provost marshall in that part of the county and so two secesh were arrested as hostages for his safety. We heard afterward that the young Wallace made his escape.

The free negroes here or rather those who have lived to themselves for negroes cant be free in Ky were very much frightened when they heard of the rebels Coming and crowded to Judge Carr's office to get possession of their free papers so they could go north if there was danger as the rebels said if they came here they would take all the free negroes and take them south for slaves.

(I made a mistake in saying no passenger train went to Louisville this evening. It did go after a delay of several hours and took a good many refugees from Richmond & other places. . . .)

1. Miss Peter possibly referred to F.W. Hunt, a Lexington lawyer educated at Kenyon College. See Perrin, *History of Fayette County, Kentucky*, 632–33.
2. Captain Charlton H. Morgan, a younger brother of General John Hunt Morgan, graduated from Transylvania University in 1858. Serving as U.S. Consul in Messina, Sicily, from 1859–1861, he became acquainted with Garibaldi. Twice captured and exchanged during the Civil War, Charlton returned to Lexington in 1865 and became steward of the Eastern Lunatic Asylum in 1871. See Perrin, *History of Fayette County, Kentucky*, 661, and Brown, *The Bold Cavaliers*, 24.
3. The commotion to which Miss Peter referred was not caused by Morgan, but rather by Morgan's lieutenant Roy S. Cluke of Montgomery County, who entered the state with about 750 men on February 4 intent on gathering information on Federals in Kentucky and supplies for his command. Cluke's men harassed the outskirts of Lexington on February 23 before falling back to southern Kentucky. Cluke eventually was captured with Morgan in Ohio and died of diphtheria in a Union prison on Johnson's Island. See Duke, *History of Morgan's Cavalry*, 363–68, and Perrin, *History of Fayette County, Kentucky*, 586–87.

TUESDAY FEB 24TH 1863

Capt Ashbury's company of the 7th Ohio Cavalry (Gen Gilmores[1] bodyguard) were out this morning and returned about 8 AM. They report the rebel pickets within five miles and brought in four prisoners one of whom was Capt Charlton Morgan. He was allowed to spend two hours at his mother's, but was not paroled. A captain and fifteen of our men whom the rebels captured a day or two ago, came in paroled this morning, the rebels having paroled them in hopes of obtaining a like favor for Capt Morgan; but Gen Gilmore told them that in paroling our captain they acted contrary to Jeff Davis' order directing that no Federal officer should be paroled and he could not on that account disobey his orders by paroling Capt Morgan.

So Capt Charlton Morgan was sent off by the evening train, to Camp Chase. It is said on good authority that he cried like a child when told that he was not to be paroled, and I dont doubt the fact as he has always had the reputation of being weakminded and childish. Mrs Morgan had a great many visitors this evening; friends and relatives coming I suppose to console about Charlton's mishap and lament over the barbarity of the Lincolnites. Gen Gilmore seems to be active, and confident of success if attacked and the men are in good spirits. He had them drawn up on Main and other streets in the centre of the town last night when he heard of the rebel pickets being so near. . . .

1. A native of Ohio, Quincy Adams Gillmore (1825–1888) ranked first in his West Point class of 1849. In 1861–1862 Gillmore served as the chief engineer for the Port Royal expedition. He commanded the Department of the South in the summer of

1863 and again from February 1865 to the end of the war. Miss Peter consistently omits one "l" from the General's last name. See Faust, ed., *Historical Times Illustrated Encyclopedia of the Civil War*, 310.

WEDNESDAY FEB 25TH [1863]

. . . The way Charlton Morgan came to be captured was this; he wrote to a Miss Mary Williams of this city, who has for some time been looked upon as engaged to him and told her he was coming on such a day and at such a time etc. to see her. Unfortunately for him the letter fell into the hands of another Miss Mary Williams who sent it to headquarters and Gen. Gilmore acted accordingly. The rebels say he would never have been captured only that in jumping over a fence he lost his pistols. The secesh seem to be making great preparations for the rebels. Yesterday the market house was crowded with secesh citizens who bought up nearly every thing in the market. And I heard of some who had provided numerous hams and cans of oysters. I am afraid they have commenced their preparations a little too soon. Their good things are likely to be spoiled before the guests arrive.

The other day a hearse belonging to J.W. Milward[1] & Son of this city, which was going to a burial was stopped on the Richmond road by a party of guerillas who took possession of the horses. The man in charge of the hearse protested against their doing so and thus leaving the hearse on the high road and when he found they paid no attention to him asked them at least to enable him to tell Mr Milward who took the horses. 'Tell that damned Abolitionist' was the reply 'that Major Steele's horse thieves took them.' This Major Steele (Dr Theophilus Steele of this city) was shortly after wounded in a skirmish The secesh say he was not shot at all he was only thrown by his horse but do not deny that some of his ribs were broken. We heard today the troops Gen Gilmore sent out had several skirmishes with the rebels and report the latter at Mt Sterling.

1. Probably Miss Peter means Joseph Usher Milward, a partner in the furniture and cabinet-making firm of Milward and Son. He was in charge of the undertaking branch of the business. See Margaret T. Macdonald, *The Milward Family of Lexington, Kentucky, 1803–1969* (Dallas: Margaret T. Macdonald, 1970), 45–46, and Perrin, *History of Fayette County, Kentucky*, 656.

THURSDAY FEB 26TH [1863]

Reported fighting at the river. Some go even so far as to say they have heard cannonading, and other reports not worth mentioning but which produced considerable excitement among timid people. . . . Two of Capt

Ashbury's men were captured by the rebels while on a scout the other day. A company of cavalry "put up" this evening in the camp of Capt Ashbury's Ohio company. They went out about dark with Capt Ashbury's company as pickets on the different roads. We heard that the cars today brought more troops and some artillery.

. . . The hospitals have turned out about 200 convalescents to aid in the defence of the city if necessary. There are not more than 800 sick here and none very sick. The rebel raid has been quite beneficial to some of them One old fellow who had been in Pa's hospital some time and never seemed to get much better, roused himself up the other morning and got his gun. 'Dr.' he said to Pa, 'Im going out to fight, the news of the rebels being so near has almost cured me!'

FRIDAY FEB 27TH [1863]

Two companies of convalescents from the Hospital in Danville came up today. They drilled this evening in the College lot. The rebels are said to have returned to Mt. Sterling with reinforcements. It is said the reason they didnt attempt to fight was that they only had a few rounds of ammunition. . . .

. . . A very heavy rain this evening and Pa said a good many people came in from Winchester in open wagons themselves and baggage all soaking wet. [They were] running from the rebels whom they feared were coming back to Winchester.

SATURDAY FEB 28TH [1863]

The Frankfort Commonwealth[1] of yesterday after mentioning that Senator Bush[2] had arrived safely in that city, from a visit to his wife says 'The rebels came into Winchester on Monday 23rd and hastened to Senator Bush's residence hoping to capture him, but his friends apprised him of the presence of the enemy and he in company with his friend S.G. Stuart, sheriff of Clark county made good his escape. We learn from Senator Bush that the rebels stole all the good horses and mules they could lay hands upon. In some cases they took every hoof of horse stock off the farms. They broke open stores and robbed the merchants of Winchester of boots, shoes, hats and such goods as they required. . . .'

. . . Senator Bush and Mr Stuart took their stand in the timber overlooking the Mt Sterling turnpike and saw the rebels pass with their horses, mules and plunder. They estimated their number at 700 or 750 with howitzers. They were armed with Springfield rifles and double barreled shot guns. Their horses looked jaded and poor except the fresh horses they had just stolen. . . .

The Observer says "the cannonading upon Richmond the other day was simply splitting logs with gunpowder." It is reported that James B Clay of Ky has gone to Liverpool. There are now no rebel forces within fifty miles of this city. The Conscription bill passed the House on Wednesday by a vote of 116 to 49. The House has voted 5000 mounted infantry for the defense of the state.

1. Edited by A.G. Hodges, this newspaper was consistently pro-Union during the war. See Coulter, *The Civil War and Readjustment in Kentucky*, 451.
2. James H.G. Bush of Clark County was a member of the state senate from 1861 to 1865. See Collins, *History of Kentucky*, 2:130.

SUNDAY MAR 1ST [1863]

Pa said the other day going to the hospital he saw Dr Payne[1] and several secesh ladies standing at a window of that gentleman's residence which is on the corner of one of the streets near the hospital [Hospital No. 1—Masonic Hall] watching the hospital very intently as if they were expecting to see him begin packing up his stores and they were going to watch and see where he put them so they could inform the rebels when they came Rebel spies are suspected of coming in very often dressed as farmers or Union soldiers. . . .

The other day a rebel surgeon was captured within our lines. He came in with three other rebels and stayed all night. The other three escaped. The 117 Ill is encamped in and around the Court house and cook upon the pavements.[2] Another regiment occupies the rooms on Water Street formerly used by John Morgan as drill rooms and armory for his Rifle company. Some 19 prisoners were brought in last night. They were all dressed in federal uniform.

1. Dr. John B. Payne resided at the northwest corner of Walnut and Barr Streets. See *Williams' Lexington City Guide*, 90, and Perrin, *History of Fayette County, Kentucky*, 854.
2. Miss Peter was evidently mistaken. The 117th Illinois was on guard duty in Memphis, Tennessee, at this time. See Thomas M. Eddy, *The Patriotism of Illinois: A Record of the Civil and Military History of the State in the War for the Union* (Chicago: Clarke & Company, 1865–1866), 2:479, and *Report of the Adjutant-General of the State of Illinois* (Springfield, Illinois: H.W. Rokker, 1886): 6:291.

MONDAY MARCH 2ND [1863]

About 27 prisoners brought in last night dressed in our uniform That is the way the rebels are able to find out so much about our movements; dressed in our uniform they can easily slip into a place like this or even pass the very sentinels or mix among our soldiers with out being suspected and learn all they want to know.

TUESDAY MARCH 3 [1863]

. . . Pa was sent for to Mrs Curds to see a man who had cut his head and had asked for him. When Pa got there young Mrs Wickliffe told him that Gen Gilmore had found the man lying on their pavement with his head cut and had had him brought into their house. That they could get nothing out of him except that he was a school commissioner from Wayne Co and knew Dr Peter. Pa dressed the mans head and tried to find out how he happened to get it cut, what was his business here and if he knew anyone or had any friends here. But the man could not tell how his head got cut nor give any connected account of himself. He asked Pa if he didnt remember him. No Pa said he didnt. Dont you remember said the man that I came to see you with Dick Prewitt,[1] but Pa could not remember anything about him. As the man was able to walk, and Pa thought if he was a school commissioner as he professed he could afford to pay his way, he had him shown the way to the Broadway Hotel. Pa thought the man was drunk but we thought it must be a crazy man from the Lunatic Asylum, especially when we heard he couldnt tell anything about himself and mentioned Dick Prewitt who used to visit at the Asylum.

1. Possibly Richard H. Prewitt, who lived on the Harrodsburg Pike between the Corporate Line and the Tollgate. See *Williams' Lexington City Guide*, 91.

FRIDAY MARCH 6TH [1863]

It is reported that after Col Runkle[1] had driven the rebels out of Mt Sterling as I mentioned before and just when he had got them in such a situation that he could easily surround a[nd] capture them an order arrived from Gen Wright[2] telling him to fall back with his command to Lexington and all because some few rebel troops had been seen hovering about the river.

Col Runkle it is said hesitated three hours whether to obey the order and then fell back. And of course the rebels regained all the ground they had lost and are said to be still near Mt Sterling and to have been reinforced by John T. Williams[,] West, Cox and perhaps others. And have stolen nearly all the horses in that part of the country. I wish we had a general that knew his business and could be trusted Gen Wright has done nothing to make the people here forget his failure last fall[3]. . . .

1. A colonel of the 45th Ohio Volunteers, Benjamin P. Runkle served from August 19, 1862, to July 21, 1864. See Thomas H.S. Hamersly, ed., *Complete Regular Army Register of the United States, 1777–1879, Part I* (Washington, DC: T.H. Hamersly, 1880), 736.
2. From June 1862 until he was ordered east in May 1863, Horatio Gouverneur Wright (1820–1899) commanded the Department of the Ohio, headquartered in Cincinnati. See Faust, ed., *Historical Times Illustrated Encyclopedia of the Civil War,* 844.
3. Possibly Miss Peter refers to Wright's order for evacuation of Lexington in the wake of the Union defeat at Richmond, Kentucky. See Wright to H.W. Halleck, September 2, 1862, in *OR,* ser. 1, vol. 16, pt. 1, 907–908.

SATURDAY MARCH 7TH [1863]

. . . I must not forget to mention that the Tableaux which the Aid Society have been preparing were exhibited last night and the night before. I only went the first night, so I can say nothing of those shown last night. What I saw were very pretty. The performance was opened by a song from the 'Thirty Four Stars,' the 'stars' being so many little girls dress[ed] in white with red and blue scarfs, with black velvet bandeaux on their heads with each a large silver star in front, and led by little Maggie Lancaster dressed as Liberty I dont know the name of the song they sung but it was sung to the tune of the rebels song 'Bonny Blue Flag['] and was a kind of parody on that song. The chorus being just the reverse of that in the rebel song and was this

> Hurra! hurra! for equal rights hurra!
> Hurra! for the Union flag
> With every stripe and Star!
> and one verse I think was thus
> The rebel forces say Hurra!
> For the hated Stars and Bars,
> But we will make them feel the stripes
> And make them see the stars. . . .

Maggie has an unusually strong voice for a little girl not more than 4 or 5 years old and could be heard all over the house and every word of the song distinctly heard. . . .

SUNDAY MARCH 8TH [1863]

Nothing new today except that some one told me that a good many of the regiments left here today going off as if on an expedition. There was no regiment in the Court House yard Thursday night when we passed there nor any signs of their having been there.

MONDAY MARCH 9TH [1863]

Today the great Union Convention appointed to take place here comes off. . . .¹

1. The Union Democrats met March 18–19 in Louisville, but historian E. Merton Coulter makes no mention of a Lexington meeting. See Coulter, *The Civil War and Readjusment in Kentucky*, 172–73, 159 n.

TUESDAY MAR 10TH [1863]

I have seen no one who has been to the Union Convention yesterday. But heard that Gen S.S. Fry made a speech, also Hon R. Buckner & others. Judge Buckners speech is looked upon as being rather 'Copperhead,'¹ and was hostile to the present administration Resolutions were passed opposing the acts of the administration but were laid on the table and delegates were appointed to attend the meeting at Louisville on the 18th inst.² The Legislature has passed a resolution calling for a convention of the Mississippi states³ with a view to determine what is best to be done for the preservation of the whole Government, and the purpose of maintaining their integrity and union etc. I dont see any necessity for such a move. I think it more likely to do harm than good. . . .

1. This term first was applied to northern Democrats who opposed Lincoln's war policy. Also referred to as Peace Democrats, these politicians proposed a negotiated peace with the Confederacy. Lincoln reportedly employed all the wartime prerogatives of the executive—including censorship and suspension of the writ of habeas corpus—to suppress them. Modern scholarship, however, "has proved, beyond any reasonable doubt, that no systematic, organized disloyal opposition to the war existed in the North." See Mark E. Neely Jr., *The Fate of Liberty: Abraham Lincoln and Civil Liberties* (New York: Oxford Univ. Press, 1991), xii.
2. The party in control of the state called itself the Union Democracy and held its state convention in Louisville, March 18–19, 1863. Joshua F. Bell and Richard Jacob were chosen as candidates for governor and lieutenant governor, respectively. A month later, however, Bell withdrew and the Union Democratic Council nominated Thomas E. Bramlette to replace him. See Coulter, *The Civil War and Readjustment in Kentucky*, 172–73.
3. This resolution passed the Kentucky House of Representatives on March 2, 1863, but was defeated in the state senate. Miss Peter was a regular reader of the pro-Union *Cincinnati Gazette*, which reported the incident on March 3. For the text of

the resolution, see *Acts of the General Assembly of the Commonwealth of Kentucky* (Frankfort: John B. Major and W.E. Hughes, 1861, 1862, 1863), 391–94.

THURSDAY MARCH 12 [1863]

. . . Several Irish people living on the edge of town near the Covington railroad have the smallpox, and it is thought likely it was brought from Richmond, Va [(]where the disease is said to have been lately) in letters. The smallpox can be carried in that way and it is certain the secesh here do get a great many letters from their rebel friends in various parts of the union. A good many such letters pass through the Lebanon post office Whether the postmaster is secesh or whether he has no means of distinguishing the rebel documents from the union ones I dont know. . . . The secesh here are said to have received letters saying that Gen John C Breckinridge and Col Pegram[1] would be here in a few weeks I hope we shall be able to give them a warm reception if they do come.

1. A native Virginian, John Pegram (1832–1865) served as chief engineer on the staffs of Generals P.G.T. Beauregard and Bragg. During the Confederate invasion of Kentucky, Pegram was Kirby Smith's chief of staff. See Faust, ed., *Historical Times Illustrated Encyclopedia of the Civil War*, 568.

SATURDAY MAR 14 [1863]

. . . The Paris Flag of yesterday says about 10 or 12 rebel cavalry attacked a forage train of Government wagons loaded with corn last Wednesday on the Flat Rock pike about 8 miles from Paris.[1] The man in charge of the train having intimation of the intended attack hastened to town and Lieut Schooler with a dozen men went to the rescue and dispersed the rebels killing two of their horses.

. . . It appears from the dispatches in this mornings paper that it was by Gen Quincy A Gilmores orders that the Frankfort Convention was broken up by Col Sam A Gilbert[2] Gen Gilmore telegraphed to Gen Boyle that he had ordered that the Democratic secesh Convention should not sit anywhere in his District but they might go to Louisville. And Gen. Boyle telegraphed back that they mustnt be sent to Louisville, that he wasnt willing to allow a Convention of Secessionists at that place who had been driven from an adjoining district as dangerous.

The members of that Convention have kept very quiet since that memorable night. We expected to hear a great outcry about Abolition tyranny and preventing freedom of speech etc. I should like to know whether anything will be done with the scamps. About 40 secesh citizens were sent off today some north; some south. I think they ought all to be sent south. Up North it is likely they will be conscripted and I dont much like the idea of there being such mean men as them in our army. They are so fond of the rebels why not send them south to their friends! The secesh ladies were very much excited and walked the streets a great deal. . . . Another Union meeting was held this morning. The court house bell was to have rung at 11 AM and most of the union men were at the court house at that time but it wasnt rung until 12 oclock from some cause or other. Judge Buckner & his principal adherents didnt show their faces. Judge Robinson[3] made a speech, the resolutions of the last meeting were voted down unanimously and strong Union ones passed instead.

The Cincinati Commercial[4] of today has a very good letter about the meeting last Monday, and says of Judge Buckners speech 'R A Buckner attacked Gen Fry, and spoke in a very contemptous manner of those whom he termed "ultra" union men He expressed great surprise at hearing certain sentiments uttered by Gen Fry applauded in the court house. It was a startling noise to which his ears were unaccustomed; that new lights were springing up in this section who in [the] future proposed to guide the direction of affairs. There was a nucleus already formed, around which he feared there would soon gather a formidable party who would be prepared to submit to Lincolns administration and if necessary to his proclamation. He wanted it distinctly understood he belonged to no such party He denounced almost every act of the Federal Congress, all of Mr. Lincoln's, called Representative Casey[5] an alien and eulogized the other members. He was in favor of the Mississippi Convention, because the rebels laying down their arms and meeting us in peacable convention was the only way to end the war except by subjugation and to that he was and ever would be opposed.' The writer thinks Mr Buckner and Mr Wickliffe[6] had the programme all laid out and the resolutions prepared before hand and regrets as all must do that Kentucky has been so woefully misrepresented by her public men and newspapers, and says 'In the name of Fayette County I can say We love thee R.A.B. but never more be representative of ours.' Mr Speaker Buckner acted a very bad part in that affair. Did he think I wonder, that that was the way to set about getting himself made a Senator? If he did he is dreadfully mistaken, he has destroyed all chance of his ever being elected to public office from this county. The union men will not join him or any like him against the administration. Though the latter may not be every thing they could wish yet they have sense enough to see that their best policy lies in supporting the government and that it is better to put up with the lesser evil of a weak administration than to bring a greater one on themselves by weakening the Union party by such a split as would be made if Mr Buckner's designs were carried out. To form a party against the administration would be to deliver ourselves an easy prey to the rebels With what face could we oppose and denounce Congress and Mr Lincoln and then call upon them for aid when the rebels invaded the state? Mr Buckner perhaps might do such a thing, but I dont think there is any true union man in the state who would not blush at the very idea of such a disgraceful proceeding Mr B is in favor of the Mississippi convention and opposed to subjugation. [He] thinks the rebels laying down their arms and meeting us in peacable convention the only way to end the war. I can very well agree to their laying down their arms but they must not only lay them down but surrender[,] acknowledge themselves in the wrong, return to their allegiance on terms honorable for us and submit themselves to the laws. This end cannot at present be obtained by a convention, the rebels refuse still to agree to any terms honorable for us. But Mr Buckner says they mustnt be subjugated. Oh no We must let the dear creatures do exactly what pleases them and just now when we are better prepared than ever to whip them we must deliver ourselves into their hands to be despised by them and all the world. Shame ten thousand times on such a mean spirited policy!

1. Military records confirm an "affair" at Paris on March 11, 1863, but provide no reports. See *OR,* ser. 1, vol. 23, pt. 1, 2, 932.
2. The convention of the Kentucky States Rights Party convened in Frankfort on February 18, 1863, to nominate candidates for state office. Colonel E.A. Gilbert, in command of Federal troops at Frankfort, refused to let the convention sit. His action was upheld by General Gillmore, the Union commander in central Kentucky. See Coulter, *The Civil War and Readjustment in Kentucky,* 170–71.
3. George Robertson (1790–1874), a Lexington resident, served in Congress from 1817 to 1821 and from 1822 to 1827 in the Kentucky House. In 1864 he was elected to the Kentucky Court of Appeals. See Kleber, ed., *The Kentucky Encyclopedia,* 776.
4. Edited by Murat Halstead, this newspaper was strongly Unionist and reported closely on Kentucky affairs. See Coulter, *The Civil War and Readjustment in Kentucky,* 451.
5. Samuel Lewis Casey represented Union County in the Kentucky House of Representatives, 1860–1862. When Henry C. Burnett was expelled from Congress, Casey was elected as a Republican to fill the vacancy and served from March 10, 1862, to March 3, 1863. See *Biographical Directory of the American Congress, 1774–1971* (Washington, DC: Government Printing Office, 1971), 715.
6. A native Lexingtonian, Daniel Carmichael Wickliffe owned and edited the *Observer and Reporter* from 1838–1865. Originally a proslavery Whig, after the demise of that party Wickliffe became a Democrat and opposed the introduction of any emancipation element into the state Constitutional Convention of 1849. Wickliffe

served as Kentucky secretary of state under Governor Robinson in 1862. See *Biographical Encyclopedia of Kentucky*, 348.

MONDAY MAR 16 [1863]

Some of Gen Carters command came in last night.[1] Gen Gilmore it seems is going to just camp all around town. He says he has a long list of rebels both male and female to be sent away from here. They are entrenching at Clay's Ferry.[2]

1. General Samuel P. Carter, an East Tennessee native and veteran of the U.S. Navy, commanded the 1st Brigade in the District of Central Kentucky. His troops were returning from operations against Cluke's command. See Dyer, *A Compendium of the War of the Rebellion*, 1:528, and Warner, *Generals in Blue*, 74.
2. Clay's Ferry crossed the Kentucky River between Fayette and Madison Counties. See Kleber, ed., *The Kentucky Encyclopedia*, 205–6.

TUESDAY MAR 17 [1863]

The 7th Ohio Cavalry passed through town this evening with their baggage going to encamp about a mile and a half out. I wonder if they will take Mr. Adam's place near the Covington depot. He is a very bitter rebel, and there was some talk of taking his place for a camping ground. The regiment went out in that direction.

WEDNESDAY MAR 18 [1863]

... Mrs Joel Higgins[1] has been ordered to leave. According to an order of Gen Rosecrans,[2] which says I think (for I only know of it by hearsay) that all rebel women having protectors in the south should be sent to them If such is the case a good many will be sent from here.

1. A native of Mississippi, Ann Louisa Higgins was the daughter of the Reverend Randal Gibson. See Charles Kerr, ed., *History of Kentucky* (Chicago: American Historical Society, 1922), 4:202.
2. William Starke Rosecrans (1819–1898) of Ohio first distinguished himself in the campaign that drove the Confederates from western Virginia in 1861. In October 1862 Rosecrans relieved Buell in Kentucky and his troops were designated the Army of the Cumberland. A crushing defeat, inflicted by Bragg at Chickamauga in September 1863, all but ended Rosecrans' military career. See Peter Cozzens, *This Terrible Sound: The Battle of Chickamauga* (Urbana: Univ. of Illinois Press, 1992), 522–28.

THURSDAY MAR 19 [1863]

The Union State Convention to nominate candidates for the next election met in Louisville yesterday at the Circuit Court room. During the afternoon session Ex Gov Wickliffe introduced the Hon J A Cravens[1] of

Indiana and on motion of Gov Wickliffe he was invited to take a seat on the Presidents platform. He was called on for a speech but excused himself as he was unwilling to interrupt the deliberations of the body, which had a large amount of business before it. He hoped they would inaugurate a policy which while it would put down the rebellion would at the same time preserve the Constitution of the country with all its guarantees sacred. He was proceeding in his remarks to the effect that the Democratic party was the only party to save the country and its members had been branded as rebels, butternuts, copperheads and traitors, when cries arose from all parts of the hall that he must be a copperhead and that this was a Union convention and they didnt want any Democratic seceshs and a great deal of confusion prevailed. The presiding officer begged that Mr Cravens might be heard but it was not until the Hon George H. Yeaman[2] begged them to respect Indiana in the person of her representative as her sons had battled manfully in defense of Ky, that Mr Cravens was allowed to proceed or rather to explain. He said he might have been unfortunate in the choice of his language he was a plain man, but if he had been permitted to proceed he should have said that all party was nothing to the great duty of restoring the country. He hoped the action of the convention would be harmonious. Great interests depended upon it. Indiana was looking with solicitude to it in common with the entire country. He thanked the convention for allowing him to make this explanation; he should go home without any harsh feelings. He knew Ky well, her devotion to the Union and the sacrifices she had made. Ky and Indiana were neighbors and had great mutual interests to protect. If any unfortunate difference of opinion or any infelicity of expression on his part caused him to fail to make his position understood he deeply regretted it, but he yielded to no one in his wish to see the Union restored and he was ardently attached to the government and fervently desired to transmit its blessings to posterity unimpaired (a voice "why didnt you say that at first.") He then "subsided," and Col Whittaker[3] then moved that as he had been creditably informed that a number of "butternuts" were in the hall who had no business there, a Sergeant at Arms should be appointed to eject them which was done.

1. Sixty-one-year-old James H. Cravens, noted Indiana congressman and abolitionist, served briefly as the lieutenant colonel of the 83rd Indiana. After his retirement, he crossed the Midwest in support of the Union cause. See *A Biographical History of Eminent and Self-Made Men of the State of Indiana* (Cincinnati: Western Biographical Publishing Company, 1880), 2:262–66.
2. George Helm Yeaman, a lawyer and judge from Daviess County, Kentucky, spoke

against emancipation while serving as a Unionist member of Congress from 1862–1865. See Kleber, ed., *The Kentucky Encyclopedia*, 971–72.
3. Walter C. Whitaker, colonel of the 6th Kentucky Infantry, retained his seat in the Kentucky Senate. He was afterwards promoted to the rank of general. See Speed, *The Union Regiments of Kentucky*, 60–61.

SATURDAY MAR 21ST [1863]

. . . Thursdays train to Nashville was thrown off the track by guerillas four miles above Richland station.[1] Locomotive, tender, and two express cars smashed. Guerillas called themselves Morgan's men. They fired into the rear car containing women and children. The passengers returned the fire killing one and wounding three. Guerillas then commenced paroling at the head of the train taking away the officers sidearms, rifles, carpet sacks, etc. The Adams Express car was robbed, but part of the contents were recovered. The mail was taken but that was recovered also. The conductor ran back a mile or two to a stockade and the soldiers from there came up at double quick, recaptured the train, drove off the guerillas and took four prisoners. . . .

. . . Two secesh who went off with Morgan[,] a Hardesty and But-ters[,] delivered themselves up to the authorities here today. A young fellow named Wallace (secesh) who came back to see his mother was taken up. Two wagons loaded with negroes were brought in today. They are some that were run off by the secesh last fall.

1. A train near Richland Station was attacked and derailed by a body of sixty to seventy-five guerrillas. Two companies of the 129th Illinois drove them off. See *OR*, ser. 1, vol. 23, pt. 1, 147–50.

SUNDAY MARCH 22ND [1863]

. . . More troops came in today. I cannot find out how many troops are here now, they are continually going and coming and it is hard to find out when they go, where to or anything about them. If the secesh know as little about them as I do, their rebel friends wont get much information.

MONDAY MAR 23RD [1863]

A part of Mt Sterling (about 15 houses it is stated) was burnt Sunday by a force of Cluke's, variously estimated at from 300 to 800. There were only about 150 Federals in the town who stationed themselves in the court house and defended themselves for five hours when the rebels set fire to the houses around them and the citizens begged them to surrende[r] to save the town from being burnt. . . .

... A spy was caught the other night trying to get over the fence at headquarters (a tolerably high fence, brickwork with an iron paling on top) near the telegraph tent. A yellow woman from one of the neighbors saw him and knew him. She asked him what brought him there, that she thought he was in the rebel army. He replied he did belong to the southern army but was a paroled prisoner. Well said she "I dont believe that," and ran and told the guard. The man ran down the street, but was stopped by another guard and taken.

A Capt Alexander a person our men have been looking for some time was captured the other night at his brother-in-law's in Woodford County. A lady overheard Dr Major say, that he didnt mind being sent North at all; he could do a great deal more mischief there than here. I hear people are getting up petitions for Dr Major and Mrs Joel Higgins not to be sent off, and Union people have signed them. I dont think that is right. Everybody knows they are most bitter rebels and Gen Gilmore has a good reason for ordering them off. I think the more of the secesh that go the better for us. The only petition I would sign for them would be that they should be sent South instead of North. ...

TUESDAY MARCH 24TH [1863]

... They have commenced fortifying Lexington, earthworks are being thrown up about a mile out on all the roads, and batteries to be planted to defend them. ...

WEDNESDAY MAR 25TH [1863]

... The 180 Federals who fought Cluke at Mt Sterling are said to have mostly consisted of convalescents and teamsters under Capt Rankin or Radcliffe of the 10th Ky.[1] Col. Walker of the 10th Ky[2] who had been in Mt Sterling had been ordered to leave the town and get between Cluke and the mountains, and Col Garrard of the 7th Ohio was to come up in front from Paris and thus surround the rebels, but from some cause or other he was too late and the plan failed. Col Walker was then ordered to Winchester. Before our men left they apprised the citizens of their intention to leave Mt Sterling, and the merchants accordingly sent off their valuables, so the rebels wont find much plunder there.

... The rebels when they burnt the houses [in Mt. Sterling] went to the hospital, bayoneted some eight or ten sick who were there and then burnt the building with the bodies in it. They went to Dr Flemings and forced him to stand by while they burnt all his surgical appartus [They] went to the house of an union man who was sick in bed and when his wife and daughter bent over him to protect him tore them off and shot him, and did as many more things of the same sort as they could. . . .

Col Walker and some of his officers came here last night; it is said their object was to get Gen Gilmore to let them return to Mt Sterling but he refused. Gen Gilmore has ordered all the sick in Hospitals Nos. 1 and 5 to be moved to the Medical Hall or elsewhere where they will not be so near the lines. . . .

Our neighbor Dr Driggs the dentist[3] was at Mrs Woolleys today. Said Mrs W was very much alarmed about the rebels coming, such a large force, etc. Asked her where the rebels could get such a large army from. "Oh" she said "all our army from the Rappahannock is coming here." Then remembering she had betrayed herself, she caught hold of the Dr's coat sleeve "I didnt mean to say I knew it certainly," she stammered, "you know I only supposed so. You mustnt think I know any thing positive, I only imagined so you know, etc," making it all the more certain by her agitation and anxiety to remove the impression she had made, that she did know what had escaped her to be true. . . .

The secesh here were very uneasy about Col Cluke when he first came in the state, as he had only joined the rebels last fall when the rebels were here (He is from Clarke Co) and said if it had been John Morgan they would not have been at all anxious but Cluke was young and inexperienced and they feared he might come to harm.

1. Captain William D. Ratcliffe and his command, Company E, 10th Kentucky Cavalry (U.S.), were captured and paroled at Mt. Sterling. See Speed, *The Union Regiments of Kentucky*, 217–20.
2. Colonel Charles J. Walker commanded the 10th Kentucky Cavalry (U.S.). See Speed, *The Union Regiments of Kentucky*, 218.
3. S. Drigg's dental office was located on Jordan's Row opposite the courthouse. See *Williams' Lexington City Directory*, 45.

THURSDAY MARCH 26 [1863]

The rebel force that invaded the southern portion of the state about a week ago are said to have been about 3000 men under Col Wm C.P. Breckinridge who issued a proclamation at Somerset calling upon all "good citizens" to join his standard.[1] All who did not do so within four days to be conscripted . . .

The counties of Fayette, Clarke, Bourbon, Woodford, Jessamine, and that part of Franklin are placed under martial law and Col S.D. Bruce appointed temporarily Provost Marshall General for the above named district;[2] and authorized to collect together as many negroes as may be wanted to work on the entrenchments, etc. by general order No. 26 of Gen. Q.A. Gilmore. Some one was arrested at Mrs. Morgans this evening.

. . . It seems the secesh here fully expected the rebels yesterday, and some of the secesh ladies went to Mr John Lee the confectioner[3] to get him to put rebel flags on their cakes. But Mr. Lee told them he would see them and their cakes in a very hot place first. . . . Mrs Brig. Gen Joe Shelby[4] who has been staying for a while at her father-in law's[,] Mr. Gratz[,][5] has been ordered to leave. Mr.Gratz wrote to Mr Lincoln to get the order recinded. Mr. Lincoln replied she might stay if Mr Gratz would hold himself responsible for her good behavior. Gen Gilmore would [not] agree to the petition to let Mrs. Joel Higgins stay, so application was made to Gen Wright who said she might either go or stand her trial and in that case if she was found guilty she would be hung. So I suppose she will go.

One of the principal things against her was a letter she wrote to her sons, in which she invited them back. [She] said now was the time for them to come, that the federals had more sick in the hospitals than men in the field That now was the time for retaliation She believed in retaliation and much more of the same sort, winding up by saying that twelve noble Southern men had been murdered in cold blood the night before. Shryock[6] who kept the ferry of that name between here and Versailles, and who aided the rebels last fall, and Whalley who made the shot and shell for them, have been taken. The latter was put in irons.

1. Colonel Breckinridge commanded a portion of the 1,550–man cavalry force led by Colonel John C. Pegram that raided Kentucky in search of cattle for the Confederate forces. The raid lasted from March 22 until April 1, 1863. See *OR*, ser. 1, vol. 23, pt. 1, 171–74.
2. Colonel Sanders D. Bruce's permanent post was in Clarksville, Tennessee. See *OR*, ser. 1, vol. 23, pt. 2, 117, 219, 240.
3. John W. Lee operated the U.S. Premium Bakery and Confectionary at Number 10, Main Street. See *Williams' Lexington City Directory*, 65.
4. Born in Lexington and educated at Transylvania University, Joseph Orville Shelby (1830–1897) was a wealthy rope manufacturer and one of Kentucky's most influential citizens before the Civil War. Shelby organized a cavalry company for the Confederacy and was active in almost every campaign west of the Mississippi River. See Faust, ed., *Historical Times Illustrated Encyclopedia of the Civil War*, 673.
5. Gratz's second wife, Anna, the widow of O. Shelby of Tennessee, was the mother of General Shelby. See Perrin, *History of Fayette County, Kentucky*, 612.
6. A former partner of Lexington architect John McMurtry, Cincinnatus Shryock

operated a ferry on the Kentucky River in Woodford County. An old friend of John Hunt Morgan and a Confederate sympathizer, Shryock assisted the Lexington Rifles in their escape after Union troops occupied Lexington in September 1861. In July 1862 Shryock assisted Morgan in crossing the river from Anderson County for his famous raid upon Midway and Cynthiana. See Thomas D. Clark, *The Kentucky* (New York: Farrar and Rinehart, 1942), 299–309.

FRIDAY MAR 27 [1863]

The fellow who was taken at Mrs Morgans yesterday was Teddy Flanagan. He was dressed in citizens clothes and they say he went first to Dr. Bush's and rang the bell and asked to see Dr. Bush, who was not at home. No doubt he did it to make people think he was an union man. I heard he was a lieutenant.

. . . There is service at the Episcopal Church every Wednesday and Friday (it being Lent) and today all the secesh ladies belonging to that church went dressed in their finest. We wondered what was 'in the wind' for they are not in the habit of going on week days Lent or no Lent. It turned out that today is the day appointed by Jeff Davis as a fast day. Some refugees from Estill [County] with their families came in today. There was a report that some of the rebels had come to Clays ferry but the river was so high they couldnt cross. Also that they were in Richmond but several wagons of sick came in this evening, I dont know exactly from what place and they said they had passed through Richmond and there were no rebels there. . . .

SATURDAY MAR 28 [1863]

. . . We don't know half as much about whats going on here now as we did when Gen Wright had command. Up in this part of the town, we dont know whether the cars bring troops, or where they take them or how many there are, or who they are or anything; we only suppose it is so, from hearing the cars whistle so continually. . . .

SUNDAY MARCH 29TH [1863]

It is said Gen Burnside[1] has dismissed Capt. Radcliffe of the 10th Ky from the service for surrendering and fighting without orders at Mt Sterling. . . . Gen Burnside sent all the officers and men who had been paroled at Mt Sterling by Cluke back to their regiments as the parole had not been rightly given.

1. Ambrose Everett Burnside (1824–1881) was an Indiana native and an 1847 graduate of West Point. He commanded the Army of the Potomac at Fredericksburg and is

generally held accountable for the Union defeat. In March 1863 Burnside assumed command of the Department of the Ohio which included portions of Kentucky. See William Marvel, *Burnside* (Chapel Hill: Univ. of North Carolina Press, 1991).

TUESDAY MARCH 31ST [1863]

... Exertions are being made by ladies and citizens to establish a Soldiers Home here on the Cincinnati model. ... Adjutant Gen L Thomas[1] made a speech to the soldiers at Cairo [Illinois] yesterday, in which he spoke of the matter of receiving colored men into the lines and reprobated the way in which some of them had been treated, instancing some cases in which they had been returned to Slavery (some of the soldiers when they get hold of a negro have been in the habit of selling them) The camp of rendezvous for blacks which is now at Cairo will soon by order of Gen Hurlbut[2] be removed to Island No 10[3] where they will be employed in tilling deserted farms. I expect when the negroes hear of this they wont feel so anxious to run off to the soldiers. Sambo doesnt like hard work especially if it has to be done regularly. And I have noticed that since Mr Lincolns January proclamation, and since they have found out that the soldiers make them work just as hard if not harder than their masters they dont take half as much interest in them and are not near as willing to do things for them, as when the army first came here. For instance when the hospitals were first brought here, they were very poorly supplied with comforts, and had to depend a great deal on the ladies. A great many of the ladies here sent food to the sick three times a day, each lady having a patient or sometimes two or three to whom she sent his meals regularly. My sister Lettie was one and sent every day just whatever we happened to have and went herself as often as possible, but if she couldnt, always sent by one of the servants. During all last winter this went on and I noticed that the servants were always willing to make bread, mush, or cook anything Lettie might want, no matter how much they might have to do, or go to the hospital at all times and in all weathers and put themselves to any amount of trouble and inconvenience to wait on the soldiers. And the servant whom Lettie generally sent with the things, would often, when Lettie thought it was too bad weather or that we had nothing worth sending beg to be sent and persuade Lettie until she consented to send. But now, (though it is very seldom there is occasion to send as the Government supplies everything) if asked to go, they seem to think it is doing you a favor for them to consent and seem to have lost all interest in it. ...

that about 150 prisoners were brought in today. Several ame today & yesterday. Some secesh men were seen walking about the regiments at the cars asking all kinds of questions to find out all about them, such as are these all of our men that are coming, how many more are coming? How many men are there in this regiment? making their inquiries as if they had been union men. . . . The rebels went to Harrods-burg about the same time as to Danville and most of the students from the college and such of the professors as would be liable to be conscripted by the rebels came to Louisville and here. A good many of the secesh sent from here to Cincinnati have been sent from that place to Camp Chase. A handbill was sent to Pa today, entitled "A Review of the Politic of Ky from 1861 to 1863," which is rather hard on Mr D.C. Wickliffe, Frank R Hunt, and W.A. Dudley former Quartermaster Gen and abuses Judge Buckner soundly.

1. Lorenzo Thomas (1804–1875), a native of Delaware, served as adjutant general of the U.S. Army from 1861 until 1869. His service in that capacity was not particularly distinguished, especially in the eyes of Secretary of War Edwin M. Stanton, who kept Thomas removed from Washington, D.C., much of the time on harmless missions. See Faust, ed., *Historical Times Illustrated Encyclopedia of the Civil War*, 754.
2. Originally from Charleston, South Carolina, Stephen Augustus Hurlbut (1815–1882), a lawyer and veteran of the Seminole War, was a Republican member of the Illinois state legislature at the outbreak of the Civil War. As a division commander in the Army of the Tennessee, Hurlbut's military achievements at Shiloh and Corinth were creditable. Illinois Republicans, convinced that their party's identification with emancipation was a political liability, cheered Hurlbut's April 1863 decision to relocate the contraband camp from Cairo to Island Number 10. See Arthur Charles Cole, *The Centennial History of Illinois, Volume Three: The Era of the Civil War* (Springfield, Illinois: Illinois Centennial Commission, 1919), 334–35.
3. Located in the Mississippi River near the spot where the states of Missouri, Arkansas, Tennessee, and Kentucky meet, this island had significant strategic value. Confederate forces fortified the area in early 1861 to block Federal navigation of the Mississippi. Union forces under General John Pope reduced the fortress in early 1862. See Larry J. Daniel and Lynn N. Bock, *Island No. 10: Struggle for the Mississippi Valley* (Tuscaloosa: Univ. of Alabama Press, 1996).

WEDNESDAY APRIL 1ST [1863]

I heard a good joke on Mr James Hannah[1] today. He went out to look at the fortifications and someone (I suppose some of the officers superintending the work) asked him what he came for, what he was doing there or something of the sort. Mr. Hannah said he wanted to get a good look at the works 'Well' was the reply, 'we can put you where you can have a much better one than from where you stand!' So they put him to work for a little while in the trenches An order [has been] issued that all soldiers found drunk or in whiskey shops should be sent to work for so many hours on the trenches. . . .

1. James Hannah had an office on the east side of Upper between Main and Short Streets. See *Williams' Lexington City Guide*, 57.

Thursday Ap 2nd [1863]

... Gen Burnside arrived on the 4 PM train from Louisville. He was driven to the Phoenix Hotel in Mrs McAllister's[1] carriage, and was welcomed by the ringing of bells and the shouts of crowds assembled to greet him. In the evening after tea he had a kind of reception, numbers of union ladies & gentlemen coming to be introduced to him. Each one came up[,] was introduced, spoke a few words and then passed out to make room for others. Gen Burnside is just like the pictures of him, that one can see in nearly all the pictorial papers, and at daguerrotype rooms. He said he was going away tomorrow but when he returned would most probably make Lexington his headquarters

1. The residence of Mrs. Sarah McAllister was located on the south side of Main Street near Mulberry. See *Williams' Lexington City Guide*, 78.

Friday April 3rd [1863]

... An Indian mound[1] (on Mr Shelton Moores place, I believe) was excavated for a magazine. In digging the fortifications a heap of charcoal and some bones were found from which it was supposed that some Chiefs body had been burnt there. There is a new provost marshall and guard (a Pennsylvania regt) and the latter are going to drill every morning at 9 oclock on Cheapside.

... The negroes will not be kept working on the fortifications any longer, soldiers will take their place. ...

1. Indian mounds were also present on Dandridge, the estate of C.C. Moore, adjacent to Meredith, the Peter family estate. In 1871 Dr. Peter aided the excavation of an Indian mound on another adjoining estate and had the artifacts sent to the Smithsonian Institution. See Ranck, *History of Lexington*, 10–11.

Saturday April 4th [1863]

... The Gazette has in it a letter from a gentleman who has lately returned from France stating that a letter was received at court on the 21st of January last (he was told this by some one belonging to the court) from Richmond Va. dated 2nd of November and signed by seventy three persons, among whom were Jeff Davis, his cabinet, a good many senators, but only two generals (Wise and Toombs), calling upon Napoleon to recognize the Confederacy and saying that when their independence had been acknowledged and their army recalled and they were at liberty to act all the non slaveholders and common white people in the south would be sent north and a nobility formed to consist of the slaveholders. And the slaves would take the place of peasants thus forming the strongest kind of a nobility since the peasant would be separated from his lord both by color and race. . . . But I would like to know if they sent all but the slaves and slaveholders north what would they do if the north still continued to wish to bring the southern states back into the Union. How would they keep them out? Do they think the fear of France would keep us out or do they think Napoleon such a goose as to agree to all their feather brained proposals?

Sunday April 5 [1863]

The 36th Massachusetts regiment that has been staying at Adams place (Eden as he calls it) received marching orders today whilst the chaplain was reading the service.[1] They at once struck their tents, packed up and started. They were very sorry to leave so soon as they said this was the nicest place they had been in for a long time and the driest as they had been in the midst of mud all winter.

. . . The secesh ladies kept a great bowing and saluting of the prisoners yesterday, and the new Provost Marshal Col. Sigfried is said to have warned them that the next time they did so they would be sent to Camp Chase or 'Dixie.'

1. The 36th Massachusetts, part of the 1st Division, 9th Corps, headed to Camp Dick Robinson. See Dyer, *A Compendium of the War of the Rebellion*, 3:1262.

Tuesday April 7th [1863]

The notorious rebel "emmissary" Miss Moon[1] was captured the other day starting from Cincinnati, and a large number of letters & papers and bottles of quinine and morphene found on her. She has made several trips south for the secesh here.

. . . Last Thursday night while Gen Burnside and a number of other gentlemen who had been invited to meet him were at Mr Davy Sayres and while the gentlemen were speaking to the crowd from the door, they were continually hissed by Mrs Hart Gibson and her sister Miss Ella Duncan, who had gone into the house without the knowledge of Mr or Mrs Sayre or their father, Mr Henry Duncan Sr. who was in the house at the time and stationed themselves by the open window of the little room over the hall, the window being just over the front door where the speakers were standing.

When the band played national airs these women sung 'Bonny Blue Flag' 'Dixie' and other secesh songs, and when Gov Robinson[2] in his speech said very warmly 'The Union must be preserved, it will be preserved, and it *shall* be preserved' the hisses were so distinctly heard that the crowd was with difficulty restrained from stoning the house. And then these creatures had the impudence to come down and send for Gen Burnside to come out unto the hall and be introduced to them.

1. Virginia "Jennie" Moon, of southern Ohio, regularly transported letters and personal papers to southerners across the Ohio River. She was arrested under Burnside's General Order No. 38. See Marvel, *Burnside*, 232–33.
2. On Robinson's difficulties maintaining his commitment to the Union and to white Kentuckians' right to hold slaves, see Smith, "James F. Robinson," 75–76.

WEDNESDAY [APRIL] 8TH [1863]

A brigade left this morning taking with them the fine band which has been delighting us for the last few weeks. . . .

FRIDAY APRIL 10TH [1863]

Straggling parties of guerillas still in the state who attack passenger trains, and commit outrages on the farmers . . .

TUESDAY APRIL 14 [1863]

Gen Wilcox[1] now commands this Post. He was serenaded last night by Saxtons band at the Phoenix hotel and made a speech. . . .

1. A native of Michigan, Orlando Bolivar Willcox (1823–1907) commanded the 1st Division of General Burnside's 9th Corps. Miss Peter repeatedly errs in spelling the general's last name.

WEDNESDAY APRIL 15TH [1863]

. . . An order received this evening for Pa to break up Hospital No 1. All the hospitals here will be broken up except No 6 (the Medical Hall) and the sick sent to Cincinnati where the hospitals are nearly empty.

FRIDAY APRIL 17 [1863]

. . . 28 prisoners taken beyond Mt. Sterling were brought in this evening. Gen Wilcox took possession of Headqr today, bringing with him besides his staff a guard of about 20 of the 48 Penn[1] who camped in the lot opposite. . . .

1. A veteran regiment of eastern theatre campaigns, the 48th Pennsylvania served as a provost guard in Lexington beginning in March 1863. The regiment later achieved fame for digging and exploding a mine during the siege of Petersburg. See Samuel P. Bates, *History of Pennsylvania Volunteers, 1861–1865* (Harrisburg: B. Singerly, 1969), 1:1191–95.

SATURDAY APRIL 18 [1863]

. . . 'Thursday,' says the Observer, 'Mr AB Gilbert[1] of Owsley Co., former member of [the] Legislature, was at our office and gave a sad account of the district in which he resides,' Clukes men robbed him of grain & stock some weeks ago and on Wednesday of last week some of Marshalls men under Jack May[2] came to his house [and] in his absence appropriated 33 blankets and other articles [They] took all the horses and robbed the bee hives, and though his wife offered them a thousand dollars not to do it burnt two dwelling houses[,] a store house and granery, not permitting Mrs Gilbert to save any clothes or anything but a bed from the flames.

Mr Gilberts two sons who were in the house sought to make their escape by running up the bed of a creek, but were discovered[,] pursued & repeatedly shot at. One of the rebels named Lacy caught up with the oldest Mr John Gilbert who was in the rear of his brother and said to him: 'God d——m you surrender or Ill hang you.' Young Gilbert drew a pistol and shot him in the arm and a second shot brought him from his horse dead. The two young men then made their escape amid a shower of balls. The rebels burnt the jail at Booneville [in] Owsley County and fired the Court house, but the latter was saved by the citizens, but the records and papers of the Circuit & County Court were destroyed They were torn up and scattered in the streets. And these same men of Marshalls in passing through Wolf County burned forty three houses. . . .

An accident occured at one of the camps yesterday. Some soldiers were extracting the fuse from a shell when it exploded wounding several. . . .

1. Abijah Gilbert represented Owsley County in the Kentucky state legislature from 1859 to 1861. See Collins, *History of Kentucky*, 2:673.
2. Colonel Andrew Jackson May commanded the 5th Kentucky Infantry. He left active service in November 1862. See Kleber, ed., *The Kentucky Encyclopedia*, 618–19.

SUNDAY APRIL 19 [1863]

Five secesh ladies were arre[s]ted this evening on the Nicholasville train I believe it was. They were taken to the Provost office and examined (they were arrested for expressing treasonable sentiments) and sentenced to be sent south to their dear rebel friends. They said they prefered staying here They didnt want to go south. They were told they must either go South or to jail and as they persisted in refusing to go to Dixie were put in jail and after a short while became quite tractable and took the oath of allegiance.

MONDAY APRIL 20TH [1863]

An immense wagon train passed through town today. A convalescent camp is or is to be established on the T.B Adams place. . . . The 48th Penn came here from Fortress Monroe[1] and is encamped near Randall's factory out Limestone Street.

1. A brick fort at the end of Virginia's Peninsula, Fortress Monroe served as a staging area for Federal attempts upon Richmond. The Ninth Corps, of which the 48th Pennsylvania was a part, departed for Kentucky from Fortress Monroe. See Faust, ed., *Historical Times Illustrated Encyclopedia of the Civil War*, 276–277.

WEDNESDAY AP 22ND [1863]

. . . Several men were at Headquarters . . . who had been driven from their homes in some of the neighboring counties and came to get arms to defend themselves from the rebels.

. . . A gentlemen from Clarke co[unty] was in town with a fine lot of horses which he sold for little or nothing, one splendid horse going for $90 as he said he would rather take what he could get for them than let the rebels have them.

THURSDAY APRIL 23RD [1863]

Gen. Burnside contermanded Gen Wilcox's order suppressing the [Cincinnati] Enquirer.[1] There was no need to stop the paper he said but if it published anything treasonable the editor would be arrested and punished. . . .

1. This incident occurred following Burnside's issuance of controversial General Order No. 38, an order that led to widespread suppression of disloyal activity. See Marvel, *Burnside*, 231–35.

SATURDAY APRIL 25TH [1863]

. . . A squad of soldiers (some of the Provost guard I suppose) went to a grocery opposite the Hospital No 1[,] emptied a barrel of whiskey into the gutter, broke bottles and destroyed everything of a spiritous caste. It would have been well if all the grog shops had been broken up some time ago. . . .

MONDAY APRIL 27TH [1863]

. . . Some soldiers from Hospital No 2, led on it was said by a citizen went to the house of a Mrs Colchazer[1] after dark this evening, broke the windows and did other damage. Mrs C. and her daughter went to the hospital, and complained of it but was told by the director, that he had no authority and they went to headquarters. I dont know what Gen Wilcox said to their complaints, but I heard the soldiers were put in the 'lock up' for the night. This woman and her daughter are both notorious secesh and women of bad character and have been in the habit of abusing the solders as they passed to and from the hospital. Its a wonder they never did anything to them before.

1. Mrs. Malvina Colclaser operated a grocery on the south side of Vine Street, between Broadway and Mill. See *Williams' Lexington City Guide*, 47.

WEDNESDAY APRIL 29TH [1863]

. . . The 2nd Maryland V.I. the "Plug Uglies"[1] as they are called from their being such an unruly, quarrelsome set came in this morning from Winchester, they will go to Frankfort tomorrow. I dont suppose they will stop there, as they are a terror to townspeople.

1. Interestingly, the 2nd Maryland's Confederate counterparts adopted the same name. The name first had been used to describe a crowd of notorious rowdies associated with the Know-Nothing Party that roamed Baltimore during the 1850s. See Harold R. Manakee, *Maryland in the Civil War* (Baltimore: Maryland Historical Society, 1961), 110–11, and McHenry Howard, *Recollections of a Maryland Confederate Soldier and Staff Officer* (Dayton, Ohio: Press of Morningside Book Shop, 1975), 28.

THURSDAY APRIL 30TH [1863]

This is the day set apart by the President as a Fast day.[1] Stores were closed and services held at nearly all the Churches. . . .

The troops here expect to move soon. They are only waiting for marching orders. An order was issued today for them to prepare eight days rations. If the 48th Penn is ordered off with the rest there will be no regiment to take their place as Provost guard, but the 1st Tenn,[2] and they have had the smallpox among them ever since they have been here. We wouldnt like at all to have them in town and some citizens are getting up a petition for the 48th Penn to be allowed to stay. The 48th dont want to go yet they say.

1. At the request of the U.S. Senate, President Lincoln proclaimed April 30, 1863, a day of national humiliation, fasting, and prayer. For the text of his proclamation, see Basler, ed., *The Collected Works of Abraham Lincoln*, 6:155–56.
2. Also called the 1st East Tennessee Infantry, or the 1st East Tennessee Mounted Infantry, this regiment of Unionist refugees from East Tennessee mustered at Camp Dick Robinson in September 1861. See Civil War Centennial Commission, *Tennesseans in the Civil War: A Military History of Confederate and Union Units with Available Rosters of Personnel* (Nashville: Civil War Centennial Comission, 1964), 375–78.

FRIDAY MAY 1ST [1863]

. . . The streets today are full of soldiers both cavalry and infantry. Probably the 1st Brigade of the 9th Army Corps, as I saw a large wagon train belonging to that brigade pass this morning. Marching orders not arrived yet.

SATURDAY MAY 2ND [1863]

. . . The 1st Tennessee, the "smallpox" regt as we call it passed by headquarters this evening. The General came out and made them a short speech. We couldn't hear what he said but it must have been cheering considering how many times the men cheered while he was speaking. Gen Wilcox always comes out and says something to the regiments passing his headquarters. . . .

MONDAY MAY 4TH [1863]

Pa went to Cincinnati this evening on business connected with the Hospital . . . Capt Radcliffe of the 10th Ky who was dismissed [from] the service for the surrender of Mt Sterling, has been acquitted by a court of inquiry and restored to his Command by Gen Burnside.

TUESDAY MAY 5TH [1863]

The 2nd Brigade of the 2nd Division of the 9th Army Corps came in this morning from Winchester, had a battery of 4 pieces. Fine looking fellows. Their flags looked like they had seen service; and had the names of a good many battles inscribed on them in gilt letters but they flapped so in the wind that it was impossible to tell what the names were.

SUNDAY MAY 10TH [1863]

. . . The alarm of fire some three or four nights ago was a false one made by the secesh. Some prisoners had been brought in that evening and the secesh thought by giving the alarm of fire to get the guards off their posts at the prisons and rescue the prisoners But the plan didnt succeed.

MONDAY MAY 11TH [1863]

... Mrs Morgans house was searched [for secesh] and a guard kept round it all last night but no one found. When they came there Mrs Morgan sent for Mr Gratz to come down which he did. Capt Ashbury gave orders to his Lieut to let Mr Gratz pass when he was ready to return home but the Lieutenant went away without giving the order to the guard and Mr Gratz was kept there until 3 oclock in the morning When Mrs. Morgan saw the guard wouldnt let Mr Gratz pass she said to him 'You see what it is to live under Yankee rule,' or something to that effect.

TUESDAY MAY 12 [1863]

... The meeting of the delegates to nominate Congressmen came off today, and Mr. J.J. Crittenden was nominated on condition of voting the last man and the last dollar to put down this rebellion. Mr C spoke last night at the Melodeon.

TUESDAY MAY 19TH [1863]

... a post is to be established at Hickman Bridge. Fortifications and a hospital erected there. Dr. Eversman has gone there to make arrangements and the stores of the hospital no 2 and perhaps others and quartermaster stores are being and to be removed from here.

I suppose the authorities have found it is no use to try to fortify Lexington. It would require much too large a force to hold fortifications around here, and after all might not accomplish the end required as there are too many weak points and too many traitors in our midst

WEDNESDAY MAY 20TH [1863]

A squad of the 1st Tennessee Cavalry[1] were here this morning. They came back to get horses. They stayed in the Lot last night lying on the bare ground just like the rebels do. Some of them went into Mrs Morgan's front yard and laid on the grass and pulled some of her flowers. If they had known whose house it was it is likely they would have done more serious damage to the place.

1. Miss Peter likely refers to the 1st Tennessee Mounted Infantry.

THURSDAY MAY 21ST [1863]

All the secesh ladies here who have husbands in the rebel army are ordered to leave within thirty days. They are not allowed to take over $1000 in money with them. . . .

FRIDAY MAY 22 [1863]

Gen Wilcox's hop[1] came off last night and was universally acknowledged to have been one of the most pleasant parties given in Lexington. My sisters describe the rooms as being beautifully adorned. Long flags curtained the windows and stands of colors mixed with sabres, guns, pistols etc. were grouped as trophies on the walls. Stacks of muskets, with piles of cannon balls, ordinance ornaments etc. adorned the corners of the rooms, the floors of which were chalked, one a blue [back]ground with a large eagle surrounded by stars on it, the other a red [back]ground with white stars; and flowers every where. The supper room was a temporary affair erected for the occasion, and ornamented like the rest. A fine band (from Newport I believe), enlivened the company with its strains, Lieut Richards was a most efficient 'maître de ceremonies,' the supper was sumptous.

Gen Wilcox made a speech and no end of loyal toasts were drank and every thing passed off as well as could be wished. The only mishap was the burning up of one of the transparencies arranged out side over the doors. I should have mentioned that the floor of the hall was painted in red and white stripes and the supper room was adorned with wreaths and festoons of flowers. I am ashamed to say that as soon as it began to get dark last evening the negroes as is their usual impertinent custom began to assemble in crowds about Headquarters. The guard dispersed them for a while when the guests began to arrive (9 PM) but they returned afterward and were a considerable annoyance to persons promenading in the gallery and when supper was over came into the supper room and robbed the table of every thing that remained Which remains the General had intended to have sent to the hospital No doubt the hotel waiters hired for the occasion thought they had a perfect right to invite all their colored friends to a share of the feast.

The secesh it is likely had in view a special treat for themselves also. Their rebel friends and admirers have been promising them another grand raid into the Blue grass region and last night was the one appointed for John Morgan to be in Lexington. No doubt they chuckled greatly over

Gen Wilcox's unwaryness in giving a party on this particular night and passed many winks, nods, and wreathed smiles among themselves thinking of what was to have happened. Perhaps they promised themselves a second edition of the battle of Waterloo [with] Morgan acting the part of [the] Duke of Wellington. . . . At any rate if the secesh looked for him they watched with a 'watery eye' for he was 'called and couldnt come' at least he didnt which is the same thing. And so Gen Wilcox and his guests danced until cock crow or after and the second edition of the battle of Waterloo turned out a complete failure. . . .

Between 12 AM and 1 PM today Hospital No 6 (the Medical Hall) was discovered to be on fire and shortly after the roof was one sheet of flame, the lurid glare of which and the dense column of black smoke arising from it showed terribly distinctive against the clear blue sky although the sun was shining in all the brightness of mid day. Assistance was promptly on the spot. A crowd of citizens, soldiers from the 48th Pennsylvania and other rgts. Gen Wilcox himself and other officers and the surgeons of course hastened to the spot. The engines were well served and officers and men worked with a will. The sick were all got out safe and were taken to Hospital No 2 and the greater part of the clothing bedding furniture etc was saved but notwithstanding all the efforts made the fire spread with such rapidity that it was impossible to stop its progress. It has been extremely hot and dry for the last week or two and the roof burnt like tinder. I never saw a fire spread so rapidly. The engines being only the small old fashioned hand engines could not reach the roof nor throw a sufficient quantity of water at once to do the least good and in one hour's time what had been the Medical Hall was only a mass of blackened ruins among which the fire continued to burn in places until night. The fire originated from a flue under the roof. The loss may be stated at $30,000; hardly more than that, perhaps not so much. . . .

1. General Orlando Willcox and his staff gave a grand dance on May 21, 1863, in the Bodley house, which served as the general's headquarters at Second and Market Streets. An elaborate dinner was catered by a Cincinnati firm in a large tent erected on the lawn. See Coleman, *Lexington During the Civil War*, 41.

SATURDAY MAY 23 [1863]

An amusing incident happened in Louisville the other night. At the theater during the intermission between the plays the band played some national airs on which a number of ladies got up and flirted out of the room. The next night the manager came on the stage and announced that

Johanna Peter's dance card from the ball General Willcox held about six weeks before the Union victories at Gettysburg and Vicksburg. (Evans Collection, Special Collections and Archives, University of Kentucky Libraries)

the band was about to play some national airs and all those who were too much opposed to the government to listen to them had now an opportunity to leave. As on the previous night a number of ladies got up and flirted out of the room but at the door they were met by the Provost guard who marched them off to jail. . . .

MONDAY JUNE 1ST [1863]

Gen Wilcox hasnt gone yet but expects to go soon. General Hartsuff has issued order No 1 making Lexington his headquarters.[1] Gen Burnside intends moving his headquarters to Hickman Bridge which is about twenty miles from here. . . .

1. General George Lucas Hartsuff (1830–1874), a native New Yorker, graduated from West Point in 1848. After suffering a severe wound at Sharpsburg in September 1862 he commanded the U.S. Army's newly formed 23rd Corps, April-November 1863, in Kentucky. See *OR*, ser. 1, vol. 23, pt. 2, 357.

TUESDAY JUNE 2ND [1863]

General Order No 84 of Gen Burnside prohibits the circulation of the New York World in this Department and suppresses the Chicago Times[1]. . . .

1. The distribution of both papers was suspended in the Department of the Ohio for expressions of disloyalty and the "tendency . . . to cast reproach upon the Government." See *OR*, ser. 1, vol. 23, pt. 2, 381.

WEDNESDAY JUNE 3RD [1863]

. . . Gen Burnside has issued an order No 87 forbidding the publication or circulation of books containing disloyal sentiment[1]. . . .

. . . The 32nd Ky Infantry nine months men were disbanded the other day at Somerset.[2] The term of enlistment of a good many regiments is nearly out, but it is likely most of them will enlist again immediately. . . .

Gen Burnside is in town tonight, bringing a good many distinguished officers with him. There are no less than six Generals in town today. . . .

1. General Burnside issued this order June 2, 1863. See *OR*, ser. 1, vol. 23, pt. 2, 382.
2. Speed records the 32nd Kentucky as having organized in the summer of 1862 at Camp Burnside and serving until November 1863. See *The Union Regiments of Kentucky*, 583–84.

THURSDAY JUNE 4TH [1863]

Quite a movement of troops going on in this part of the state. The Cincinnati cars are in the employ of the military today and there is quite a stir among the troops here. . . . Mr Lincoln has countermanded Burnsides order respecting the Chicago Times and then Gen Burnside revoked that part of it respecting the New York World. Its a pity Mr Lincoln hadnt let Burnside alone. . . .

FRIDAY JUNE 5TH 1863

. . . The jails here are full of rebels. The soldiers say that hardly a night has passed but a rebel has been taken up in some part of the country between here and Somerset.

SATURDAY JUNE 6TH 1863

Gen Wilcox leaves by the 2 PM train. He is going to Indianapolis to take command of Indiana and Michigan. . . . The Union citizens here got up a petition the other day for him to be allowed to stay here but I havent heard that any answer has been made to it, and I suppose there were good reasons for his going. The people here did not like much to lose him just when they were getting well acquainted with him and his men and would like to have had a better opportunity of entertaining them. Gens Hartsuff & Wilcox and their staffs were invited to Mr. Henry Duncan Jr (just above us) Saturday night and up to Mrs McFarlans[1] either Monday or Tuesday of this week. . . . Gen Hartsuff's corp consisting of all the troops in the state except Gen Carters Division and the 9th Army Corp and being scattered over the state has yet to be formed. Someone asked him what troops belonged to his corps. The General replied that was just what he would like to know himself, as it would save him a good deal of trouble. He proposes visiting the camps of his command and during his absence General Sturgis[2] will command here. Gen Sturgis has brought his wife with him, as also has Col Poe of Hartsuff's staff, the latter lady is said to be the grand-daughter of Mr Ross Wilkins of Detroit, an old acquaintance of Pa's. . . .

Quite an accident happened at Nicholasville today. A train of cars was about starting from there when the boiler of the engine (the Kenton I think the engine is called) burst. There was a considerable crowd around it at the time and four were killed and a number injured some soldiers among the rest. We got the news this evening that Dr Eversman and Mr. Jamison started to go to Nicholasville to see about the soldiers but got a dispatch on the way saying they would be sent here.

The following places have been designated by the Governor of Ky as camps for the organization and instruction of the troops raised under the act of Congress calling for 20,000 twelve months men for the defense of Ky.[3] First District, Owensboro & Greenville. Second District, Russelville and Lebanon. Third District, Eminence. Fourth or Covington District, Falmouth. Fifth District, Camp Dick Robinson. Sixth District, Camp Dick Robinson and Irvine. Seventh District, Cattlettsburg and Olympian Springs. . . .

1. This might have been the wife of John McFarland, whose home was on the north side of High Street between Rose and Mulberry Streets. See *Williams' Lexington City Directory*, 69.

2. General Samuel Davis Sturgis (1822–1889), a Pennsylvania native and West Point graduate, commanded a division in the Ninth Corps. See Faust, ed., *Historical Times Illustrated Encyclopedia of the Civil War*, 729–30.

3. Following negotiations between Governor Robinson and the federal government, the U.S. Congress allowed Kentucky to raise twenty thousand troops with the understanding that the recruits would remain within the state. Though designed to soothe Kentuckians' anger over the draft, this effort failed miserably. Few Kentuckians answered the governor's call. See Coulter, *The Civil War and Readjustment in Kentucky*, 189–96.

MONDAY JUNE 8TH 1863

. . . Did I mention that when Capt Ashbury moved his camp he left the small stable in which he and his lieutenants kept their horses and which was nearly opposite to our front door still standing. When the warm weather came it was a great nuisance and Pa and Mr Gratz applied several time both to the Capt himself, to the Quartermaster in Chief Capt Van Ness,[1] and then to the Provost Marshall Col Sigfried to have it removed but it was not until today that it was done.

1. Captain William W. Van Ness served as quartermaster on the staff of Colonel N. Bowen, the assistant adjutant general in Lexington. See *OR*, ser. 1, vol. 23, pt. 2, 277–78.

THURSDAY JUNE 11TH [1863]

Gen Burnside in town today. Two squads of prisoners, one 28, the other 14 in number were brought in today from the vicinity of Somerset. The band belonging to the 48th Penn arrived today. The guard over in the lot, consisting of about thirty men belonging to the 48th Penn got new tents today.

SATURDAY JUNE 13TH [1863]

. . . Heard this evening that the rebels had made a raid on Mt Sterling.[1] We expected "something was up" for no less than six couriers arrived at headquarters within three hours.

. . . The members of the Quartermaster department were all arrested today Mr Davidson,[2] among the rest. There has been cheating going on there. We heard some time ago that there was secessionists among the clerks employed, and it was mentioned to some of the officers, but received no attention at the time. Of course Mr Davidson will not suffer by this as everyone knows he is an honest man and a loyal citizen.

1. General Morgan's cavalry entered Kentucky on June 2, 1863, and captured Mt. Sterling on June 8. See Duke, *History of Morgan's Cavalry*, 518–24.
2. Prior to the Civil War, James T. Davidson had been a bookkeeper for the Northern Bank of Kentucky. A strong Unionist, he held the position of quartermaster's clerk in Lexington during the war. See Perrin, *History of Fayette County, Kentucky*, 595.

SUNDAY JUNE 14TH [1863]

A battery stopped by our house for some time this morning between 4 AM and 5 AM. I could not learn what battery it was or where it came from. The men looked very tired. The secesh said they had been driven in from Mt Sterling. . . . Dr Eversman has been having a garden made at the hospital No 2, has got a good many flowers there already. He is going to have a minature fort erected in front of the house with small cannon mounted in it. I believe the guns intended for the purpose were some little old ones left by the rebels last fall. . . .

MONDAY JUNE 15TH 1863

. . . A report today that Maysville had been sacked by a body of rebels[1]. . . . A company of the 14th Ky mounted Infantry came in about 4 PM. Stopped about half an hour near our house. Said they had come from near Mt Sterling and had been to Big Hill after a body of rebels whom they had heard were there but had not found any. . . .

1. As Morgan approached Mt. Sterling, he deployed parts of his command around Lexington to confuse the defenders. Captain Peter Everett was assigned the task of raiding Maysville. See Duke, *Morgan's Cavalry*, 523.

TUESDAY JUNE 16TH 1863

. . . On Sunday [June 14] a body of 250 rebels under Peter Everett dashed into Maysville remaining several hours in the town and retiring without molestation taking with them a large amount of government and private property.

WEDNESDAY JUNE 17 [1863]

. . . A few days ago the 1st Massachusetts negro regiment was to pass through Cincinnati. The free colored people there made great preparations to receive them and had a very handsome flag ready to present to them on their arrival. A large number of the citizens determined to put a stop to these proceedings. A large crowd went to the store of Shiltoe & Co. [Shillito] in whose front window the flag was hanging and threatened to demolish his store if the flag was not taken away. They also went to the market house where the supper for the regiment was to be set out and declared if the supper was set out it should be the last that that regiment would ever eat. So the negroes gave up the idea of receiving their friends and the officers of the black regiment smuggled it through during the night. About that time a good many negroes from here ran off to join that regiment.

THURSDAY JUNE 18 [1863]

Lieut Tom Fry of the 11th Indiana was here tonight. He is now a Captain of Quartermasters. He was promoted by the President for gallantry at Fort Donelson. He is the nephew of Gen S.S. Fry. He says the people of Indiana dont like Gen Wilcox. They dont want any Generals. They think their Governor can attend to everything that is necessary. Gen Wilcox it seems returns the compliment, for in a letter to some one here he said he wished he was back here he liked this place much better than Indianapolis and as for his staff they looked like so many theological students.

FRIDAY JUNE 19TH [1863]

. . . About noon today the Nunnery was burnt. As usual the soldiers took an active part. The Catholic church which is just adjoining and which everyone thought would certainly be destroyed as it is an old building with a great deal of wood work about it was saved by them though. I heard the organ was injured by some person trying to get it out at one time when the end of the church caught fire. I believe the Sisters did not lose anything of any value except one piano which got broken in letting it down out of a window. The house can soon be repaired. The fire originated from a spark from one of the chimneys. . . .

... The secesh are in high glee about the raid into Pennsylvania[1] and seem to expect the rebels will be here shortly. I suppose they will try to come here in August as they did last year. ...

The 8th and 9th Michigan under Col Decourcy and the 10th Ky under Major Foley whipped the rebels under Peter Everett near Owingsville on the 16th.[2] That was the same body of rebels that was at Maysville.

1. Reference is to General Robert E. Lee's northern invasion that culminated in the battle of Gettysburg, July 1–3, 1863.
2. Colonel DeCourcy drove Peter Everett's company from Trippletts Bridge in Rowan County on June 16, 1863. See *OR*, ser. 1, vol. 23, pt. 1, 381–84.

MONDAY JUNE 22ND [1863]

... A soldier was telling us about a visit he made to the graves of the rebels at the cemetery here. When he went there there were several finely dressed ladies busy about them and the graves were adorned with a quantity of all kinds of fine flowers, arranged in every imaginable way. While he was looking at the graves of our soldiers which a[re] near those of the rebels, one of the ladies spoke to him and said 'Only see what a difference there is between these two places; that one (pointing to our soldiers graves, which had no flowers or ornaments) so mean looking and this other so beautifully adorned with flowers.' 'Yes ma'am' he replied 'I was just observing them, they are indeed beautiful flowers, in fact they are magnificent. But pray my dear lady[,'] he continued feigning ignorance[,] 'can you tell me why there is so much difference made between the graves?' 'Why' said she 'dont you know these are the graves of the rebel soldiers?' 'Rebel soldiers!' he said, 'do they allow *rebels* to have a place of burial in a Christian cemetery?' The secesh lady retired. 'Ah,' he said to Ma when telling this 'I have seen a great deal of rebel ladies, and had very often to guard them and have had them to spit on me and abuse me and never said anything rude to them; but this time I couldnt help it.[']

TUESDAY JUNE 23RD [1863]

... The 1st Carolina negro regiment mutinied against their officers lately When ordered to start on some expedition one of the negroes threw down and severly bruised the commanding officer and killed another; he was shot. There have been some other cases lately in which the negro has attacked the white. I am afraid now that the negroes have got arms in their hands, and so many notions of freedom in their heads that before the war is over it is not improbable that we may have to fight them as well as the secesh

WEDNESDAY JUNE 24 [1863]

. . . Mr D.C. Wickliffe's paper the [Lexington] Observer and Reporter seems to be getting Copperhead. It endorses the resolutions of the Copperhead meeting held at Springfield Ill on Wednesday last.

SATURDAY JUNE 27 [1863]

. . . Tonight two of the 48th Pennsylvania were taken to the hospital wounded. Three of them it seems got drunk and had a fight and these two were wounded one of them mortally.

MONDAY JUNE 29TH [1863]

. . . There are several men in the hospital here—deserters from the rebel army who jointed Tennessee regiments One of them died lately He said the rebels treated their soldiers worse than dogs sometimes making them march fifty miles a day and thinks that is what killed him

FRIDAY JULY 3RD [1863]

A squad of nine or ten guerillas under Capt Hines[1] attacked and destroyed a train of cars on the Lexington & Louisville railroad near Christiansburg about twenty miles from Frankfort yesterday morning The train was bound from Louisville to Lexington. The passengers were unarmed. The guerillas robbed them of their watches and money, rifled the safe of the Adams express and the mail bags, burnt the cars and the baggage they couldnt take with them, and threw the locomotive down an embankment The daughters of the rebel Gen Wm Preston[2] were on the train returning from paying a visit to a relation in Louisville, and had in their trunks besides a quantity of new things they had purchased[,] a good deal of jewelry and other finery which their relatives had given them, she being in mourning and having no intention of wearing them again. The guerillas destroyed the Misses Prestons baggage with the rest although they made known to them that they were Gen Prestons daughters The Misses Preston were very much incensed as it was really a great loss to them. Nothing the rebels could do would be so apt to turn them against the Confederate cause as destroying their valuables. . . .

1. Captain Thomas H. Hines, 9th Kentucky Cavalry (C.S.), played a key role in Morgan's Indiana and Ohio raid and engineered the general's escape from the Ohio

State Penitentiary. Hines later became a secret agent for the Confederacy and sought to initiate anti-Union activity in the Northwest. See Cecil Fletcher Holland, *Morgan and His Raiders: A Biography of the Confederate General* (New York: Macmillan Company, 1943), 232–33; James D. Horan, *Confederate Agent—A Discovery in History* (New York: Crown Publishers, 1954); and Edward M. Coffman, "The Civil War Career of Thomas Henry Hines" (master's thesis, University of Kentucky, 1955).
2. Preston had five daughters: Jessie Fremont, Mary Owen, Caroline H., Margaret H., and Susan C. See Preston-Johnston Papers.

SATURDAY JULY 4TH [1863]

We did not have much of a 4th. By order of Lieut Colonel Pleasants[1] of the 48th Pennsylvania who now commands this post (Gen Hartsuff & staff are still here but the General is too busy organizing his corp to have time to attend to Post duties) two salutes were fired from the fort one at dawn, one at 2 PM. The 48th marched through the streets and had a battallion drill on Cheapside about eight o clock and had a display of fireworks at their camp at night. The Catholics had a picnic at Ashland to get money for some purpose but that was all that was done except to ring the bells. I think the citizens ought to have given the soldiers a picnic or dinner or something. With the band that they have we might have had a very nice time but it seems nobody thought of it. . . .

1. Lieutenant Colonel Henry Pleasants resided in Schuylkill County, Pennsylvania. See Bates, *History of Pennsylvania Volunteers*, 1:1191, 1211.

MONDAY JULY 6TH [1863]

The city was thrown into a state of excitement this morning by the news that the rebels 5000 or 6000 strong were at Laurenceburg. Dr Shumard stopped at the door on his way to or from the hospital and told us that it was true and the rebels it was thought might come here and if they did they would come today. That was about eight A.M. Capt Lyon of Hartsuffs staff was here shortly after and said that a dispatch had been received at Headquarters to the effect that Morgan's gang was at Laurenceburg and might come this way. . . . Dr Jackson was here several times during the morning as also was Doctor Eversman who was packing up and sending away things from the hospital and getting all ready to send off the sick if the rebels did come. Dr Jackson did not like the idea of leaving at all, but he said there were not enough troops here to hold the place if the rebels came in force. . . . They knew a week ago that the rebels might come here and had telegraphed repeatedly to Cincinnati for troops but could get no answer. . . . That all the troops here had been sent out to Fort Clay ready to repel an attack. And a great deal more. Altogether he seemed very much "put out," though some of it might have been put on for the occasion to see if he couldnt scare us a little. As for us we did nothing but sit in the front door. Annie & Miriam Gratz and ourselves and talk about the news and what we would do if they did come, and had a deal of fun. . . .

. . . Gen Hartsuff issued an order before he left this morning, published in handbills that for every union citizen that was injured in his person five rebel sympathizers should be punished according[ly] and similar retaliation was to be made if the property of union citizens was destroyed. . . .

Mr Morgan Vance came today from Harrodsburg with his family and says the rebels were there when he left early this morning. A good deal many people left here but I dont think there is any danger of the rebels coming. Dr Eversman sent 50 convalescents to the fort from the Hospital this morning.

TUESDAY JULY 7TH [1863]

. . . Col Alston,[1] Morgan's Chief of Staff was taken prisoner at Lebanon and arrived in this city this evening. He reports that Thomas Morgan[2] was killed at Lebanon on Sunday. Mrs Morgan was dreadfully distressed. William Doroughty one of Ashbury['s] men (he served in the Crimean war) told Ma that as he was passing there this evening he heard such shrieks and cries that he stopped and asked one of the servants what was the matter and the servant said one of his young 'marsters' had been killed, but didnt know which one. . . .

1. R.A. Alston was a native South Carolinian who served as John Hunt Morgan's assistant adjutant general. Alston was the second editor of *Vidette*, published by Morgan's men in Tennessee. See Holland, *Morgan and His Raiders*, 13 and 141.
2. Favorite brother of John Hunt Morgan, Thomas served as a lieutenant in his brother's command. He was captured twice by Union forces before his death at the third battle of Lebanon, July 5, 1863. "Tom" was described by Cecil Fletcher Holland as "a gay, laughing youth with a clear tenor voice, who led the raiders in song as they passed along the highroads." See Holland, *Morgan and His Raiders*, 12, 47, 229, and Duke, *Morgan's Cavalry*, 426.

WEDNESDAY JULY 8TH [1863]

A salute of thirty guns was fired at noon today in honor of the taking of Vicksburg. . . .

Friday July 10th [1863]

With the two boats (Alice Dean & J. T. McComb) he had seized on the night of the 7th, Morgan crossed the Ohio at Brandenburg Ky. on Wednesday night with a force of 6000 and took possession of Corydon. Gen Burnside has a large force in Morgans rear and another in front. The Indiana militia are pouring from all parts of the state; one regiment is said to have been raised in Indianapolis between dark and bedtime. The object of Morgan in going to Indiana is thought to be either because he was forced to by our forces or to prevent troops being sent to interfere with Buckner who is said to be coming into this state[1]. . . .

1. Morgan initially entered Kentucky with orders to attack Louisville and disrupt Federal supply lines. See *OR*, ser. 1, vol. 23, pt. 1, 817–18.

Saturday July 11 [1863]

The last heard of John Morgan he was at Orleans Ind. aiming it is thought to get back to Ky. . . .

. . . The trains to Louisville are running again. For a day or two they did not run between Louisville & Frankfort on account of guerillas. It is said that a train with soldiers concealed on it and with a small cavalry guard was sent out as a decoy to the guerillas, the latter took the bait and the road was cleared of them. I give this for what it is worth. A new weekly paper the Ky Loyalist[1] has just commenced publication in this city. . . .

Todays number contains a copy of the journal of the rebel Col Alston giving account of the movements of the rebels from the time they entered the state to the time of his capture at Lebanon. Confirmed the death of Col Chenault, praises the bravery of the 20th Ky[2] and says, after Col Hanson[3] had surrendered Caley Morgan took him by the beard and cursed him and might have shot him if he had not been prevented. Says the rebels behaved very badly every where they went and altogether writes in a very desponding tone as if he had some presentiment of his own capture. Says Tom Morgan was shot charging at the head of his men but Col Hanson who is in town today says that is not so that the rebels made no charge at all. There were several other of the Lex young men among the rebels wounded at Lebanon. There are several of the 20th Ky in town, and say they had been ordered to leave Lebanon and Col Hanson had sent off his ammunition train and they were about following it when the order was countermanded and thus they had to fight the rebels with no ammunition but what they had about them. Col Hanson was very reluctant to yield

even when his ammunition was nearly gone as he had sent for reinforcements and wished if possible to hold out till they arrived and it was not
until the rebels set fire to the houses his men occupied that he surrendered.
The rebels robbed our men of money (of which they happened to have a
good deal having just been paid) watches, boots, hats, in short anything
they happened to fancy. . . .

1. The *Kentucky Loyalist*, "a frail little news sheet," first appeared on July 4, 1863. It
was published at the offices of the suppressed *Kentucky Statesman* by Private William
P. Atkinson, Company C, 48th Pennsylvania Volunteers. See Coleman, *Lexington
During the Civil War*, 42.
2. Colonel D.W. Chenault died while leading the 11th Kentucky in an assault on
Tebb's Bend Bridge, July 4, 1863. See Brown, *The Bold Cavaliers*, 181.
3. Lieutenant Colonel Charles Hanson of the 20th Kentucky commanded the defense of Lebanon against Morgan. See Brown, *The Bold Cavaliers*, 182–85.

MONDAY JULY 13TH [1863]

Martial law has been proclaimed in Cincinnati, Newport &
Covington.[1] Morgan went to Vernon Ind on the 11th and demanded the
surrender of the place. Col Burkham refused and Morgan finding our
forces intended to give battle and probably hearing of Gen Love's approach skedadled.[2] Nineteen of the rebels were captured. The rebels
destroyed the Madison & Indianapolis railroad and a portion of the Ohio
& Mississippi railroad west of Vernon, cut the telegraph and arrived at
Versailles [Indiana] at 1 o clock on the 12th. Gen Hobson is only a short
distance in Morgan's rear. . . .

. . . There is a rebel Capt Hutchcraft at the Hospital a notorious
scoundrel who at one time forged a note to a considerable amount in his
fathers name. (His father is a Union man and wont have anything to do
with him) He was nearly well at one time but the rebel ladies sent him so
many things to eat that he got sick again and this evening when Mrs
Lancaster sent him supper it was sent back to her. . . .

Two of the Lexington rebels wounded at Lebanon, young Logwood[3]
and Mrs Priscilla Brands son have been brought here. They were not
allowed to stay with their mothers but young Brand was sent out of town
to Mr Alex Brands and Logwood was taken to the hospital. Mrs Logwood
(a very common woman) made a great ado about this, and the secesh troop
up there every day to see him some of them pretending to be union. Fine
ladies who before this war commenced wouldnt have touched him with
the hem of their garments much less take any notice of him.

1. Martial law was proclaimed in these three places earlier on the thirteenth as Morgan entered Ohio from Indiana. See *OR*, ser. 1, vol. 23, pt. 1, 632.
2. Colonel J.H. Burkham, commanding officer at Vernon, refused to surrender to Morgan. The raider withdrew upon learning of the approach of General John Love's forces. See *OR*, ser. 1, vol. 23, pt. 2, 727, 730, 736, 740.
3. Prior to the war, Thomas S. Logwood, a clerk, boarded on the south side of Constitution Street between Mulberry and Walnut Streets. See Perrin, *History of Fayette County, Kentucky*, 650, and *Williams' Lexington City Guide*, 650.

TUESDAY JULY 14TH [1863]

. . . There is in todays Gazette an account of Morgans fight at Lebanon and the other movements that agreed pretty well with what I have heard from persons who had conversed with those of the 20th Ky now here. The reason reinforcements did not reach Hanson in time was this. Col David who had been sent from Stanford & Hickman with the 8th and 9th Michigan by Gen Hartsuff with orders to hold Morgan until Gen Hobson could come up, arrived at Lebanon just as Morgan was leaving and instead of obeying his orders he contented himself with throwing a few shells into Morgans rearguard and then in despite of the entreaties of his officers and soldiers fell back and allowed the rebels to escape. The rascal has been put in irons to await his punishment. Morgan marched his prisoners on the double quick to Springfield through a broiling sun. On the march three men fell with exhaustion. One of them was dragged before the artillery which passed over him, crushing him to death. The other two had their brains knocked out with muskets and when Henry Brennan[1] (who is a captain in the 20th or an officer of some kind) was nearly worn out with fatigue Cally Morgan would have shot him if he had not been prevented by Howard Smith.[2]

Cols Jacobs[3] and Wolford were so exasperated at hearing all this that Jacobs took off his cravat and hoisted the black flag and Wolford promised six months furlough and the thanks of the country to any one that should bring Morgan dead or alive.

Morgan sent a small detachment to Harrodsburg 67 of whom fell into Col Saunders hands and the rest dispersed to the houses of their numerous friends in Mercer and Woodford Counties. Morgan with his main body moved towards Shepherdsville pursued by Gen Hobson. There he divided and part went to Brandenburg and one went to Litchfield.

Gen Hartsuff has established a system of patrol[s] who are bringing in prisoners taken in the highways and byways and in secesh houses. Some of the secesh say Morgan did not go into Indiana himself but staid in Ky. . . .

1. Captain Henry C. Brennan commanded Company E, 20th Kentucky Infantry. See Speed, *The Union Regiments of Kentucky*, 485.
2. Colonel D. Howard Smith commanded the 5th Kentucky Cavalry (C.S.), a regiment new to Morgan's command. See Brown, *The Bold Cavaliers*, 175.
3. Colonel Richard T. Jacob, a Louisville native and member of the Kentucky legislature, commanded the 9th Kentucky Cavalry. See Speed, *The Union Regiments of Kentucky*, 209–10.

WEDNESDAY JULY 15 [1863]

. . . We Lexington ladies were in hopes when we heard of the capture of the 20th Ky by Morgan at Lebanon that the flag we presente[d] to them on their entering the service had escaped capture Col Hansen[1] it seems did send it away with a guard but there seems to be no doubt entertained that it fell into the rebels hands. If it had been taken by any other than Morgans gang we wouldnt have cared so much but to fall into the hands of such highway robbers was too bad. . . .

1. On July 5, 1863, Colonel Charles S. Hanson, with 300 men of the 20th Kentucky Infantry, bravely defended Lebanon for seven hours. Hanson was forced to surrender when Morgan's cavalry, fighting on foot, set fire to the railroad depot where his troops had taken refuge. See Kerr, *History of Kentucky*, 2:903, and Collins, *History of Kentucky*, 1:125.

FRIDAY JULY 17TH [1863]

. . . Several very ill looking men, evidently strangers, passed here this morning. Dr. Henry who was at the door when they went by said it was probable they were some of the New York cut throats as a gang of rascally fellows had been discovered hiding in Warfields Woods who were suspected to be some of the New York mob come here to escape the draft. Especially as several persons had had things stolen from them during the last two or three days. Pa, for one had six dollars stolen out of his drawer in the study. . . .

Capt James C Morris formerly of the 20th Ky[1] who resigned when the Presidents Proclamation was issued and whose resignation was accepted for the good of the Country, woke up this morning with the discovery that the union and the Constitution could only be saved according to the Copperhead platform and offers himself as a candidate for the Legislature from Fayette. If I am not mistaken Fayette would not have him for a gracious gift. . . .

1. Captain Morris commanded Company D of the 20th Kentucky. See Speed, *The Union Regiments of Kentucky*, 485.

SATURDAY JULY 18 [1863]

Yesterday evening an attempt was made by the prisoners at the jail to lock up Mr W.H. Lusby[1] the County Jailer so that those confined there might make their escape. The scheme failed but two of the prisoners James Maloy who was under arrest for stealing Mr Henry Duncan['s] horses, and B.F. Barnes made their escape. . . .

1. City Marshal William H. Lusby lived on the south side of Main Street between Lower and Cox Streets. See *Williams' Lexington City Guide*, 77.

WEDNESDAY JULY 22ND [1863]

. . . The English papers are getting insufferable and yet it is ludicrous too the way they are letting the Confeds lead them by the nose. But England has never been able to forgive us our prosperity and would no doubt go as far as she dared to destroy us. That iron clad fleet that is being fitted out there ostensibly for the Emperor of China but really as every one knows for the rebels. Wouldnt she make no end of noise if the North were to allow ships to be fitted out in our ports for one of her enemies? It would be an intolerable outrage then, a causus belli, a violation of the laws of nations. But Madam Brittania thinks she is at liberty to do what she pleases no matter if it is against the laws of nations but nobody else must dare to do it[1]. . . .

1. Under mounting pressure from the U.S. government, Britain began to suspend the construction of ironclads for the Confederate Navy. Miss Peter may have referred to the April 1863 case of the *Alexandra*, in which a British court decided the construction of the ship did not technically violate its nation's neutrality laws. See Warren F. Spencer, *The Confederate Navy in Europe* (Tuscaloosa: Univ. of Alabama Press, 1983), 100–104.

SATURDAY JULY 25 [1863]

. . . The Richmond papers are urging the propriety of killing all the dogs in the Confederacy as they consume too much bread. It would be a good thing if they would kill all the two legged as well as the four legged ones.

TUESDAY JULY 28TH 1863 (BETWEEN 1 AND 2 P. M.)

Another scare. The rebels at Richmond this morning; were fighting there at 8 AM with Col Saunders force which is said to be 300. The rebels have 1500. Col Saunders was forced to retreat. . . . Baggage was packed up and sent off from headquarters at noon and the stores from the hospital sent to the fort. . . . Gen Haskall[1] has taken command during Gen Hartsuffs absence and has declared martial law. All citizens between 18 and 45 to be armed and put under Command of Col Will Scott. . . .

7½ P.M. Two regiments of cavalry the 5th Tenn.[2] and 19th Michigan[3] and a battery just came in from Hickman. Gen Hartsuff is to be back tonight, his staff have just gone out to the cars to meet him. They say at headquarters that enough troops will be here by 8 PM to catch the whole rebel forces. . . . Cannon has been placed on most of the roads, and trees felled across the road by the cemetary. As usual a good many people came in from Richmond. They say the rebels did not behave as badly as they sometimes do. . . .

1. General Miles Smith Hascall commanded the District of Indiana at this time. See Faust, ed., *Historical Times Illustrated Encyclopedia of the Civil War*, 348–49.
2. There is no record of the 5th Tennessee Cavalry or the 5th Tennessee Infantry in Kentucky at this time. See Civil War Centennial Commission, *Tennesseans in the Civil War*, 329–33, 385–87.
3. The 19th Michigan Cavalry never existed and the 19th Michigan Infantry was in Tennessee at this time. See Dyer, *A Compendium of the War of the Rebellion*, 3:1289–90.

WEDNESDAY JULY 29TH [1863]

. . . The Secretary of War[1] is said to have issued an order that Morgan & his commissioned officers should be confined in the Columbus Penetentiary[2]. . . . Mrs Morgan went to Cincinnati to see John but was refused permission. . . . Gen Hartsuff was a good deal displeased at Gen Haskalls declaring martial law, and issued an order today saying martial law was not declared which order was printed on hand bills the same size as those Gen Haskall's order was on and ordered to be posted over the latter where ever found. . . . A regiment of cavalry passed by here about 3 AM going to headquarters. . . . It is a grand thing to hear one of our cavalry regiments pass. The regular stamp of the horses in the dead stillness of the night was like the rush of many waters. . . .

1. It was General-in-Chief Halleck, not Secretary of War Stanton, who requested that Governor David Tod of Ohio secure a prison where Morgan might be held. See Ramage, *Rebel Raider*, 183.
2. During his Ohio raid of July 1863, Morgan was captured (July 26) near West Point, Ohio. He was incarcerated at the Ohio Penitentiary in Columbus. Morgan and six of his officers escaped on November 27. See Ramage, *Rebel Raider*, 178–94.

THURSDAY JULY 30 [1863]

... This morning as I was looking out of my window a soldier from
the hospital with his gun and Knapsack passed and called to me "was I
afraid of the rebels coming." No, I said, did he think they would come. He
said he didn't know but they said the rebels were coming this way from
Winchester. He said he had seen some ladies the other day very much
frightened about the rebels coming, but the soldiers werent going to let
them come in town. They were just going to fight like "bludgeons". ...

There is an old captain staying at the hospital now, a very common
looking man, who is seldom or never seen with an officers uniform on, and
would never be supposed to be anything but a common soldier, who has
done a good deal of service (and is still) in the way of a spy and in arresting
the rebels who are continually sneaking into various parts of the state and
hiding in the house of their sympathizing friends. ...

It is said tonight that martial law has been declared in Nicholasville as
it was thought the rebels were coming there.

FRIDAY JULY 31ST [1863]

There is a law setting forth that any person who has served the
Confederacy, or the Provisional Government of Ky., in either a Civil or
military capacity, or given voluntary aid and assistance to those in arms
against the forces of the United States, or of the State of Kentucky, since
the 10th of April 1862 cannot exercise the right of voting, and is deemed
to have expatriated himself, which law is being published in the papers by
Gen [Governor] Robinsons direction.[1] We will see Monday how it will be
carried out and if any one will attempt to elude it. Gen Boyle offers
himself as a Candidate though his name was rejected by the Convention
that nominated Mr. [Brutus] Clay.[2] The only good he will do by it will be
to assist the Copperheads by dividing the vote of the Union party. ...

1. Issued by Governor Robinson on July 10, this proclamation was part of the Federal attempt to ensure the election of Unionist candidates to office. See Coulter, *The
Civil War and Readjustment in Kentucky*, 176.
2. General Boyle's assessments against Confederate sympathizers and employment
of Federal soldiers in influencing elections earned him the disrespect of many Kentucky Unionists already at odds with the Lincoln administration. Following the death
of Union Democratic Party candidate John J. Crittenden on July 26, 1863, Boyle
announced his candidacy for Congress. He was defeated by Brutus J. Clay. Many
considered Boyle responsible for military interference in the election. See Coulter,
The Civil War and Readjustment in Kentucky, 176–78.

Saturday Aug 1st [18]63

... Gen Burnside has declared the state under martial law in consideration of the avowed intention of the rebel force in the state to interfere with the election, and orders the military to assist the civil authorities in preventing unlawful voting. ...

Sunday Aug 2nd [1863]

260 prisoners were brought in tonight. Mr. B. Gratz and Mr. Augustus Hawkins[1] went out to Hickman today and met these men coming from there. ... They are mostly Louisianians and Texans. Villainous looking fellows and said their object in coming into the state was to get six hundred horses that were said to be at Lexington. ...

1. Augustus F. Hawkins, cashier at the Northern Bank of Kentucky, lived on the northwest corner of Market and Short Streets. See *Williams' Lexington City Guide*, 65.

Monday Aug 3 [1863]

Election day has been unusually quiet.[1] As far as I could learn the votes in this district are ten to one in favor of the Union candidates. Up to 10 PM the returns from such of the other districts as have been received mostly show large majorities for the Union ticket. ... Tonight a large bonfire was lighted in the public square, and the band went down and played and the boys fired off innumerable crackers and everyone was rejoicing over the good news (all the Union people that is, of course the beaten party were not in the most charitable of humors). While the band was playing Red, White and Blue, the Reverend Mr. Brank, Presbyterian minister passing remarked in the hearing of a good many union men standing near that that was the "dirge of human freedom." Whereupon Mr. Tom Dolan, who is always foremost when anything pertaining to the Union is to be defended gave him a good "setting down." The idea of Mr. Brank who has all along been thought such a good Union man saying such a thing as that! But these are times that try men's souls. I only hope everyone is satisfied now that Kentucky loyalty does not go half way, and that she really is the good Union state she pretends to be and it is no use for traitors to think of inticing her from her allegiance. ... Mr Lincoln has issued a proclamation, stating that the government intended to protect all its soldiers, black or white, and that for every black soldier imprisoned a rebel shall suffer like punishment, and for every black soldier sold into slavery a rebel shall be in [the] future set to hard work in some prison until the negro is regained[2]. . . .

1. The state gubernatorial election pitched Thomas E. Bramlette (Union Democrat) against Charles A. Wickliffe (Peace Democrat). High levels of interference by Federal military authorities marked this election. Bramlette won by fifty thousand votes. See Coulter, *The Civil War and Readjustment in Kentucky*, 177–79.
2. In response to reported murders of U.S. Colored Troops by Confederate soldiers, Lincoln issued General Order No. 100. See Cornish, *The Sable Arm*, 168–72.

TUESDAY AUG 4TH 1863

. . . The Gazette today has in it . . . a piece copied from the Dayton Journal about Mrs John Morgan[1]. . . the substance of which seems to have been obtained from letters of hers that have been intercepted. It says she had to run the blockade to Nashville last November aided by her sister Mrs. Cheatham[2] who is now imprisoned at Alton, Ill., to get her wedding clothes and quotes a letter of hers written when she joined Morgan at Tullahoma after the rebels were driven from Murfresboro about the ball in which she was "the belle" in her "beautiful green silk dress which my dear husband brought to me from Kentucky, and it is the favorite dress of my dear husband." And she had a "bewitching bonnet which my noble husband brought me when he came back from his last raid." But she was almost out of shoes, she couldn't get more until her "noble husband went on another raid." No doubt John brought her a great deal of stolen finery and expected to take her no end of pretty things in this last raid but if she dont get any shoes until John brings them to her I am afraid she will be in a bad way. . . .

1. John Morgan married Martha "Mattie" Ready on December 12, 1862. See Ramage, *Rebel Raider*, 134–35.
2. Mary Ready, the sister of John Hunt Morgan's wife, was married to William A. Cheatham, a Nashville lawyer. See Ramage, *Rebel Raider*, 57.

WEDNESDAY AUG 5 [1863]

The Observer is very bitter this morning over the results of the election. Says "For the first time in the history of the Commonwealth, Kentucky at this election was placed under martial law, and the vote of the state was cast under that extreme measure. . . . The result of this election, when all the returns are in will we think show, that little less than one half the vote of the State has been polled. The voters were intimidated in the first place by the military orders which preceded the placing of the State under martial law. By those orders it was declared that whenever the necessity existed for the pressing of private property, that of rebels and rebel sympathizers would be first taken, and that a vote for the 'no more men and no more money' ticket[1] would be regarded as evidence of such sympathy; and that Gen Fry's order to the Provost Marshall here for 150 slaves taken from the disloyal persons to be sent immediately to Camp Nelson to work on the roads in his department and Gen Burnside declaring martial law had intimidated half the state from voting. . . ."

When the vote of Kansas was taken, whether she would be admitted to the Union as a free or slave state, the proslavery democrats of Missouri fearing the day would go against slavery went to Kansas and took possession of the polls. And John C Breckinridge and other heads of the democratic party in Ky collected a number of young men under age, who really had no right to vote . . . whom they took with them to Kansas, where they went the rounds of the state voting in all the precincts thus carring the state for slavery against her will.[2] No doubt if martial law had not been declared and Gen Fry's order issued, the same thing would have been tried at this election. . . . Perhaps he [Wickliffe, *The Observer*] would not have thought this anything but constitutional, especially as he doesn't say a word about the shabby manner in which J T Boyle's friends got a good many votes for him by telegraphing false news about the way the election was going. That Mr Clay was getting so few votes, everyone was voting for Boyle etc. . . .

Saw the old scouting captain Bernhardt this evening. He had been out after a deserter. He is a queer old man, a thorough German. Stolid dull looking and would never be suspected of taking any notice of what was going on around him but very sharp for all that; with an eye that takes in everything without seeming to do so and a quick perception and ready wit for putting this and that together. He said he put on his "butternut" suit and went to the house of a rebel where he suspected this man would go and arrived just as they were sitting down to breakfast. He knew the man of the house well (and the man most likely looked upon him as the secesh he pretended to be). So he went in and sat down with the rest and noticed that (to use his own expression) "there was one plate with no one sitting to it," which circumstances confirmed his suspicion that the fellow he was in search of had been there and also made him think he was not far off. The host noticed him looking at the vacant seat and told him that Mr ———— naming the deserter had been there last night but had gone away early that morning, but he could send some one after him. No the Capt said he wouldnt trouble him, it was of no consequence, he would just light his pipe and go on. So after a little while he went out into the yard behind the house to two small log cabins that stood by the cornfield fence. And in one of them he found his man. The deserter ran at his approach first from one cabin to the other and then across the cornfield, when the captain fired at him and he allowed himself to be taken and marched off with the man at whose house he had stayed.

1. Peace Democrats mobilized in Kentucky for the August 3, 1863, election against what they considered the "usurpation" of the U.S. government and the "crimes" committed by the U.S. Army. See Coulter, *The Civil War and Readjustment in Kentucky*, 173–75.
2. The Kansas-Nebraska Act of 1854 permitted Kansans to vote to determine whether their territory would be free or slave. An influx of free-soil and proslavery partisans flooded Kansas to influence the voting, precipitating the hostilities known as "Bleeding Kansas." John C. Breckinridge did not participate in this aspect of the crisis. See Davis, *Breckinridge: Statesman, Soldier, Symbol*, 135–37.

THURSDAY AUG 6TH [1863]

Thanksgiving day passed very quietly. Few of the churches were opened. Mr. Matthews (1st Presbyterian) did not open his principally I suppose because one of his daughters is very ill, was not expected to live at one time. Mr Shipmans (Episcopal) church is having an addition built to it and being repaired generally, and the Odd fellows Hall where he has been having service being on Main St. in the midst of the business part of town it would be almost impossible to make himself heard for the noise. It is bad enough on Sundays and on a week day of course it would be much worse. Mr. Brank (2nd Presby) made a pitiful excuse about being afraid of dividing his Congregation if he had service today, and some of the other churches have secesh ministers. They say Mr Dandy, the minister at one of the Methodist churches made a very strong union sermon. . . . The jail on Broadway opposite the Hotel was discovered to be on fire today, and a good many of the prisoners were taken out and sent off on the cars to Louisville fearing the building might be destroyed but only a small portion of the roof was burnt. People are beginning to think it was set on fire in order to give the prisoners a chance of escaping in the confusion, and that there must be an incendiary about since this is the third large building that has caught fire on the roof. It looks rather suspicious. . . .

MONDAY AUG 10TH [1863]

Gen Burnside is in town today. The band came in from camp to escort him to his hotel and he made a short speech to the people saying among other things that he was sorry so many rebels had been allowed to vote here and that Ky was the most loyal state in his department. . . . Gen Grants sister was in town today (she lives in Covington) She was at Mrs Judge Paynes[1] tonight and Lettie and Jo and some others were asked to meet her. They say she is a very nice sensible girl.

1. Miss Peter refers to the wife of Judge Hugh B. Payne. The Little College Lot map located the residence of Judge Payne adjacent to Dr. Peter's garden on Market Street. See Evans Papers.

TUESDAY AUG 11TH [1863]

. . . A report was out today that the rebels had taken Col Wolford prisoner, but that is all bosh. Apropos of Col Wolford, Mr Lincoln offered him a brigadiership as a reward for his service in this Morgan raid, but the Col refused. One regiment was trouble enough, he said, without having a whole brigade to manage. But Mr Lincoln wouldnt take his refusal and said he should be a brigadier whether he took the brigade or not. . . . The band of the 48th [Pennsylvania] is out tonight playing at headquarters.

WEDNESDAY AUG 12 [1863]

The band played some time at Headquarters last night and Gen Hartsuff spoke to them and took them in and entertained them and afterward they went to one of the depots and played and hurrad and had a great time. I suppose the cars brought up some of their friends or comrads . . .

. . . There are conflicting orders out about taking negroes to work on the railroads. Gen Fry's orders [were that] the negroes of rebels, rebel sympathizers and 'no more men and money' men [were] to be taken first. But Gen Boyle's [orders] say take all negroes between 16 and 45 without making any difference between Union and rebel. A large number of the New York rioters[1] (4000 the soldier said that told us of it) have been arrested in this and adjoining counties and set to work on the roads. No one doubts that these fellows have been set out here by the New York Copperheads to influence the election; for such a number of poor men could not have afforded to come so far unless they had been supplied with money for the purpose.

The Copperheads expected that by sending these men out here to vote they could carry the state for the Copperhead candidates. They knew well that that was the only way they could hope to defeat the Union candidates and but for the timely declaration of Martial law by Gen Burnside they would have got possession of the polls and carried the State by illegal voting. Kentucky is too valuable a state to the secesh for them to leave any stone unturned to get her. . . .

1. The Enrollment Act, passed by Congress on March 3, 1863, met harsh resistance in New York City. Draft riots resulted, July 13–16, 1863. Police failed to contain the mob of fifty thousand protesters against the draft. Mostly Irish workers, the rioters terrorized and murdered blacks as well as damaged much property before they were subdued by militia and regular army units. See James Barnet Fry, *New York and the Conscription of 1863* (New York: G.P. Putnam's Sons, 1885); Eugene C. Murdock, "Was It a 'Poor Man's Fight'?" *Civil War History* 10 (September 1964): 241–45; and Iver Bernstein, *The New York City Draft Riots: Their Significance for American Society and Politics in the Age of the Civil War* (New York: Oxford Univ. Press, 1990).

FRIDAY AUG 14TH [1863]

Gen Hartsuff is gone. The guard in the lot broke up their camp this morning and went this evening out to the camp of the 48th [Pennsylvania] They were very gay all the morning and laughed more than they have done all the while they have been over in the lot. I suppose they did not like to make a noise so long as the General and his officers were at Headquarters for fear of disturbing them, but now they were gone the men had a fine time. They played drilling the "awkward squad" and sent out scouts and had a skirmish with some imaginery rebels in which some of them got wounded and had to be carried off the field in stretchers and after they had retreated stragglers would come in wounded and the doctors would be very busy attending to them. Then half of them took off their coats and put on their India rubber blankets wrong side out, so as to look like the white linsy coats the secesh wear and pretended to be rebels and tied an old piece of gauze to a stick for a flag; and the others were Federals and mounted an old pump stalk that was lying by the well at the top of the lot, on a barrel for a cannon and the rebels came up and fought them, and the Federals took the rebels prisoners and marched them off to their camp, the secesh looking very sulky. . . .

One of them, Mr White,[1] came to tell us goodbye before they went. He is very amusing . . . he uses a great many hard words in the wrong places. He for instance said to Ma "I exhonorate you Madam as having been very faithful to the Union and truly kind to us soldiers." "Exhonorate" seems to be a favorite word as he uses it on all occasions and when about to speak to anyone always first draws himself to his full height (and he is pretty tall) turns out his toes and sticks his thumbs in the armholes of his waistcoat as if he was going to make a stump speech.

1. This might be a reference to Private Paul White of Company K, 48th Pennsylvania. See Bates, *History of Pennsylvania Volunteers, 1861–1865*, 1:1235.

SATURDAY AUG 15TH [1863]

. . . One would have thought from the way the papers speak of Dr. Watson, the new Medical Director, being so active in collecting and sending off convalescents and going about to the various hospitals around here that he was all that could be wished for in a Medical Director, but it turns out otherwise when the facts are known. This evening Mr Jamison the head steward of the hospitals stopped at the door wanting to see Pa who had gone over to Mr Gratzs for a few minutes. While waiting for Pa to return Mr Jamison told Ma and me that Dr. Watson had come up to the hospital that evening perfectly intoxicated and had given all kinds of ridiculous orders, and had made Mr Jamison write orders from his dictation which he would tear up on reading. Wanted to have the oath administered to all the hospital officers, which was of course entirely unnecessary, though the officers being Union men would not make any objection to taking it fifty times a day if need be. . . . Then he wanted some one for a new ward master and Mr Jamison recommended Mr Chas Cochran a very clever, honest young man and a great favorite with all who knew him. Dr Watson asked him how long he had been at the hospital and on being told called Mr. Cochran a sneak, and a coward who merely stayed in the hospital because he was afraid to go back to his regiment and said a good many other abusive things to him. All of which were very trying to poor Charley Cochrans feelings, not less so because they were all undeserved, and he vowed vengeance against Dr. Watson and Mr Jamison was afraid he might even attempt to kill the Dr he was so much hurt at being called a coward.

Mr Jamison told Pa he wished he had been up there to help him as he began to get rather provoked himself. But Pa was very glad he hadnt been there as he had no desire to be ordered about or get into a quarrel with such a man. And Mr Jamison and he agreed that whilst Dr Eversman was absent in Cincinnati it would be best to be polite to Dr Watson, and for Mr Jamison to obey his orders only so far as they agreed with the instructions he had received from the Secretary of War for Mr Jamison having been appointed and received instructions from that functionary was not amenable to any Medical Director and that Mr Jamison should keep an account of all Dr Watson said and did and report it to Dr Church or Dr Shumard and try to get them to appoint another Medical Director who was not in the habit of getting beside himself from drink.

TUESDAY AUG 18TH [1863]

Last night the neighborhood was disturbed by a great piece of impertinence on the part of some of the negroes who assembled in the negro quarters at Headquarters and had a ball [as they] danced on the porch, stamped[,] shouted, got drunk and kicked up a great row until a very late hour. If Capt Ashbury's Cavalry had rode their horses over the porch they couldnt have made more noise. Where was the watch You may say that they did not interfere Ah, my dear sir or madam you might watch with a watery eye before you would see the watchmen attempt to do anything so unheard of in the annals of the present Lexington. . . .

I dont know who the negroes were that gave the party . . . but whoever it was it was very insolent of them to take such advantage of headquarters being deserted. Pa saw the Mayor about it who promised to have it looked into. They might have burnt the house down. The small guard left there were afraid or didn't think they had any right to interfere but Pa told them they ought to have done so, for if anything had happened to the building they would be the ones blamed for it. There are a great many bad negroes in this neighborhood and our boy is one of them. It is very likely he was down there as he was gone after 12½ PM, and no one knows when he came home. . . . Mr Chas Cochran is going to Vicksburg tomorrow to join his regiment as he said he couldnt stay in the hospital after he had been called a coward for doing so. The hospital will lose a good ward master in him. He has been in the hospital ever since before the rebels came last fall and has always been kind to the sick. The band of the 48th Pa. gave another concert last night at Odd Fellows Hall.

WEDNESDAY [AUGUST] 19TH [1863]

About noon today Mr Perciciles Scotts house on Broadway caught fire. The roof was burnt off but the rest I believe was not much injured thanks to the efforts of the soldiers. One captain was among the first to mount the roof and stood within a few feet of the flames holding the hose and was perfectly drenched in doing so . . .

Gen Nelson's body is expected to arrive here tomorrow morning on the Louisville train on its way to Camp Dick Robinson. Preparations have been made by the Council to give it a fitting reception and a Committee of

Citizens appointed among whom are Mr. Gratz and Pa to meet it at the cars. . . . One of the soldiers from the hospital stopped here this morning to rest himself . . . said his wife was with him now. She had come all the way from Tennessee on horseback to see him.

THURSDAY AUG 20TH [1863]

. . . Gen Nelsons body arrived on the Louisville train at 11 oclock AM. A salute was fired from the fort as the cars entered the town and a procession of citizens and 1st Ohio and 48th Pennsylvania escorted the herse from the Louisville to the Nicholasville cars which were to take the body part of the way to Dick Robinson. . . .

FRIDAY AUG 21ST [1863]

A lady came here this morning stating she had lost her baggage and purse and wished to get enough money to take her home. Ma thinking she might be one of the many unfortunate persons who had been forced to leave their homes in Tennessee and southern Ky to escape the rebels, asked if she was a refugee. What is that? said she rather sharply. Ma said she meant was she flying from home. She replied indignantly she was not flying from home. She was Mrs. Sarah Jane Miller of Trimble Co. She had been on a visit to some friends in Quincy Ill and had lost her baggage and with it her money at one of the stations between that place and Cincinnati. . . . When asked if she was Union, she replied she was not anything, she left politics to the men. (An answer which has got to mean secesh, as it is generally the one given by secessionists or Copperheads when they are with Union people and do not wish or are afraid to own to their true sentiments) but she afterwards said the Union never could be restored. . . . Ma told her that in times like these people had to be very cautious how and to whom they gave money, and that we had seen enough of rebels to make us wary of strangers, and hinted that it was not much in accordance with the character of a lady to be going around begging of strangers, for Ma doubted the story she told especially when she found she was not Union, and refuse to give her anything, which Mrs. Sarah Jane Miller thought very uncharitable. We did not know whether to think her a spy, a person collecting money for rebel use, a rebel mail carrier who was cloaking her designs by pretending to be in need of help or one of the inmates of the Lunatic Asylum, but we could hardly trust her story. . . .

MONDAY AUG 24 [1863]

. . . Mr. Davy Sayre was here this evening. He was in New York when the [draft] riot broke out but did not stay to see much of it. What he told us of it was very much what we had seen in the papers but his manner of telling a story would make the most tiresome, amusing. He is almost equal to Mrs Partington[1] in the wrong use of words. He said he had never expected to see a "prescription" (conscription) going on at the north. They were obliged to have "prescriptions" in the South, had had a good many, but he never thought it would be necessary to have a prescription in the North.

1. "Mrs. Partington" was a literary character created by the nineteenth-century humorist Benjamin Penhallow Shillaber. "Mrs. Partington" represented conventional wisdom and made humorous mistakes like the "prescription"/"conscription" example Miss Peter cites. See Shillaber's *Life and Sayings of Mrs. Partington, and others of the family* (New York: J.C. Derby, 1854).

FRIDAY AUG 28 [1863]

... There are said to be 30,000 troops in and around New York City. I was sorry to see in the papers that a good many of their officers were Copperheads or secesh, but in New York and most of the Northern states the people are not so strict with that class as we are in Ky. The New York people keep a Copperhead Governor[1] in office and allow him and his friends to give offices in the militia to copperheads. And allow secesh and Copperheads to express their opinion freely in their public halls and market places.

There are said to be more rebels in New York City than in the whole state of Ky. and there is not the least doubt about their having more privileges there than here. Does any one suppose for instance that men like Gov Seymour or Fernando Wood[2] would be allowed to speak publicly in Lexington and express sentiments against the administration and the Government? I know they would not; we have had to struggle too hard to keep ourselves in the Union and under the old flag ever to let Copperheads grow and flourish; we know it is necessary to beware of them as of the reptile whose name they bear. ...

... It has been a very wet, chilly day, everything looks dreary and dripping, and the wet tents of the guard and soaking wet grass in the college lot recall the time last winter when Capt Cliffords cavalry occupied the lot and the men and horses had tramped it into a perfect quagmire with not a blade of grass to be seen. I wonder if the same fate will be its this coming winter, or if the war will be ended by that time? Wont it seem strange to have no war and no soldiers to look at. It will be extremely uninteresting. . . . I shouldnt be surprised if we should get up a quarrel with some one else just to pass the time. England for instance, or we may have trouble with the negroes now they have arms in their hands they may one day turn them against the white people in hopes of conquering them. They are conceited enough for anything . . . The people around here are bringing in their negroes to work on the roads pretty fast. There are a good many in town today and the work is said to be going on well . . . of course the union people get paid for the use of their negroes while secesh and sympathizers dont.

1. Horatio Seymour (1810–1886) was elected governor of New York on the Democratic ticket for the second time in 1863. Politically opposed to Lincoln and his strong war powers, Seymour severely criticized the president's alleged violations of individual liberties. As governor he was especially opposed to the federal government's conscription policy which he considered unfair to residents of New York City. See Stewart Mitchell, *Horatio Seymour of New York* (Cambridge: Harvard Univ. Press, 1938).
2. A longtime leader in New York City's Democratic "machine," Tammany Hall, Fernando Wood (1812–1881) used his position as mayor to encourage Irish opposition to abolition, blacks, and the Lincoln administration in 1861 and 1862. Like Clement L. Vallandigham, Wood was a leader in the Peace Democrat movement. See Samuel A. Pleasants, *Fernando Wood of New York* (New York: Columbia Univ. Press, 1948).

SATURDAY [AUGUST] 29 [1863]

. . . The Observer and Reporter this morning devotes nearly a whole page to a letter from that notorious rebel Proff Morse, advocating the doctrines of the rebel Vice president. Pa said this was the last time the Observer should enter his house and gave orders that if the boy brought it on Wednesday he should not be allowed to leave it. . . . Pa is by no means the only one that has ceased subscribing for it. It has dwindled down into a very mean affair not worth reading and probably will in the course of time entirely disappear. . . .

Our new neighbors, the guard in the college lot, are very quiet and orderly, and the weather being so cold as to make indoors more pleasant than out, we have seen little of them and have not yet discovered exactly what regiment they belong to. We have only exchanged civilities so far as to send them milk every day for their coffee and once or twice to send something at meal times to one of the sergeants who looked rather "pale and interesting" as if he had been sick. That there are Scotchmen among them is fully proved by their manner of speaking. . . .

SUNDAY AUG 30TH [1863]

. . . Tonight about 8 oclock a knock was heard at the side door. It happened that none of the servants could go to the door at that moment so Ma went. On opening the door what should she see but . . . a respectable looking man of about forty years of age well dressed with white vest and neat coat, and bushy red whiskers, looking like he might be a drover, who politely asked if he could remain here for the night. Ma told him this was a private house, a gentlemans house, and she couldnt accomodate him. "But madam," he persisted "I will pay you well." Ma told him again she couldnt take him in, that if he would go a little further down town he would find a hotel. No doubt he took our house for a tavern, from its straggling look and numerous windows with lights. It was in fact used as a boarding house by the person who built it and was partly built for that purpose.

MONDAY AUG 31ST 1863

. . . The Covington train did not get in tonight until 9 oclock so we didnt get the Times, not that I expected it would have anything in it, but the gentlemen always seem to think so and throw away many a five cents upon it, and dont get much satisfaction even if the paper has news in it for they say themselves they cant rely upon what the Evening Times says. Never know whether to believe it or not until the Gazette or some of the other papers confirm it. But for all that they cant do without the Times. . . .

It is reported that our dishonorable and much to be ashamed of relative, the rebel Gen Floyd is dead.[1] I don't know whether to hope it is true or not considering what a bad man he was, but I think it would be a good riddance, and the best thing I ever heard of his doing. I never saw him, and know very little about him. But all I ever heard of him was not to his credit and I could not if I tried recall any circumstance favorable to him, or any good deed he had performed, or anything to make me wish to remember the relationship.

1. Virginian John B. Floyd (1806–1863) served as governor of Virginia (1848–1852) and U.S. Secretary of War (1857–1860), and he was accused of transferring war materiel to the South as the war approached. Appointed a Confederate brigadier general, Floyd deserted his command at Fort Donelson in February 1862 and was relieved of command a month later. Floyd's relationship to the Peters is unknown. See Robert W. Barnwell, "General John B. Floyd," *Confederate Veteran* 39 (April 1931): 141–42.

TUESDAY SEPT 1 [1863]

. . . Gov Bramlette will be inaugurated today at Frankfort. What a different 1st of Sept from that of last year, everything so quiet and peaceable, with no danger to be feared; a bright day and the citizens all quietly pursuing their daily avocations. While last year it was a day of anxiety and suspense, a day never to be forgotten. A dispersed defeated army, retreating reluctantly before the conquering rebel hoards. A surrendered city, expecting with dread, the arrival of tyranny and a feeling as if Egyptian darkness was covering the land. No one that has ever experienced the misery of being ruled by secessionists would ever wish to see that day return when they would get into power. . . .

Mr Jamison and my sisters went down to the Melodeon to help dress the hall for the festival or rather fair which is to be held there. After they returned Mr Jamison stayed awhile and among other things told us of his late trip to Washington to take some soldiers to the Lunatic Asylum there. He gave an amusing account of the trouble he had with them during the journey and when he got to Washington, not knowing where to go, as he had not been told to report to anyone, and did not know the address of the Asylum and not being able to discover it from anyone at the depot he went at once to Mr Lincoln to get orders. He said Mr Lincoln received him very politely and talked with him, and told him where to go. He said Mr Lincoln talked with everybody and always had something to say, but he looked very careworn. "Just like," to use Mr Jamison's words, "he had lost all his relations and every friend he had in the world." And that he was very tall and awkward and very much like the pictures of him, but was a man whom no one could help liking. Had a very winning way about him. . . .

WEDNESDAY SEPT 2ND [1863]

. . . Fuel still continues very scarce, wood is used almost entirely, very little coal to be had for any price, either because there are not enough men at the mines to work . . . or because transports are not to be had, to bring it. If this state of things continues into the winter there will be a great deal of suffering here.

THURSDAY SEPT 3RD [1863]

. . . The Lex secesh had a report this morning that Gen Burnside had been whipped at Kingston.[1] His army was totally routed; the men ran just like sheep, said Mr & Mrs Secesh. But the Union people on the contrary said this meant that we had taken Kingston. We have learnt to interpret rebel reports pretty well by this time. Generally when they say we have been badly whipped it is only necessary to put our army in the place they put theirs, to get the truth. They generally tell just the reverse of the real facts. . . .

1. General Burnside advanced into Eastern Tennessee in autumn 1863. Confederate forces planned resistance at several places, including Kingston, Tennessee. Nevertheless, Burnside captured Knoxville on September 2. See Marvel, *Burnside*, 272–76.

FRIDAY SEPT 4TH [1863]

On Wednesday about noon a party of some seventy or eighty guerrillas entered Flemingsburg, Ky and robbed the bank of some $500 and robbed many of the inhabitants of the money they had about them. . . .

Mr. Lancaster (who keeps [the] shoe store)[1] went to Chicago not very long ago to see his son who was taken with Morgan and was allowed to see him. So a few days ago Mrs Morgan Mrs Duke and some others with Mrs Lancaster started on a like errand. They have all returned. Mrs Lancaster took Lizzie Skillman[2] and Maggie Lancaster with her and was allowed to see her son chiefly she said through little Maggie's means. Mrs Morgan went to Columbus and was allowed to see John through a grating but not to speak to him. She said she wished she had not tried to see him as he was so changed she hardly knew him and had his hair and beard cut close.

1. M.P. Lancaster, a dealer in shoes and boots, had his store at 25 Main Street. See *Williams' Lexington City Directory*, 64.
2. Elizabeth B. Skillman, age eighteen, lived with her mother and other members of the Skillman family next door to the Bain family. See Eighth Census of the United States for Fayette County, 1860, Schedule 1, 600.

SATURDAY SEPT 5TH [1863]

· John Morgan and his followers in the Penetentiary have hitherto been allowed to receive any little thing their friends chose to send them but now it is said this will no longer be allowed. I suppose the large boxes and baskets of luxuries sent from Ky made the Penetentiary too little like a place of punishment. . . .

. . . There is any quantity of land for sale around here and still more has come into the market lately, as it is said that rebel property is to be confiscated soon and secesh are selling out. Ashland[1] is to rent, (it cant be sold thats one good thing) with all the furniture. . . .

1. The former estate of Henry Clay was purchased in 1853 by his son, James B. Clay. A Confederate sympathizer, James resided in Canada at this time. See Elizabeth Simpson, *Bluegrass Houses and Their Traditions* (Lexington: Transylvania Press, 1932), 403–4, and Kerr, *History of Kentucky*, 3:6–7.

TUESDAY, SEPT 8TH [1863]

... Never in the annals of the worlds history has any nation or people resorted to so much falsehood and deceit of all kinds to preserve their existence as have these Confederates. Their whole system is but a tissue of lies from the very beginning. How can they possibly hope to stand when they have built their house on such an insecure and sandy foundation? ...

WEDNESDAY SEPT 9TH [1863]

... Gen Sturgis said he wanted to come to Lexington to live he felt more at home here, even than in Cincinnati and was looking for a place to buy. Lettie told him perhaps he could get Mrs Morgan's house as she had wished to sell it last year and it was not improbable she would still be of the same mind. The General said he would like to have that place very well, thought it a very nice one. I wish he would get it. Expect Mrs. Sturgis and he would make very pleasant neighbors. ...

SUNDAY SEPT 13TH [1863]

I have just been looking at a very pretty picture or rather a "tableau vivant." I have been looking from Ma's window at the soldiers in the lot. How prettily they are grouped, some standing some sitting around their camp fire, where their evening meal is cooking. If I were but artist enough what a nice sketch in colors it would make! The soldiers in their blue uniforms, surrounded by the white tents, the blazing fire with its column of blue smoke rising up amid the tall black stemmed locust trees, against some of which a shining rifle or two is leaning, and the carpet of "Blue" grass looking so fresh and green after the rain and contrasting with the bare brown space around the fire. ...

MONDAY SEPT 14 [1863]

... More men came over in the lot today, to join those of the 79th NY[1] already camped there.... A friend, Mr Patterson told us we ought to think a great deal of these men, not because they were countrymen of his (Mr P. is Scotch) but because they had seen so much active service. The 79th had been the right wing of the right division of the right wing of the Army of the Potomac in nearly all the great battles in Virginia and had been very severely handled in most of them. And had almost always had the place of honor and were good soldiers and clever men which is saying a great deal. They have certainly behaved very well and kept a very orderly camp since they came to be neighbors of ours. I dont know how many of them there are in the lot but there are about twenty tents in all. . . .

1. The 79th New York, part of the 9th Corps, was composed of Scotsmen. The regiment had campaigned extensively in the Eastern theater and along the Atlantic coast before going west. See Frederick Phisterer, comp., *New York in the War of the Rebellion, 1861–1865* (Albany: J. B. Lyon Company, 1912), 2841–42.

TUESDAY SEPT 15TH [1863]

. . . Lord Russel says he cant find any proof that the ironclads building in England are intended for the rebels. Cant some kind and considerate person lend him a telescope or a spy glass and an ear trumpet so that he may see and hear what is going on under his very nose?[1]

1. During the first week of September 1863, Charles Francis Adams, U.S. Minister to Great Britain, pressured Lord John Russell to confiscate ironclads built in Glasgow for the Confederate States Navy. Constrained by a strict reading of British confiscation law in the *Alexandra* case, Russell replied that there "was no legal evidence sufficient to seize the vessels." See Spencer, *The Confederate Navy in Europe*, 110–11.

SATURDAY SEPT 19TH [1863]

. . . It is quite cold and there was a slight frost last night. The worst of it is, fuel is so high and scarce. The river still continues low so that no coal can be brought from Pittsburg. And they are selling coal here for 50 cts per bushel and hardly to be had at that. I think if this state of things continues (and I have heard people say that the Ohio river has been known to stay low until after Christmas) . . .

. . . Gen Fry had better take his negroes when they have done working on the railroad and set them to mining the coal on the Big Sandy. It would be a very good thing if he was to think of it. But I think it would shame the Ky people because they ought to have done it themselves years ago.

SUNDAY SEPT 20TH [1863]

It is said that some of the New York rioters ("Dead Rabbits" as they are called) four car loads of whom were sent south to work on the roads (and some of them to the roads in Ky to judge from what I hear) came into an eating house here last night and behaved so outrageously that they had to be arrested. The 2500 rebels under Gen Frazer captured at the Gap by Gen Burnside[1] are expected here either this evening or soon, and

Hospital No 3 (now unoccupied) and a warehouse on Water St. are being got ready for them to stay in while awaiting transportation to Ohio.

1. Confederate Brigadier General John W. Frazer surrendered his brigade to General Burnside's advancing troops on September 9, 1863. See *OR*, ser. 1, vol. 30, pt. 2, 607–15.

MONDAY SEPT 21ST [1863]

. . . The prisoners from Cumberland Gap arrived this evening. As they were being taken into Hospital No 3 a secesh lady (or rather a rebel individual of the feminine gender, for she disgraced the name of lady) dressed to represent the "Bonny Blue Flag" . . . began talking to the rebels and singing rebel songs for them. The guard tried to make her stand back and not come near the prisoners, when she abused him and used very insolent language. She went off at last and the guard followed her. . . . Some of the secesh said the guard hurt her with his bayonet, but that was not true . . . but she ran a great risk of being hurt going home, for a number of people who had witnessed her behavior, collected together, followed her, and began throwing stones and would have mobbed her . . . if they had not been prevented.

An old acquaintance came with the soldiers who guarded the prisoners, a mulatto who used to be a waiter in the Gault House [in] Louisville,[1] and had waited on Pa and Dr. Bush and the other Proffessors of Transylvania during the winters they lectured in the Louisville Medical College.[2] "Uncle Tom" or "Miss Nancy" as he was called very often by the boarders at the Gault House on account of a strange fashion he has of wearing his hair tucked up at the back of his head with a comb like a woman, and speaking in a very soft insinuating tone of voice, had always a great liking for "the Doctor" as he calls Pa and came to see him whenever he visited Lexington, and always amused us children very much by his queer ways and speeches. But we had not heard anything of him for several years and had thought him dead and Lettie told him so. "La! Miss Lettie" he said "did you think Uncle Tom was dead. Why I've been at Cumberlands Gap Cooking for a mess of eight and one of them a Captain and I've walked all the way from Cumberlands Gap". . . .

He said Gen Frazer who commanded the rebels at the Gap seemed as if he wished his men to be taken, for they hadnt made any attempts to escape although they knew plenty time enough that "Mr Burnside" was coming and when our men entered the Gap the rebels were unprepared for them and a good many were playing cards in their tents. . . .

The 1st Georgia is among the rebel prisoners. That regt. it will be remembered was here this time last fall when the rebels had Lexington. . . .

1. A well-known Louisville hotel, the Galt House sat on the corner of Second and Main Streets. See Kleber, ed., *The Kentucky Encyclopedia*, 363.
2. The Kentucky School of Medicine in Louisville, founded in 1850, shared faculty with Transylvania University. Dr. Peter and other members of the medical staff spent winter months teaching at the Kentucky School of Medicine. The Louisville Medical College was a competing institution. See Dwayne Cox, "Medical Education in the South: The Case of Louisville, 1837–1910," in *A Mythic Land Apart: Reassessing Southerners and Their History*, eds. John David Smith and Thomas H. Appleton Jr. (Westport, Conn.: Greenwood Press, 1997), 43, 49.

SATURDAY SEPT 26TH [1863]

. . . Mrs Wm Preston & daughters are getting ready to start for Washington to get passes to go to Georgia to see Gen Preston. . . .

SUNDAY SEPT 27TH [1863]

Mrs. Preston has received intelligence (from whom I could not ascertain) that Gen Preston was not wounded at Chicamauga[1] and it was not necessary for her to come. Some people thought this might mean that Gen Preston was dead, and that they were afraid to tell her. Time will show. . . .

1. General Preston commanded a Confederate division at Chickamauga and was not wounded. See Peter J. Sehlinger, "General William Preston: Kentucky's Last Cavalier Fights for Southern Independence," *Register of the Kentucky Historical Society* 93 (summer 1995): 257–85.

TUESDAY OCT 6TH [1863]

. . . The Ky rebels are said to have suffered dreadfully in the battle of Chickamauga.[1] Breckinridges Corp is said to have come out of the battle with only 300 men. Bragg's[2] animosity to Breckinridge is well known. He puts the Ky troops, always in the most exposed positions, and seems to wish nothing better than that every Kentuckian in his army should be killed. . . .

1. This battle occurred on September 19–20, 1863.
2. North Carolinian Braxton Bragg (1817–1876) graduated from West Point in 1837. He commanded the Confederate invasion of Kentucky, August-October 1862. Victorious at Chickamauga, the controversial Bragg was forced to retreat to Georgia after his failure at Chattanooga. Bragg then served as military adviser to Confederate President Jefferson Davis, 1864–1865. For aspects of the stormy Bragg-Breckinridge relationship, see McWhiney, *Braxton Bragg and Confederate Defeat, Volume 1*, 378, and Judith Lee Hallock, *Braxton Bragg and Confedeate Defeat, Volume II* (Tuscaloosa: Univ. of Alabama Press, 1991), 150, 246.

Robert Peter (1805-1894) in later years. (J. Winston Coleman Photographic Collection, Transylvania University Library)

THURSDAY OCT 8TH [1863]

On Monday night a gang of outlaws calling themselves rebel soldiers went to the house of Major Wileman[1] of the 18th Ky near Knoxville[,] Pendleton Co[.,] Ky and carried the Major off with them. Major Wileman had been wounded at Chickamauga and was home on a furlough. Intelligence of his capture reached Capt Dyas of the 40th Ky[2] at Falmouth who immediately dispatched a force after the marauders, who found Major Wilemans dead body about a mile and a half from his own home It appears his captors stripped him of his clothing, tied him to a tree and shot him. His face was disfigured with blows as if from the butt of a musket. Five citizens of Pendleton [County] have been arrested and brought to Covington.

This outrage is only one of many others that have been committed by the people of Pendleton and the neighboring counties. The secesh of Pendleton are perfect savages but I should not advise them to come in contact with the 18th Ky Oh, how enraged they will be when they hear of this! The Germans in Missouri it seems are just as bad to the secesh there as the Pendletonians are to Union men. Some one writing from Missouri to a friend here said that within full view of their house, were the dead bodies of sixty rebels whom the Germans in the neighborhood had hung on the trees and which no one was allowed to take down and the Germans killed the secesh whenever they had an opportunity[3]. . . .

1. Major Abram G. Wileman, 18th Kentucky Infantry (U.S.), was wounded on the first day of the Chickamauga campaign. See *OR*, ser. 1, vol. 30, pt. 1, 475.
2. The 40th Kentucky (U.S.) apparently did not have a "Captain Dyas." However, Captain Robert J. Dyas served in the 32nd Kentucky (U.S.), Company A, which may have been in the area at the time. See Speed, *The Union Regiments of Kentucky*, 584.
3. Violent guerrilla activity characterized the war in Missouri. Miss Peter refers to the Federal regiments of German-Americans mobilized in the state. See William L. Burton, *Melting Pot Soldiers: The Union's Ethnic Regiments* (Ames, Iowa: Iowa State Univ. Press, 1988), 103–9; Michael Fellman, *Inside War: The Guerrilla Conflict in Missouri During the American Civil War* (New York: Oxford Univ. Press, 1989), 10, 39–40; and Christopher Phillips, *Damned Yankee: The Life of General Nathaniel Lyon* (Columbia: Univ. of Missouri Press, 1990), 164–65.

FRIDAY OCT 9TH [1863]

. . . Lieut Col King of the 35th Massachusetts is Post Commandant and has issued his orders No 2 dated the 7th for the regulation of soldiers and citizens generally. Among other things his order said people had complained to him of their cows being milked and beaten, and said if he caught any one whether citizen or soldier, milking the people's cows he would make them drink so much milk that they would wish they had been weaned from the love of it. . . .

SATURDAY OCTOBER 10 [1863]

All the unmarried free negro men between the ages of 16 and 50 as well as those having slave women for wives are to be impressed to work on the military railroads in Ky by an order of Gen Boyle. The impressment will be made only in those counties specified in the original order. . . .

SATURDAY OCT 17 [1863]

Gov Bramlette[1] has issued an order saying that if at least one company be not raised in every county of Ky. before the 14th for the purpose of putting down guerillas he will enforce a draft. . . .

1. In the antebellum years Thomas E. Bramlette (1817–1875) had served as a commonwealth's attorney and had represented Cumberland County in the state legislature. During the Civil War Bramlette served as colonel of the 3rd Kentucky Infantry (U.S.) until 1862 when he became U.S. district attorney for Kentucky. In 1863 he was elected governor on the Union Democrat ticket. See Kleber, ed., *The Kentucky Encyclopedia*, 112–13.

MONDAY OCT 19TH [1863]

There has been an unusual degree of housebreaking & stealing going on lately: the latter art being not confined to professional artists but women and even ladies, whom one would not think of suspecting of such meanness have been detected in the act of purloining hats, dress goods etc. from the stores. One lady was detected by a shopkeeper in carr[y]ing off several pieces of dress goods, and the merchant knowing who she was followed her home[,] accused her of it before her father and made them pay him the value of the goods. I could not learn whether she was union or secesh but I could hope not the former

Several houses have been broken into and silver stolen but the persons could not have been citizens or very well informed as to the wealth of the persons whose houses they robbed, for they did not go to the most wealthy citizens as might have been expected. Perhaps the 'Dead Rabbits' are exercising themselves a little The President has issued a proclamation calling for a draft of 300000 additional men; and it is reported that an order will be issued for enlisting colored men in Ky, Maryland and other states. . . . I for one would not be at all disgusted at having Ky slaves emancipated. . . .

It is an undoubted fact that we are much nearer emancipation now, than even last year People are getting more accustomed to the idea, and do not think it near so terrible as they used to. It is rather significant that at the present writing it is considered nearly if not quite as cheap to buy negroes as to hire them. Clothing and food being so much higher than in former times. Every thing is tending to decrease the value of the negro as a servant, and to make a great many people look forward to the time when this state will be a free one. The time is not yet come for such a change; but unless the 'signs of the times' are very deceptive, it will be affected in due course of time.

SATURDAY OCT 24TH [1863]

. . . Richardson's guerrillas stated by the Louisville Journal at 400, were at Columbia and Greensburg on Wednesday and Thursday night made their appearance at Bardstown robbing stores etc and burning the depot, a locomotive and cars. Local news this PM is that they have been to Danville and Harrodsburg and that cavalry has been sent from Louisville after them. . . .

TUESDAY OCT 27 [1863]

. . . When the guerrillas went to Harrodsburg they went at once to Mrs. Thompsons where Mr Morgan Vance[1] and family were staying, saying they knew he was in the house; that they had certain intelligence that he was there only a short while before, and looked for him everywhere. As they said, Mr Vance had been there just before they came, but when they came to the house, he got out upon the roof, knowing well how bitterly the rebels hated him because he was a commissioner in the Federal service and had had secessionists arrested, and shown himself faithful in aiding the Union cause, in that nest of secession (for Harrodsburg deserves no better name). But even on the roof he was very nearly discovered, for one of the rebels was just about to look from a window which commanded a view of the roof when Mrs. Vance called his attention away by making some sharp remarks. It was a narrow escape.

. . . It will be remembered that last fall when the rebel army was here, the rebels burned Mr. Vance's house, forcing him and his family to fly to Lexington for safety, with such few things as they could snatch in their hurry, and plundered him of all the fine furniture, etc. the house contained, cutting up his carpets and dividing his silver among their secesh friends. And now a second time he came to Lexington to avoid them, though this time they did not do him so much damage, of course. It is thought the rebels in the neighborhood of Harrodsburg, Bardstown and other similar secesh holes, have regular meeting places at which they collect when such a raid as this last is contemplated. And that they expected this time to collect some thousand or so, instead [of] the small number they did. Nothing but very stringent measures can put a stop to such proceedings. We are beginning to see that it is very little use to be kind to secessionists; they dont appreciate kindness. They wont let us be kind to them, and the resident secesh are much more cruel, and oppressive when they have the power than the Confederate soldiers ever are. . . .

1. Morgan Vance, while a resident of Harrodsburg, Kentucky, served as a Federal commissioner and was responsible for the arrest of several secessionists. See Evans Papers.

TUESDAY NOV 10TH [1863]

. . . Pa has received orders to take charge of the hospital as Dr Eversman is ordered to Louisville.

SATURDAY NOV 14TH [1863]

. . . There were two fires this morning notwithstanding a smart rain was falling. Mr Drummond Hunt's on Broadway and Dr Payne's on upper corner of Bar Street[1]. . . There was a large fire tonight some frame houses on Limestone St They made a terrible blaze and burnt for a long time. I never saw such a cloud of sparks as rose while the roof of one of the houses was burning; it covered the whole sky like a shower of stars, and if it has lasted long would have set other houses on fire, but fortunately the roof soon fell in and put an end to the danger.

1. Dr. John D. Payne's home was on the northwest corner of Walnut and Barr Streets. See *Williams' Lexington City Guide*, 90.

MONDAY NOV 16TH [1863]

. . . There has been rain for the last three days and there is hope the river may soon be high enough to bring down coal. . . .

FRIDAY NOV 20TH [1863]

. . . HW Beecher was entertained by his society on Tuesday night and made a speech which is published in todays Gazette for those who choose to read it.[1] I rarely ever read any of his speeches myself. Mr Beecher is too ultra an Abolitionist for me. He says this war is to abolish slavery and that it ought to be continued (even after the rebels have surrendered) until slavery is utterly exterminated from this country. Now, I always understood that this war was undertaken merely to put down rebellion, and that the government was forced to resort to arms to save the Union and all our national institutions, not for the purpose of abolishing slavery though, the latter has been greatly undermined and broken up by the war. But to say that this war is carried on for the purpose of abolishing slavery is to give the rebels just cause of complaint and give them a strong point to base a case upon. The rebels say, "the Yankee government is fighting to take away our negroes." Mr Beecher says we are carr[y]ing on this war to abolish slavery, which is the same as saying that we intend to take away the southerners negroes and we are fighting for that purpose. Where is the difference between the two statements? Now I always understood that the war would stop as soon as rebels laid down their arms and returned to their allegiance to the Union, and thought this was all right. But Mr Beecher would have the war prolonged until all the slaves are set free. And so I suppose if the rebels laid down their arms tomorrow he would still have the war continue. Now I think with Gov Bramlette that a man who wont have the Union, unless the negroes are out of it, is just as bad and as much an enemy to the Union cause, as the secessionist who wont have the Union unless he can have the negro too. For my part I say whip the rebels first and then let the ballot box decide the slavery question if there are any slaves left.

1. Henry Ward Beecher, prominent minister and abolitionist, was in England on a speaking tour at this time. See Lyman Abbott, *Henry Ward Beecher* (Boston and New York: Houghton, Mifflin and Company, 1903), 244–63.

SATURDAY NOV 21ST [1863]

. . . It is a curious fact and one I never mentioned before not thinking I had proof enough of its truth, that in a great many cases, the bodies of the rebel soldiers killed in battle turn black, or lurid purple in the face and sometimes all over. There is not the least doubt of this and it is ascribed to the practice the rebel officers have of giving their men whiskey mixed with gunpowder before going into battle, so as to make them go into the fight fearlessly. The effect upon the men is to almost craze them. They get almost beside themselves and rush into the thickest of the fray, screaming and yelling and fight like fiends, regardless of any danger, and seemingly uncon[s]cious of any. It has been ascribed to the "gunpowder whiskey" because that delectable mixture has been found in the canteens of those whose bodies blackened after death, and there is nothing else apparent that could have had that effect. . . . I shouldnt like to be a rebel soldier; he is one of the most abused creatures I ever heard of, a perfect slave to his officers, and too ignorant to know how much he is imposed upon. . . .

SUNDAY NOV 22ND 1863

. . . The secesh here are very gracious today and appear to be in the best of humors, going about smiling and nodding condecendingly to their Union acquaintances; which is a sure sign that they have been furnished with some great sensation[al] story by the 'grape vine' telegraph.[1] For when they havent heard any news or have heard bad news they stay at home or if they happen to be on the street take very little notice of Union people, or even show them the cold shoulder. You never see them laughing and talking in groups on the streets unless 'something is up.' . . .

1. Apparently the secessionists anticipated a victory by Confederate General James Longstreet who, on the eve of the battle of Chattanooga, began an attack on Burnside's force at Knoxville. Longstreet's expedition proved disastrous. He abandoned his seige of Knoxville on December 3. See Marvel, *Burnside*, 314–31.

MONDAY NOV 23RD [1863]

There was another fire today, Yeisers Stables.[1] It is thought it was set on fire by some of the rowdy boys about town. When the guard came in from camp this morning, they had the band along with, which they have not had for some time, some of them being not always well enough to play. Hearing the unusual music we thought the regiment must be going to leave Lexington, and ran out to have a farewell look at it, and were surprised to see only the guard. The 7th Rhode Island is still doing guard duty, and expects to stay some time longer as the officers are busy recruiting.[2] And a good many of the men both at the camp and the artillery men at the fort have been sick. . . . We have a new neighbor Mrs Col Byrd (or Bird) wife of Col Bird of the 1st Tennessee. She occupies the house on the street back of us formerly owned by Isaac Scott. My sisters have been to see her and like her very much.

. . . A great many people have come to Lexington from various places around here, to live, and houses are in consequence scarce, and rent, high. . . .

1. Miss Peter possibly refers to P.E. Yeiser's leather, hides, and oil store on the southwest corner of Main Street and Broadway. See *Williams' Lexington City Guide*, 118.
2. Veterans of the eastern theater and Vicksburg campaign, the 7th Rhode Island relieved the 48th Pennsylvania as Lexington's Provost Guard on September 10, 1863.

The regiment was barracked in Randall's Hemp Factory. See William P. Hopkins, *The Seventh Regiment Rhode Island Volunteers in the Civil War, 1862–1865* (Providence: The Providence Press, 1903), 129–31.

THURSDAY NOV 26TH [1863]

Thanksgiving day dawned as bright and beautiful as one could wish not a cloud in the sky and the weather mild and pleasant. At an early hour servants with baskets and waiters covered with white napkins were to be seen making their way to the hospital shadowing forth, what was to the Union people, the attraction of the day, the dinner which was to be given to the soldiers at the hospital and for which the union ladies had been preparing for some time. . . .

Towards 9 oclock the ladies began to go to the hospital and about 9 oclock the band of the 7th Rhode Island arrived and took its stand on the College (hospital) porch and commenced playing. All morning the soldiers dressed in their best were seen walking about the hospital grounds and crowds of ladies coming and going either busy about the dinner or bent on seeing the decorations which the soldiers had put up in the dinner hall and sick wards. Then at eleven oclock came the glorious news that "boasting Bragg" had once more "cut stick and run," and that our army at Chattanooga had won a great victory after a three days fight and driven Bragg from all his fortified positions[1]. . . . This was indeed something to be thankful for and very suitable news for the day. The number of ladies going to the hospital increased as the dinner hour (1½) approached, as they were all desirous of seeing the tables and know how the soldiers enjoyed themselves. The dining room with a room ajoining it which had been opened to give more room were hung with wreaths of evergreen with mottoes such as "Secession is Treason" "Kentucky loyal to the Union" "Thanks to the loyal Ladies of Lexington" etc. and adorned with little flags and bunches of small arms. The wards upstairs were likewise hung with wreaths, and in one of them was a large beautiful anchor, made of evergreen, with the mottoe "Hope."

The tables were loaded with provision of all kind, and the kitchen shelves and tables were piled up with pies and cakes and such things as there was not room for on the dinner tables. And besides this the shelves in the small kitchen allotted to the Matron Mrs McEwing were full of jellies and delicacies for such as were too sick to eat solid food. The dishes on the dinner tables were ornamented with bunches and wreaths of roses, which had been made for the purpose by the chief cook Mr Prairie and some of the men acting under his directions. These roses were carved out of carrots, beets and turnips. . . . The turnip roses especially might at a little distance have been mistaken for camellias, and yet nothing but a common penknife was used in making them. . . .

I may safely say, there could not be neater nor more beautifully clean kitchens desired than those at the hospital. In fact, all the attendants and officers of the hospital must be very attentive to their duties, for I have heard numbers of persons say that this hospital, from the garret to the cellar, was the cleanest nicest place they ever saw. All the sick wards and beds [are] so tidy[,] the men so well attended to and everything [is] in such nice order. In fact we take great pride in our hospital. . . .

. . . At half past one oclock the dinner began, and when the soldiers at the hospital were done, the tables were filled again and the artillery men from the fort were invited up and given dinner also. Still there was a quantity of provisions left especially pies and cakes, so Mrs McAllister had them packed up to take out to the soldiers at the fort and camp. The citizens had sent the soldiers at these places enough turkies to give them a good dinner but still the ladies thought the pies would not be amiss.

The soldiers were delighted with the dinner at the hospital. They said they never expected such a dinner. "Why" said some of the ladies "if you didn't expect to have a dinner what made you take the trouble to make so many decorations?" "Oh," was the reply, "we knew you would send us something, but we never expected anything like this." One of them said he hoped the Lexington ladies would live forever. Some people thought perhaps they would have enjoyed themselves more if there hadnt been so many ladies there but the soldiers said no. They liked it all the better for that very reason, and paid the ladies all kinds of compliments. The band played in the office all the time the dinner was going on, which was until after 4 PM and then on their way back to camp passed through some of the streets playing. Pa sent a notice of the dinner to the Observer & Reporter and Mr. Jamison said he was going to write an account of it for the Cincinnati Commercial.

1. On November 25, 1863, General U.S. Grant drove the besieging army of Braxton Bragg from the heights surrounding Chattanooga, Tennessee. See Faust, ed., *Historical Times Illustrated Encyclopedia of the Civil War*, 133.

SATURDAY NOV 28TH [1863]

... The news arrived this evening that John Morgan and six others had made their escape from the Penetentiary. $1000 reward has been offered for Morgan.[1]

... The Observer & Reporter did not publish Pa's notice of the hospital dinner [on Thanksgiving]. I dont see any reason for that, as there was nothing relating to politics in it, being really a short piece, mentioning the dinner and thanking the ladies.

1. On November 27, 1863, Morgan and six of his officers escaped from the Ohio Penitentiary by digging holes in walls, traveling through air vents, and climbing over the outside wall. In addition to the $1000 offered by Governor Tod, Secretary of War Stanton offered $5000 for Morgan's recapture. See Ramage, *Rebel Raider*, 193–95.

MONDAY NOV 30TH [1863]

... The Gazette contains ... an account of the manner in which John Morgan and six of his men escaped from the Penetentiary which said Morgan and the other six were not under the charge of the persons having charge of the Penetentiary though they still occupied cells there, but had been handed over to the charge of the military authorities. ... It said they escaped through an air chamber under their cells, but I expect they had help from without, and that some bribing was done among the guards. ... We were much vexed that they should have been allowed to escape but did not much trouble ourselves about them, as they are very likely to be caught again. ...

TUESDAY DEC 1ST [1863]

... in the Gazette ... one or two pieces describing the destitute condition of the people in Dixie, one of which contains an advertisement by a lady who wishes to dispose of a half worn black dress for $250 in Confederate script. It shows how much the rebels money has depreciated that such prices should be asked.

Pa came home tonight in great glee. He had been down as usual when the 7 PM train from Covington came in, to get the news. And he had got some very good news as we all knew when he came in, it was written plainly in his face even if he hadnt rubbed his hands together and waved his hat round his head, in his great satisfaction. Longstreet was whipped he said and it was reported that 5000 cavalry had been captured[1]. ... The Union men were all jubilant over the news.

... There is an old store box on Cheapside that is called the Abolition stand, because the Union men go there to talk or speechify, and I expect there were a great many stump speeches delivered tonight. ...

1. Lieutenant General James Longstreet (1821–1904) was a leading Confederate corps commander. He was credited with engineering the Confederate victory at Chickamauga but failed in his attempt to capture Knoxville after the Union triumph at Chattanooga, November 23–25, 1863. Longstreet's two-week siege of Burnside's troops culminated in an unsuccessful attack on Fort Saunders. Longstreet withdrew his divisions five days later on December 4, 1863. See William Garrett Piston, *Lee's Tarnished Lieutenant: James Longstreet and His Place in Southern History* (Athens, Georgia: Univ. of Georgia Press, 1987), and Faust, ed., *Historical Times Illustrated Encyclopedia of the Civil War*, 420–21.

WEDNESDAY DECEMBER 2ND [1863]

... The Gazette copies from the Indianapolis Journal a call made by several gentlemen of Indiana for persons to join them in the work of freeing the prisoners in the Libby Prison. ...

... It is enough to rouse anyone, to hear the numerous tales of the sufferings of the inmates of Libby and Belle Island[1] that appear in the papers. The cruel treatment of the Richmond prisoners has had a great effect upon our soldiers. They fight much more desperately, having such a prospect before them if they are taken prisoners, and do all they can to avoid capture. ...

1. These were two of the Confederacy's chief prisons. Libby Prison in Richmond, Virginia, was a former tobacco warehouse converted into a compound for captured Union officers. Bell Island, located on the James River and consisting of "a maze of tents" in an unhealthy environment, housed enlisted men captured by the Confederates. See Emory Thomas, *The Confederate State of Richmond* (Austin: Univ. of Texas Press, 1971), 60, and Frank L. Byrne, "Prisons," in *Encyclopedia of the Confederacy*, ed. Current, 3:1266.

FRIDAY DEC 4TH [1863]

... There was a great sensation story in town this morning. The news came last night that the rebels or rather guerrillas who had been at Mt Sterling and burnt the court house there and stolen some horses, were coming this way. The military prepared to meet them and pickets were placed on all the roads. This morning Madam Rumor had it that the rebels were at the Ky river; they were 5000 strong, and no doubt they were either Wheelers Cavalry or some of Longstreets men. The secesh were in a very good humor, and there was some excitement among the timid of the Union side. The people of Winchester and Booneville were much alarmed and it was said that numbers of them were getting ready to fly from their homes to places of greater security. . . . The military however could find no traces of the rebs, nor meet any one that would tell of their whereabouts, and the number of the guerrillas dwindled down gradually until from 5000 it got to 200, which was the most probable number.

WEDNESDAY DEC 9TH [1863]

. . . The Providence R.I. Journal of Dec 5th contained a notice of the dinner given at the hospital here on Thanksgiving day. [It was] written by a member of the 7th Rhode Island expressing the greatest gratification at the attention paid them and the other soldiers here. . . . I am sure the union people here were more than paid for what they did, by the pleasure it seemed to give the soldiers, and we only wished we had been able to do more. The soldiers are always so grateful for any kindness shown them, that we would be mean indeed if we did not feel pleasure in doing what we could for them. . . .

. . . Our Post Commandant Col King seems to be much excited at present on the subject of salutes.[1] The soldiers lately, had fallen into a way of frequently not saluting officers when they met them, the soldiers from the hospital especially. Col King was annoyed at this, no doubt very properly, and issued several orders containing articles referring to salutes, which he sent to Pa as surgeon in Charge. Pa had them read in all the wards of the hospital, but still deriliction was complained of, and now Col King says if the hospital soldiers dont learn to salute officers they shall not be allowed to come in town. I suppose this will settle the business.

1. The Rhode Islanders in Lieutenant Colonel William S. King's (35th Massachusetts) regiment seem to have considered him a martinet. See Hopkins, *The Seventh Regiment*, 135.

THURSDAY DEC 10TH [1863]

. . . I think Mr. Lincolns message[1] a very sensible one. We did not think much of him at first and he only got one vote in Lexington, but the more we see of him the better we like him. If he runs for President next election as there is little doubt he will be obliged to do to satisfy his friends, he is almost certain to be reelected. I know a good many people here will vote for him. . . .

1. Miss Peter refers to Lincoln's "Proclamation of Amnesty and Reconstruction," issued on December 8, 1863. It specified that whenever 10 percent of a Confederate state's 1860 voting population had taken an oath of allegiance to the Union, that

element could reestablish a state government along republican lines. Certain high-ranking Confederates were excluded. For the text of the proclamation, see Basler, ed., *The Collected Works of Abraham Lincoln*, 7:53–56.

SUNDAY DEC 13TH [1863]

... The darkies met with a great mishap this evening. Just as their churches[1] were being dismissed a number of soldiers who had been stationed out side rushed upon the unsuspecting negroes capturing all the men they could lay hands on. The darkies in great terror ran in all directions, some jumping out of the church windows and all doing their best to elude pursuit, sometimes in a most laughable manner, stout, hale men pretending to be crippled & hobbling along with their canes. The soldiers however caught a good many whom they sent off to Camp Nelson[2] to work on the wagon road they are going to make to Cumberland Gap until they can get hands enough to finish the railroad. It was right mean of them to be 'pressing' the darkies on Sunday and all dressed in their 'go to meetin' clothes, and not even give them time to take off the latter. ... The hospital is full. Some of the sick had to be put on the floor, as there were not enough beds.

One old fellow from Camp Nelson had his hand in a kind of a sling and when Dr. Bush[3] came to examine it, held it out with the fingers all cramped up, pretending he could not straighten them. Dr. Bush pretended to examine them with a great deal of attention. At last he turned to one of the soldiers near him and told him to bring his dissecting knife, for said he 'I shall have to cut the tendons of this mans hand.['] He had no sooner said this than a most wonderful cure was effected. The man's fingers straightened themselves instantly and he became well enough to be sent to his regiment. There have been two cases of this kind in the hospital lately, sneaking fellows who pretend to be disabled, so they may get a discharge, and make money by hiring themselves for substitutes or by reinlisting.[4] But the doctors here have seen enough of such tricks to know pretty well how to detect them.

1. Lexington had three African American churches: the First African Baptist on the south side of Short Street, between Spring and Lower (now Patterson) Streets; the Second African Baptist, southeast corner of Back (now Deweese) and Short Streets; and the Independent African, southwest corner of Main and Locust Streets. See *Williams' Lexington City Directory*, 17.
2. Established in 1863, Camp Nelson was the principal site in Kentucky for the enlistment and training of black soldiers. Located in Jessamine County at the mouth of Hickman Creek near Ariol on the Lexington and Danville Pike, it had a fortified circumference of ten miles. See John G. Fee, *Autobiography of John G. Fee* (Chicago:

National Christian Association, 1891), 174–83, and Marion Lucas, "Camp Nelson, Kentucky, during the Civil War: Cradle of Liberty or Refugee Death Camp?" *Filson Club History Quarterly* 63 (October 1989): 439–52.

3. In 1839 Dr. James M. Bush accompanied Dr. Robert Peter overseas to London and Paris to purchase books and equipment for the Transylvania Medical College. See Robert Peter, *The History of the Medical Department of Transylvania University* (Louisville: John P. Morton and Company, 1905), 114–20.

4. County, state, and national bounties for enlistment could amount to $1000. Some men, known as "bounty jumpers," enlisted, received their bounty, then deserted or obtained a discharge, with the intention of reenlisting again somewhere else for another bounty. See McPherson, *Battle Cry of Freedom*, 605–6.

TUESDAY DEC 15 [1863]

. . . The Medical Inspector has been paying Lexington a visit. He expresses himself as being much pleased with the appearance of the hospital. . . . There was a report here last night that rebels were at Mt Sterling, and pickets were put out on all the roads . . .

THURSDAY DEC 17TH [1863]

. . . There are a great many men in Lexington at present who have come in to get exempt for the draft[1]. . . .

. . . Mr Laschelles, Pa's Orderly, came after Pa tonight to see a rebel who had been brought to the hospital from the Provost Marshalls office. Pa found the fellow to be one of the Tanksleys,[2] a family who work a good deal for the Prestons and are great rebels.

1. Unlike southerners, northerners could not receive an exemption from military service based on occupation. They could, however, receive an exemption by claiming dependent relatives, hiring a substitute, or paying the commutation fee of $300. See McPherson, *Battle Cry of Freedom*, 601.

2. Fountain Tanksley, a peddler, lived with George Tanksley on the south side of Second between Broadway and Jefferson. See *Williams' Lexington City Guide*, 102.

SATURDAY DEC 19 [1863]

. . . The draft in Ky has been stopped; and it is doubted now whether we will have any at all, as some mistakes have been made in reckoning up Kentucky's quota, and it is thought probable it is not so large that we cant fill it by volunteering. . . .

. . . There was a hop going on at the Phoenix the other night when Gen Burnside arrived, and the General did not stop for ceremony but went in just as he was, and danced in his riding boots and spurs. . . .

1863

WENESDAY DEC 23RD [1863]

. . . A rumor is prevalent in town today that Longstreet is coming through the [Cumberland] Gap. We thought the secesh had some news on hand from the way they were flocking to Mrs Morgan's today and yesterday evening and collecting in groups on street corners. . . .

TUESDAY DEC 29TH [1863]

. . . The race horse John Morgan escaped on is thought to have come from Victor Flournoy's place, which is not at all improbable.[1] Mr. Flournoy is in the south at present and his place which is about seven miles out on the Newtown pike is in charge of Mr Standiford a very bitter secessionist. Mr S. does not reside on the place, but in town, and there is generally only the Dutch gardener (who is also a rebel) and the blacks on the place. Now Mr Flournoy is a rebel and his place has generally been as one might say headquarters for the secesh in the neighborhood, which is mainly rebel, and if J Morgan did come into that part of the country, that is the place he would be most likely to go to as a quiet place where he could meet his rebel friends, without having his presence known in the neighborhood. Now a short while after Morgan escaped from the Penetentiary, it was whispered in that neighborhood that several of the secesh had been seen at night going to Mr. Flournoy's. That Mr Standiford had been out, and a stranger had been there who had got a horse from Mr. S. and this gave rise to the story about J Morgan, which may or may not be true.

1. Victor M. Flournoy, a wealthy "planter & farmer," lived with his wife and three white servants. See Eighth Census of the United States for Fayette County, 1860, Schedule 1, 335.

WEDNESDAY DEC 30TH [1863]

There has been a considerable amount of stealing going on lately in this part of the country. People have been detected going out from town with wagons, to the country, and stealing loads of wood, fowls, corn, etc. from the farmers, which they afterward bring to town and sell, either to groceries, or at the camps. Today a free colored man named John Taylor,[1] who has kept a livery stable here for some years, and been considered a respectable person, was sentenced to the Penitentiary for stealing a wagon load of corn worth twenty dollars. He went during the night to the farm of Mr Jerry Tarleton[2] about seven miles out on the Newtown road, and filled a wagon which he had brought for the purpose, with corn. On the way back the wagon broke down near the tolegate, and Taylor went back to town and got another. The delay gave Mr Tarleton time to follow him up pretty closely, the wet, muddy corn was found in Taylor's loft which was perfectly dry & clean, and the fact was proved on him too clearly for doubt. . . .

1. John H. Taylor's livery stable stood on the south side of Church Street between Mulberry and Upper Streets. See *Williams' Lexington City Guide*, 102, 103.
2. Fifty-two-year-old farmer Jerry Tarlton lived with his wife and two sons. See Eighth Census of the United States for Fayette County, 1860, Schedule 1, 331.

THURSDAY DEC 31ST [1863]

Last night some person, or persons unknown broke into Pa's mill,[1] on Elkhorn Creek, stole 300 lbs of flour and cut the curtains off his mill wagon. . . .

1. The flour mill, one of Dr. Peter's several business interests, was supervised by his son, Benjamin, at this time. See Evans Papers.

FRIDAY JAN 1ST 1864

There was only a slight fall of snow last night, but the wind blew fiercely from the northwest all night to the imminent danger of chimney pots, window shutters, and worse that all the tents of the soldiers, which must have suffered as well as the soldiers themselves for it was a terribly cold night and the wind was keen as a razor. The thermometer was 8 degrees below zero, in the middle of the day and I was told it was at 18 below zero early in the morning . . . several persons had their ears and noses frozen . . . things freeze even in rooms where there is fire, and the water might be said to freeze as it came out of the pump. Old citizens say there hasnt been such cold weather since the year '35. . . .

TUESDAY JAN 5TH [1864]

. . . Three federal soldiers were frozen to death at Camp Nelson on Saturday night . . .

. . . The Department Headquarters have been ordered to be moved from Cincinnati here and Mrs Vertners house[,] the former headquarters[,] is being got ready for them. Mr Jefferies[,] Mrs Vertners son-in-law, or rather the husband of her adopted daughter[1] is here from New York and objected greatly to this and obstinately refused to give up the key. As he did not give any sufficient reason for refusing and as he was a secessionist the door was broken open. . . .

1. A noted poet, Rosa Vertner Jeffrey, was born near Natchez, Mississippi. Her mother died when Rosa was nine months old and a maternal aunt and her husband, Daniel Vertner, adopted her. The Vertners purchased the Bodley house (see also note 2 for November 8, 1862, and note 1 for May 22, 1863) and moved to Lexington in 1836. Alex Jeffrey was Rosa's second husband. See Simpson, *Bluegrass Houses and Their Traditions*, 159–60, and Perrin, *History of Fayette County, Kentucky*, 634–35.

WEDNESDAY JAN 6TH [1864]

. . . Some secesh prisoners were employed today cleaning the snow off the pavement at Headquarters. . . .

THURSDAY JAN 7TH [1864]

. . . We saw yesterdays [Cincinnati] Commercial today. Gov Bramlette has issued a proclamation ordering military commands throughout the

State in any instance when a loyal citizen is taken off by Southern guerillas, to immediately arrest at least five rebel sympathizers in the vicinity of the outrage. . . .

FRIDAY JAN 8TH [1864]

Two young men, clerks from headquarters were here this morning wanting to get boarding here. Lettie knew one of them, he had been in the hospital here a few months ago. They said about one hundred staff officers, clerks etc. would be here but the General would not. They were very anxious for Ma to take them as they said they did not wish to board at any but a Union house and there were several others who would like to take day boarding here. Ma would have liked very well to have had them if she had been able to accomodate them, but had no room to offer them. . . .

TUESDAY JAN 12TH [1864]

Gen Grant was in town yesterday.[1] He took breakfast at our neighbor's Mrs. Payne and my sisters & M[iriam] Gratz were asked up to see him. . . .

1. On Sunday, January 10, 1864, Grant arrived in Lexington and stopped at the Phoenix Hotel. He had journeyed from Big Hill, near Berea. While in the city he was showered with attention by a crowd of admirers and friends. See Perrin, *History of Fayette County, Kentucky*, 464–65.

WEDNESDAY JAN 13TH [1864]

. . . The draft is postponed until the first of March. The secesh say Gen Grant came here from Cumberland Gap flying from Longstreet. The latter had been strongly reinforced and had whipped the Yankees and was coming right on into Ky, which story was founded on the fact the Gen Grant came here on horseback, without his escort and no baggage, not even a change of clothing, as he said himself. . . .

SATURDAY JAN 16TH [1864]

Congress is debating about expelling Mr. Garret Davis[1] of Ky from the Senate. He used to be a good Union man, but lately he has become exceedingly Copperish and delivered some very treasonable resolutions in the Senate. . . . The chief characteristic of Mr Davis' reply [to Senator Henry Wilson of Massachusetts] was abuse of his adversary. The speech was filled with denunciations of Abolitionists in general and Mr Wilson[2] in particular. He reiterated his denial of treasonable intent, and like the offending child who threatens to 'go tell his mother' said he would go home to the people of his loved native Ky and 'raise the cry of oppression, tyranny, usurpation, and revolution against the faithless who had charge of the Government.'

Mr Davis had better try it. I should like to see him make the experiment and if his 'loved Ky.' does not set him down as completely as ever she did traitor[s], then I am mistaken in her. Mr Davis appears to have lost his senses. I truly hope the Senate will kick him out without more ado. I believe the State has no power to remove him but it is very certain she does not endorse his resolutions, and that he has misrepresented her too long already.

1. Born near Mt. Sterling, Kentucky, Garrett Davis (1801–1872) represented his state in the U.S. House of Representatives, 1839–1847. He was elected to fill the senate seat left vacant by the expulsion of John C. Breckinridge in 1861 and served until his death in 1872. Once a strong Unionist and Lincoln supporter, by January 1864 Davis had become a severe critic of Lincoln and his "war party." Davis asserted that the conflict was "enriching hundreds of thousands of officers, plunderers and spoilsmen, in the loyal States, and threatens the masses of both sections with irretrievable bankruptcy, and infinite slaughter." On January 5, 1864, Davis urged Americans in the North and South to end the war and revolt against the administration. See Coulter, *The Civil War and Readjustment in Kentucky*, 208–9, and Kleber, ed., *The Kentucky Encyclopedia*, 255–56.
2. Henry Wilson (1812–1875) served as U.S. Senator from Massachusetts, 1855–1873, when he resigned to become vice president under U.S. Grant. A Radical Republican leader who considered the speeches of Senator Garrett Davis treasonable, Wilson demanded the Kentuckian's expulsion from the Senate. See Richard H. Abbott, *Cobbler in Congress: The Life of Henry Wilson, 1812–1875* (Lexington: Univ. Press of Kentucky, 1972).

Wednesday Jan 20th [1864]

Ma was standing in the front door this morning when one of the 48th Penn V.I. came by whistling as merry as a bird and bid her good morning gaily with a face all smiles. "Well" said Ma, after she had shaken hands with him, "I should like to know what has put you in such good humor. I should like to share your gaiety." "Oh" said he "the 48th have all reinlisted and are going home on a furlough, and they are at Camp Nelson, and we're coming to Lexington when we come back from home. Isnt that enough to make one feel glad?" . . .

Thursday Jan 21 st [1864]

Some 200 or 300 prisoners of Longstreets command arrived here last night from Knoxville. They are wretchedly clad, dirty, miserable, and half starved. The secesh ladies with Mrs. Curd and Mrs McCaw at their head, have been busily engaged, supplying them with food and clothing.

Gazette publishes a letter from Gov. Bramlette [to Captain Edward Cahill] about negro recruiting in Ky.[1] "Yours of the 10th inst informing me that you had been ordered to recruit 'free colored men' for the Army of the U. S. and asking my consent for so doing is before me. You do not inform me by what authority you come to Ky to recruit 'free colored men.' I know of no act of Congress requiring such service, nor have I seen any order from the War Department directing it. On the contrary I am well assured that in deference to our peculiar position, and to avoid unnecessarily aggravating the troubles of the loyal men of Ky, the authorities at Washington do not contemplate recruiting 'colored men' in Ky. We are ready to fill our quota from the 'free' white citizens of Ky. We will unhesitatingly comply with the requirements for men to defend our Government. We claim the right to furnish from the citizens whose duty it is to make that defense and who are ready to comply with the requirement of duty. The duty of defense devolves upon those who enjoy the benefits of our Government. From such we will fill the call upon us. We presume that white men who owe the duties of citizenship to the Government will be accepted for its defense. We will furnish them. If therefore you come to recruit 'colored men' for the benefit of Ky, we decline your services. If you come to recruit for the benefit of another State we deny your right to do so and forbid it. No state has the right under any law or order, to enter Ky to recruit white, or 'colored' men. We do not intermeddle with any State that chooses to recruit 'colored' men within its own limits. But no State that is not willing to meet the measure of duty by contributing its quota from its own population, shall be permitted to shelter from duty behind the free negro population of Ky. We shall meet the call upon us without enlisting colored men, and your State must meet its call from its own white, or colored men, as may best suit its people, and not assume to recruit either white, or black in Ky"....

A correspondent from Paducah Ky to the Gazette writes "A scout that went from here recently into Graves County, captured some rebel officers and soldiers on one of whom was found a couple of letters to men in the rebel army. The letters were from ladies. One is written to her husband in the rebel army, under date of Dec 30th, and seems to be in a very despondent mood. After speaking of this "troublesome world," she says, "I dont see anything we should want to live for." She complains bitterly about not hearing from him, and his neglect of her and says, "You have wanted to be in this war ever since it began, and I reckon you will get your fill before it is done. I have my fill already. I am willing to have peace in any way. I believe the South will go up and it is the general belief here. Oh! I would give anything I possess, or ever expect to, if you hadnt gone in this war. If I had known everything as I do now I would have tied you and kept you tied to have made you know I never did want you to go." She had seen the "Yankees" and like most of the rebel women has been agreeably disappointed in them. She says "The Yankees have been kinder to me than I could expect." She expresses her fears that she will never see him again, and says "I tell you it makes me feel awful to think that I will be left in the world with two little children with no way to make a support." She here expresses what will be the condition of thousands upon thousands of women and children, whose husbands, and fathers have died, or been killed in the rebel army. . . . She is much afraid the men will all leave and says "I cant see what all the women will do if all the men are taken from here. I am more troubled now than I ever have been". . . .

. . . The [Cincinnati] Gazette's Frankfort letter rates the Conservatives well and expresses a wish which all Union people here will join in, namely that we had a loyal paper edited in Kentucky that would express the true sentiments of the Governor and people. The Louisville papers and the [Lexington] Observer & Reporter here are all conservative. So are I believe the Frankfort papers except the Frankfort Commonwealth. Conservative is a disgusting name. I would much prefer an out spoken rebel to a Conservative, because, with the former you know how to deal and what to expect, but the latter are false friends.

1. Kentucky congressmen had opposed the inclusion of blacks in the Conscription Act of 1863. Public outcry in Kentucky over the enrollment of slaves and free blacks was so extreme that in June 1863 the Provost Marshal General ordered the cessation of enrollment of free blacks in October. Lincoln assured Governor Bramlette that no blacks in Kentucky could be enlisted. Many blacks, however, continued to be impressed for labor and many fugitive blacks enlisted in regiments of other states. Governor Bramlette wrote his letter to Cahill on December 14, 1863. See Howard, *Black Liberation in Kentucky*, 45–51, 189 n.

FRIDAY JAN 22ND [1864]

Cincinnati Gazette contains a good deal of Southern news. John Morgan's address to his troops calling on them to rally to him once more. I suppose he intends resuming his former trade. If he lets us get hold of him again his neck will not be so safe as last time. . . .

. . . Regiments are reinlisting rapidly and returning home on furlough of thirty days. Not a day passes but one or more pass through here. . . .

. . . There was a case of varioloid discovered at Headquarters this morning, but I suppose the Post Surgeon, Dr Sprague has had the man removed to his smallpox hospital, at the camp of the 7th R.I. at Randalls Factory by this time. A good many of the 7th Rhode Island had the smallpox not long ago but it was not until lately that the fact was known in town as the officers were afraid to say anything about it until the men were well. It is very probable there may be more cases out at that camp as everyone knows it is very hard to get entirely rid of such a disease, especially in a crowded place like a camp.

MONDAY JAN 25TH [1864]

Rumors of a Rebel invasion of Ky prevail in Louisville. The Paris Citizen of Friday says that reports were on the streets of that place that 2400 rebel troops had entered Eastern Ky. and 400 of them had advanced to Salyersville between 65 and 70 miles from Paris. Rumor added that this advance had reached Owingsville . . . Some of the young men at Headquarters have announced it is their intention to at their leisure moments [publish] a small paper called the "Mailbag," the first number of which appeared today.

WEDNESDAY JAN 27TH [1864]

The [Kentucky] Legislature has passed the Military bill.[1] It is probable that most if not all the Ky regiments will reinlist, and it is thought doubtful whether any new ones will be required. Gov Bramlette will take no action in the premises until he has consulted Gen Grant. . . .

As for Morgan's being 'the favorite son' of Ky and our officers being delighted to see him, I never saw a more barefaced lie in a rebel paper, which is saying a great deal[,] for these documents stand first in that accomplishment.[2]

In the first place I have always heard that Morgan was born in Alabama, and as for favorite! his character here was always that of a gambler and libertine, and before this war no gentleman in Lexington would associate with him, and none would, now but those who have placed themselves on the same level with him by becoming secessionists. And what loyal Kentuckians are there that would be delighted at the escape of the traitor who pillaged their families, destroyed their homes, and persecuted them in every way. The outlaw whom they so often pursued to bring to justice, and who could never be called a brave man. It is disgusting to hear such a thing mentioned. I mention these things merely as a note. I should not be surprised if Morgan wrote that piece himself. It sounds like some of his vainglorious boasting.

The Radicals, as the secesh now call the strong Union men (Abolitionist has lost its effect) intend holding a meeting at Louisville on the 22nd February to try and pass resolutions for emancipation. People here are beginning to think it must come to this some day or other, and as Missouri, Maryland, Tennessee and Arkansas are holding meetings for this purpose, I suppose Kentucky ought not to be behind them. A Mr Stephens preached at the Methodist church lately, who had just been travelling through a good many of the surrounding counties, and he said that every where he went the principal slaveholders seemed to think that slavery was destroyed and never would be restored; and the best thing they could do was to come to emancipation at once, for the negroes were dissatisfied and idle, and not content at home and it was best to settle the affair at once. In fact the negroes throughout the country are no longer the humble servants that they used to be. They are restless, impertinent and discontented, neglect their work, and run off in great numbers. . . .

Not very long ago the Methodist minister, Mr. Dandy, lost two of his servants; two whom he thought a great deal of and to whom he had been very kind and indulgent. One was a man and the other a girl who nursed his children. This girl came to Mrs Dandy one evening and asked to be allowed to go to the "singing" that evening, some of the colored people having agreed to meet together to sing, most likely to practice for the church as negroes do sometimes. Mrs Dandy asked what company she had, and said she might go if she had good company to go with her. The girl said her brother was going with her. "Well" said Mrs D. "you may go." The girl left the room and after Mrs Dandy thought she was gone she went down stairs where she found the girls brother. Mrs D told him she thought he had gone with his sister to the singing. "Oh" said he, "she wouldnt let me go. She told me to stay and mind the children." Mrs Dandy thought nothing of this but next morning the girl did not make her appearance and was no where to be found. And what was more Mr Dandy found that his rockaway and man servant were gone also. It seems that Mr D's servants and those of another family took the rockaway and decamped the same night, some of the men disguising themselves in womens clothes the better to escape detection. They did not take the horse, probably because he was well enough known in the neighborhood, & most of the towns around here, to be recognized. But they stole three horses from someones pasture to get off with. They were traced to Versailles and then all clue was lost. It was thought beyond the possibility of a doubt that it was a preconcerted scheme and that very likely they had help from some of the Abolitionists who are scattered through every northern regiment. Mr Dandy did not mind the loss of his servants so much as of his rockaway, as the latter he would hardly be able to replace though he might the others. . . .

1. The "Military bill" to which Miss Peter refers was entitled "An Act Empowering the Governor to Raise a Force For the Defence of the State." It was passed January 26, 1864. See *Acts of the General Assembly of the Commonwealth of Kentucky, 1863–1864* (Frankfort: Commonwealth Office, 1864), 20–21.
2. This is in response to an article in the *Richmond Enquirer* describing Morgan's visit to Libby Prison.

MONDAY FEB 1ST [1864]

. . . The Louisville Journal has further advices of the recent guerrilla raid on Scottsville Ky. Capt Gillum of the 48th Ky[1] was commanding at Scottsville with 150 men. Hamilton with 500 rebels attacked him, and after a desperate fight Gillum surrendered on condition that private property should be respected and himself and men paroled. Hamilton assented but afterwards fired the courthouse destroying all the public documents. . . .

The 18th Ky, Col Warners old regt. now commanded by K Milward[2] of this city, arrived about five oclock P.M. There were about 400; all the regiment I believe but one company which either had not, or did not intend to reinlist. The 400 veterans were marched into the little College lot to receive their furloughs and be dismissed. . . . in the deepning twilight the regiment was drawn up in line and one by one the furloughs were distributed and with a cheerful hurra the men broke ranks, and dispersed to their various homes.

After supper, the surgeon of the 18th Dr Elliot (the same who had charge of one of the hospitals here at one time) came to see us. Coming in he met Ma and my little four year old sister in the passage. After speaking to Ma he asked Dollie to shake hands with him, which she did at once to Ma's surprise, for she is generally very shy of strangers. Ma asked her afterward "Dollie why did you shake hands with Dr Elliot. Why were not you afraid of him?" "Oh," said Dollie "I had to shake hands with him because he said he was a *veteran*." I dont know what she thought a veteran meant but she seemed to think it must be an uncommonly good Union man.

Dr. Elliot had been taken prisoner at Chicamauga, and taken to Richmond. He was confined in a large tobacco warehouse with about 1000 other officers. He said what we had heard about the living in the Richmond prisons was true, but that while he was there they had got boxes from home and had a pretty good time. The officers used to amuse themselves in all sorts of ways, sing, make speeches and have theatre, and used to tease their rebel guards every way they could think of. Once they were left without fire, and they kept themselves warm by forming themselves into companies and running double quick up and down the room. One of the guards came up and told them not to make such a noise, but as soon as he was gone they began running again. Again the rebel came and repeated the order, and again he was disobeyed as soon as his back was turned. When the rebel came up a third time he drew his pistol and told them if they didn't stop that noise he would fire into them. One of the officers stepped forward and told him to do it if he dared and they'd skin him in no time. So he thought discretion was the better part of valor and retired. . . .

1. Miss Peter likely refers to Captain John D. Gilliam of Company B, 52nd Kentucky Mounted Infantry (U.S.). See Speed, *The Union Regiments of Kentucky*, 650–52.
2. Twenty-nine-year-old H.K. Milward made harnesses and read law prior to the war. He served in several Kentucky regiments before he assumed command of the 18th Kentucky. See Perrin, *History of Fayette County, Kentucky*, 659.

THURSDAY FEB 4TH [1864]

. . . Four or five guerrillas were brought in yesterday from Mt Sterling. They were sent in by Col John Brown of the 45th Mounted Infantry[1] stationed at Mt Sterling, and had been captured by some of the 45th while in the act of putting a rope round the neck of a Union man for the purpose of hanging him.

1. Colonel John Mason Brown commanded the 45th Kentucky Mounted Infantry. The 45th mustered in October 1863 and was assigned to repel raiders from Kentucky. See Speed, *The Union Regiments of Kentucky*, 624, 627.

SATURDAY FEB 6TH [1864]

. . . The Ky correspondent of the Cincinnati Gazette writing under the head of Kentucky Politics puts a question that all Union Kentuckians would like to have answered. Why is it, that Geo D. Prentice,[1] the old friend of Henry Clay, a Union man as most people think, and the Senior Editor of the Louisville Journal, allows that paper to publish pieces in favor of Vallandigham[2] and the conservatives, and articles against the Government? Why does he, if he is a Union man lend his name to a paper that publishes pieces in favor of traitors? I hope he will give an answer explaining his position. His name has a great deal of influence, and is doing harm while at the head of a rebel paper. . . .

1. An ex-Whig, George D. Prentice (1802–1873) professed to place preservation of the Union above all other interests. However, certain actions of Lincoln's government, including the Emancipation Proclamation and the recruitment of black soldiers, cooled the fiery editor to Lincoln's administration. See Coulter, *The Civil War and Readjustment in Kentucky*, 28, 41, 180–82, 202–3. For Prentice's pre-war career, see Betty C. Congleton, "George D. Prentice and His Editorial Policy in National Politics, 1830–1861" (Ph.D. diss., University of Kentucky, 1961).
2. Clement L. Vallandigham (1820–1871) was a controversial Democratic congressman from Ohio. He symbolized the "peace at any price" opposition to Lincoln that formed a menacing "fifth column." In 1863 Vallandigham denounced the government for needlessly refusing to end the war by mediation. The Ohioan was deported to the Confederacy but returned to the North to oppose Lincoln in the 1864 political campaign. See Frank L. Klement, *The Limits of Dissent: Clement L. Vallandigham and the Civil War* (Lexington: Univ. Press of Kentucky, 1970).

MONDAY FEB 8TH [1864]

. . . News from Southern papers goes to show that the value of negroes is greatly depreciated. The hire of a servant for one year, being nearly, or quite equal to his fee simple value. This is pretty much the case here. The negro is not a very marketable article at present. People do not care to risk buying a species of property which if it does not 'take wings and fly away,' like riches, at least of late years, often makes good use of its legs and runs off. And that is generally the last his master sees of him unless he should take it into his head to return of his own accord. So most persons prefer hiring to buying. Only yesterday a likely negro man was sold for $250. . . .

WEDNESDAY FEB 10TH [1864]

. . . The Unionists in the Ky Legislature yesterday defeated the two-faced resolutions on Federal relations to the sorrow of the Copperheads, and delight of all good & loyal Kentuckians.[1] The ladies are preparing to give a dinner to the returned veteran Ky regiments, at the Masonic Hall, on Friday next.

1. Defeated on February 19, 1863, the resolution stated that Kentucky did not need to reaffirm its loyalty to the Union, that Kentucky opposed the enlistment of blacks, that Kentucky opposed the Lincoln administration's contention that Confederate states should rewrite their constitutions before reentry to the Union, and that Confederate states had the right to resume their relationship with the Federal government based on pre-war conditions. See *Journal of the House of Representatives of the Commonwealth of Kentucky* (Frankfort: Commonwealth Office, 1863), 495–497.

THURSDAY FEB 11TH [1864]

The Frankfort Commonwealth has taken up the cudgels in defense of the Union, Mr Lincoln and Hon G. Clay Smith,[1] against the attacks of the Louisville Journal. I am glad to see that there is still one of our leading papers that has sense enough to stand up for the right, and I hope the Commonwealth will remain firm to its present position, and deserve & receive the support of all loyal men. . . .

. . . There is an order out, that henceforth hospitals will be in charge of commissioned officers. In consequence Pa has been relieved from charge of the hospital here. His successor Dr Micham of Ohio arrived today. Pa will still be retained as Assistant Surgeon. The country people are sending in any quantity of provisions ready cooked for the dinner tomorrow, and all the confectioners in town are at work preparing for the same.

1. A native of Richmond, Kentucky, Green Clay Smith (1826–1895) served in the Mexican War, graduated from Transylvania University, practiced law, and was elected to the Kentucky House of Representatives in 1861. As colonel of the 4th Kentucky Cavalry (U.S.), Smith helped rout Morgan at the May 5, 1862, battle of Lebanon, Tennessee. Appointed brigadier general in June 1862, Smith was assigned to the 2nd Division of the Army of Kentucky, Department of the Ohio. He was elected to the U.S. Congress in 1863 and served until 1866. See Kleber, ed., *The Kentucky Encyclopedia*, 829–30.

FRIDAY FEB 12TH [1864]

The day broke cloudy and misty with threats of rain, a wet day for the soldier's dinner. A slight rain fell and the sky remained cloudy, as if the "clerk of the weather" had not decided whether it should rain, or not. But before the dinner hour arrived, the clouds broke and the sun came out and the day became as pleasant as one could wish. There were not as many Ky soldiers present as had been expected, but still the dinner, large as it was, was disposed of.

A Home Guard company from Bath County came in; a wild looking, rough set of fellows. But of course they were ordered to fall into line, and came into the hall with the others. When they got to the table they literally got down on their knees, as if they expected to be occupied so long that standing would be too irksome. And though they did not gormandize, they made the provisions fly, and seemed to enjoy themselves highly.

There being not yet enough to dispose of the quantity of eatables on hand an invitation was sent out to the 11th Michigan Cavalry.[1] Their officer received it just as the regiment was going out to drill (they generally go out to some of the lots around town where there is room for their evolutions) and without saying a word to the men about it, he marched them on, as if nothing had happened until he reached the Masonic Hall. Then to the surprise of the men the order to halt was given and they were told what had occurred and told to fall into the line of invited guests. No doubt the "boys" enjoyed it all the more from the surprise. . . .

That secesh scamp John Dudley and his son Tom have come back. They got released from Camp Chase, Ohio, where they were confined, by taking the amnesty oath. I dont believe in a man like John Dudley being allowed to take an oath of any kind because I don't believe he would consider it at all binding on him. He would say he was in prison when he took it, and such oaths were not binding as they were made under compulsion or that he only did it to get out of prison, and never meant to keep it. I shall be surprised if he doesnt do all he can to help the rebels yet. There is no sense of honor in such men, and he would think it a clever trick, most likely, to cheat the Yankees, and do all he could to harm the Union, while he screened himself under the cloak of loyalty.

1. The 11th Michigan Cavalry mustered on December 10, 1863, and was in Lexington to prepare for assignment in the field. Colonel Simeon B. Brown commanded the regiment. See Robertson, *Michigan in the War*, 729–30.

MONDAY FEB 15TH [1864]

. . . I believe what an officer said to me once is true, that Gen Halleck did not like for any one but himself to get any glory, and was jealous of his inferior officers. I have never met an officer, or soldier yet who liked Gen Halleck. They all have some fault to find with him, and some have even gone so far as to say he is a Copperhead. All the soldiers I have heard express any opinion on the subject, despise or distrust him, especially those who have known him. If it was put to the vote among our armies whether Halleck should be Commander-in-Chief I dont think he would be their choice. . . .

THURSDAY FEB 25TH [1864]

. . . The 45th Ky Col Brown has been assigned to Owen County, Lebanon and Bardstown for the suppression of guerillas (Col Brown is in Lexington at present) Col Maxwell[1] has been ordered back to his old post at Bowling Green. Hobson again takes command of his old headquarters at Glasgow. The 2nd Heavy Artillery have been sent to Fry's old district headquarters at Camp Nelson. The 26th Ky have been mounted and by order of Gen Grant assigned to Russelville. These assignments and others in contemplation by Gen Burbridge,[2] commanding Department of Ky, it is expected will secure the people from guerillas.

Dr Micham [Meacham] has been to Louisville, and returned today bringing with him his family and a company of the Invalid Reserve Corp.[3] All the hospital officers, ward masters, cooks, etc. are to be sent to their regiments and their places supplied by this company of Invalids. The Ky University at Harrodsburg was burnt Thursday morning.[4]

1. Colonel Cicero Maxwell commanded the 26th Kentucky Infantry. See Speed, *The Union Regiments of Kentucky*, 540.
2. General Stephen Gano Burbridge of Scott County succeeded Boyle as commander of the District of Kentucky in February 1864. See Faust, ed., *Historical Times Illustrated Encyclopedia of the Civil War*, 95.
3. In April 1863 the War Department created the Invalid Reserve Corps, composed of soldiers disabled from wounds or disease. These troops performed guard duty and served in hospitals behind Union lines, freeing able-bodied men for service at the front. In March 1864 its name changed to the Veteran Reserve Corps. See Faust, ed., *Historical Times Illustrated Encyclopedia of the Civil War*, 383.
4. Established in September 1859 by John B. Bowman in Harrodsburg, the school burnt down on February 16, 1864. It merged with Transylvania University in 1865. See Kleber, ed., *The Kentucky Encyclopedia*, 515.

MONDAY FEB 29TH [1864]

. . . The Invalid Corp promise to be troublesome. This morning they rushed into the breakfast room at the hospital and eat up all the rations prepared for the old wardmasters, cooks, etc, who have not yet left and grumble about being put on guard, about various other things, and seem rather untractable. But perhaps they do so because they are unaccustomed to such things and will do better after a while. . . .

WEDNESDAY MARCH 9TH [1864]

. . . The Ky Contributor to the Gazette states that George D. Prentice has ceased to have any connection with the Louisville Journal except to let the real proprietors, Henderson & Osbourne,[1] have the use of his name.

Paul R. Shipman[2] is now the Senior editor. Prentice has nothing to do with it. It is a shame for him to lend his name to such a mean paper. His doing so may be called a deception for most persons did not know that his connection with the Journal had ceased and thought they were following the footsteps of Prentice when it was in fact only Paul R. Shipman that was leading into the marshes of Rebellion like a deceitful Jack o lantern.

The enrollment bill goes into force today and slaves are to be enrolled here and all over the country.[3] Col Frank Wolford's division is stationed in Ky. Wolford is to be presented with a sword here tomorrow at 11 AM at Odd Fellows Hall by the Citizens. We have heard from cousin James Coleman (Col in CSA). He wrote to his mother that he was in Richmond, Va. with Breckinridge (on whose staff he is). He did not tell anything about the state of affairs there as his letter came by flag of truce and had to be left unsealed for inspection.

The rebels are going to make a desperate effort to get into this State.

. . . It is generally suspected that a great many rebels have come into the state, who, pretending to be tired of the rebellion and anxious to take the amnesty oath do so just to aid the rebels and get a chance to recruit for the rebel army in a quiet way.

1. John D. Osborne and Isham Henderson published the *Louisville Journal* on the west side of 3rd Street between Jefferson and Green Streets. See Henry Tanner, comp., *The Louisville Directory and Business Advertiser for 1859–1860* (Louisville: Maxwell & Company, 1859), 109.
2. Paul K. Shipman served as assistant editor of the *Louisville Journal*. See Tanner, comp., *The Louisville Directory*, 211.
3. In December 1863 radicals in Congress amended the Conscription Act to ensure that all blacks, slave and free, regardless of location, would be enrolled and be eligible for the draft. Provost Marshal General James B. Fry ordered Kentucky's provost marshal to begin enrolling blacks on March 7, 1864. See Howard, *Black Liberation in Kentucky*, 56–57.

THURSDAY MARCH 10TH [1864]

. . . We had a fight in the streets here last night. The 6th Ky Cavalry (Col Watkins)[1] it seems had received permission to have the liberty of the town. This was contrary to Col King's orders, which do not allow soldiers to roam about the streets without passes, and so the guard refused to let them enter the town. The Kentucky soldiers persisted in their attempt to get by the guard, and Col King threatened if they did not obey orders and return to their camp, that he would have out the artillery and force them to obey. The Kentuckians would not yield, and a fight ensued between them and the guard. Several volleys were fired and the artillery brought out but it was not used. . . .

Col Wolford came up today, after making the people assembled at Odd Fellows Hall wait a long time, and made a long speech in reply to the sword presentation. His speech caused much surprise & indignation among the Union men. They had thought him an unconditional Union man and a true patriot, and behold he delivered such an address as none but the vilest Copperhead would make, abusing Mr Lincoln, telling Kentuckians that they ought to arm themselves to resist the enrolling of negroes and setting himself in opposition to the Government.

. . . The Union men were perfectly astounded [at Colonel Frank L. Wolford's[2] speech]. Was this the good Union man, and gallant soldier, whose services to the country they wished to acknowledge in public by a present? Was this the man to whom they would be proud to bestow a sword? Why had they not known this before? Why had they been deceived into giving to a traitor the sword intended for a gallant patriot whom Ky wished to honor? Why had they been put to the blush before all the world, and what possessed him that he dared to talk of treason, before Union men? Had he been bought over by the rebels; or had he caught the negrophobia and knew not what he did? One or maybe both, and whichever it is that has caused this mad behavior it is bad for him. Is it not strange that in these day[s] few Kentuckians can get high in public favor and authority and remain true to the Union? Are we to be always deceived, and must our public men always turn traitors when they feel themselves secure in a little brief authority? Much better would it be for us if they would be bold and avow themselves outspoken rebels; but to turn Copperhead, especially those who have commissions in the army, is not a sign of much spirit to say the least. But let not such men as Wolford think that they can persuade Kentucky to resist the Government on account of the negro. She will not follow any such lead, and the only thing they will do by preaching such a doctrine will be to destroy all hopes of getting compensation for the slaves that are taken by the Government.

1. Colonel Louis D. Watkins commanded the 6th Kentucky Cavalry (U.S.). See Speed, *The Union Cause in Kentucky*, 145.
2. Frank L. Wolford (1817–1895), a successful criminal lawyer before the war in Kentucky's Green River region, served as colonel of the 1st Kentucky Cavalry (U.S.) and distinguished himself at the battle of Mill Spring in early 1862. On March 10, 1864, Wolford was honored by the citizens of Lexington for his brave service. He

used the public assembly at Melodeon Hall as a forum from which to denounce the enlistment of black troops in Kentucky. Wolford openly criticized Lincoln's emancipation policy and urged residents of the commonwealth to resist recruiters who sought to enlist their slaves. Continuing his anti-administration speeches, Wolford soon after was placed under military arrest and, ultimately, was dishonorably discharged from the service. See Hambleton Tapp, "Incidents in the Life of Frank Wolford, Colonel of the First Kentucky Union Cavalry," *Filson Club History Quarterly* 10 (April 1936): 82–99.

SATURDAY MARCH 12TH [1864]

. . . Basil Duke it is said was feted by the Copperheads at the Continental Hotel, Philadelphia, when he and Major Johnson who was in charge of him stopped for the night on their way to Ft Monroe, or wherever it was Duke was to be taken for exchange.[1] A Kentuckian in Philadelphia to whom the proceedings at the Continental were known gives to the Press an account of Basil Dukes behavior in Ky. in the fall of 1862. How he shelled a town (Augusta Ky) without giving the least notice to the inhabitants of his intention, nor allowing any time for the removal of the women and children, and when the citizens resisted him, sheltering in the houses, he fired the houses, burning up the wounded in them, and shot down the men after they had surrendered and ordered every Union citizen in the place to be killed, which order would have been carried out but for the arrival of aid to the citizens. Then Duke took the Union officers whom he had made prisoners to Lexington and shut them up in the "negro pen" and would have shot them if Kirby Smith had not interfered. The citizens went to Duke and requested that the officers & their guard might come and stay at their houses, but he refused.

This reminds me of what I have heard of Duke's grandfather Col Beauford. It was said of him, that in the Revolutionary war, he for a bribe paid him by the British allowed his men to be cut to pieces, he running off and leaving them. Col Beauford had six children, three sensible and three idiot ones. And some people thought this was a judgement on him for betraying his countrymen. Truly the sins of the fathers are visited on the children into the third and fourth generation. Basil Duke is more like old Col Beauford than his own father, who I have always heard was a very clever, mild, old gentleman.

Col Wolford was arrested today by order of the Provost Marshall General. It is just what he deserved for if all we hear be true his speech here is not the worse he has done.

... Dr Barnes,[2] Senator from Bath Co[unty] Ky. told Pa not long after Kirby Smith was here that he was taken prisoner by the rebels and kept at one of their camps for some time, during which he had a good deal of conversation with a very intelligent rebel soldier. One day this man said to him 'Our General Morgan is carrying on a correspondence with your Col Wolford, and we expect to have him on our side before long.' The rebel's prediciton has come true. It is strongly suspected that Wolford was bribed by the rebels. The Observer & Reporter endorses Wolfords speech and thinks [it] is just the thing. If the Observer had been wise, he would have examined the signs of the times before he committed himself. If he upholds such doctrines as Wolford preaches, he should not be surprised if he should share the same fate.

1. While being transferred from Camp Chase, Ohio, to Fort Delaware, Colonel Basil Duke stayed in a hotel with his escort in Philadelphia. Major Johnson took Duke to visit friends in Philadelphia. See Basil W. Duke, *Reminiscences of General Basil W. Duke, C.S.A.* (1911; reprint, Freeport, N.Y.: Books for Libraries Press, 1969), 365–70.
2. Dr. Joshua Barnes represented Bath County in the state senate, 1862–1865. See Collins, *History of Kentucky*, 2:46.

MONDAY MARCH 14TH [1864]

Longstreet is reported preparing to come into Kentucky. The secesh are jubilant what with Wolfords speech and the promise of the rebel army invading the state. I suppose they think there will be a counter revolution here against the Government which will greatly aid the rebel army in taking the state out of the Union Times look stormy, but the old ship of state weathered the first storm in 1861 and I expect she will weather this one also. We dont know yet what side Gov Bramlette will take but if he is wise he will support the Government and not attempt to resist the enrolling of negroes. Mr Lincoln did not make that enrollment law. It was Congress and as Congress decided that all persons from 20 to 45 without regard to color should be enrolled we cannot resist the carrying that law into effect, without being as much in a state of rebellion as any of the Confederates, and having a Civil War in our midst.

Such a course would be fraught with evil to us in every way. We would have our slaves set free, as was the case with the Confederate States, and would have no hopes of compensation. Our Kentucky troops would be sent out of the State; the whole State overrun with armies and devastated by war. Do the Copperheads think that the Union men will bring about such a state of things just for the sake of the negro? Never. If Gov

Bramlette attempts to resist Congress he will find that the Union men have not forgotten how they put down Magoffin[1] in '61 and they will put him down in the same way.

Does Col Wolford think because the Union men have been proud of his bravery against the rebels, and have thought him a true friend to the country, that he can come here and advise the Governor before an assembly of the people, to call out the Ky troops, to resist Congress [?] [Can Wolford] call Mr Lincoln an usurper and traitor, and advise the people to put all the officers who attempt to enroll negroes in the penitentiary, and say that he does not intend to obey orders unless he thinks them right, and expect that the people will follow his lead and go over to the rebels because forsooth Col Wolford advises it? Is the man a fool? Who is Col Wolford I should like to know, that he should attempt to advise Kentuckians what they should do? If he had made this speech before instead of after, the sword was presented to him, he would not have received it.

And why did Governor Bramlette sit quietly by, on the same stage and allow himself to be advised to call out Kentucky troops against the Government, and hear Mr Lincoln abused and military authority defied, and say nothing, nor show the least signs of indignation? Is it because he endorses Col Wolfords sentiments? Some people think so, but I hope time will show that he has more sense, than to do so. The secesh will make one more attempt to get Ky It may be a bloody one, but come and cost what may[,] Ky stays in the Union, and will never side with those who resist the Government. These are [times] to try mens souls and sift the wheat from the chaff. . . .

Col Wolford was not formally arrested as reported the other day, but evidence is being collected against him previous to such a step.

A negro man and woman were sold at the Court house today for $300. Prices are very high in every thing else. Turkeys from $1.50 to $2.00 Fowls 40 cts apiece, butter 50 to 60 cts, bacon 15 cts per lb, Kid gloves $2.00[,] shoes from $1.25 to $3.00. [The] coarsest negro shoes not to be had for less than $1.25 and other things in proportion. . . .

1. A graduate of Centre College, Beriah Magoffin (1815–1885) practiced law before becoming governor of Kentucky in 1859. His attempts at compromise short of war (January-April 1861) and his declaration of Kentucky neutrality in May 1861 failed. Magoffin resigned in August 1862 after the legislature passed pro-Union acts over his vetoes. See Edward Conrad Smith, *The Borderland in the Civil War* (New York: Macmillan Company, 1927), 302–3.

Friday [Tuesday] March 15th [1864]

... The order that arrived the other day for the 11th Michigan Cavalry to be ready to start at three oclock turned out to be a trick. The officers sent to headquarters to know if such an order had been issued and found that nothing had been heard of it there, and it was ascertained that some of the 6th Ky Cavalry sent the order by telegraph just to plague the Michigan men whom they heartily despise.

Not very long ago a body of men went to the house of Mr Uriah Offort in Scott Co., and telling him they were Union soldiers, who wanted a nights lodging, were admitted. No sooner had they gained admittance than they seized Mr Offorts son, took him into the yard, and binding him fast to a tree, they robbed the house of the silver & other valuables. Before leaving they told Mr. Offort what no doubt he had discovered by this time, that they were not Union soldiers. Mr Offort is a Union man. ...

Thursday March 17th [1864]

... Dr [Robert] Breckinridge has a letter to Col Hodges, editor of the Frankfort Commonwealth, which appears in that paper, in which he thanks God that there is one good, true, loyal paper in Ky. (meaning the Commonwealth) It has indeed spoken out strongly for the Union cause and deserves the encouragement of all good Union men. Gov Bramlettes proclamation appears also. It advises the people to support the laws of Congress and if redress is needed, to resort to the authorities etc. Altogether it is as mild as milk & water and sounds like the production of a timid schoolboy who has seen his play fellow whipped for disorderly conduct and is much afraid his own turn may come next, and is looking innocent & trying to be Uncle Sam's good boy now. It was much feared at first that he would take sides with the Copperheads for he was not heard to express any indignation or disapproval of Wolfords speech and was present at the entertainment which the Copperheads gave Wolford. It was said that he had an address ready in type advising the people to resist the drafting of negroes, but after he had talked with Gen Burbridge and Dr Breckinridge he changed his mind. Col Wolford has been ordered to report to Gen Grant. He was arrested by request of the citizens, who collected testimony against him and even waited until he had made a Copperhead speech at Mt Sterling. ...

FRIDAY MARCH 18TH [1864]

... [The] second meeting of the Sociable Club (a club formed for the purpose of dancing & amusement by several of the young ladies of Lexington) [was held]. None but ladies can be members but each member has the privilege of inviting & bringing with her any gentlemen whom she may chose, always providing that it is not one whose society is disagreeable to any of the other members. The refreshments are limited to three kinds to be left to the choice of the member at whos[e] house the club happens to meet. Ladies are not allowed to come in evening or party dresses, but must wear promenade or 'at home' villetes. No music to be engaged, but dancing is allowed if there is a piano. The Club met at our house tonight. (It meets once a week at the house of each member in turn.) ...

SATURDAY MARCH 19TH [1864]

... A Washington dispatch of the 17th says "There is a rumor of a conspiracy embracing several counties and cities of Ky having for its object the annexation of Ky to the Southern Confederacy. That its leaders had headquarters in Monticello, and were corresponding with Longstreet in Tennessee, and that Ky members of Congress in Richmond had social correspondence with parties in London, Monticello, Mt Vernon, Danville etc (Ky) and it is feared that a central Committee has been established in every county, that will attempt to compell the inhabitants to join the rebel Confederacy as soon as Longstreet or Breckinridge enter the State. This infamous conspiracy was discovered by the seizure at the Post Office of letters addressed by Ky members of the rebel Congress to some leaders of the plot". . . .

SUNDAY MARCH 20TH [1864]

Co B of the 40th Ky Cavalry encamped today in the College lot opposite us.[1] This is all of that regiment here at present. They were sent up to the lot by Col More at the Provost office. They might just as well have been sent to some of the [other] lots around town, but we had no fault to find with the men as they were very quiet and well behaved.

1. Miss Peter probably means the 40th Kentucky Mounted Infantry (U.S.), engaged in scouting in eastern Kentucky. Captain Simon Rice commanded Company B. See Speed, *The Union Regiments of Kentucky*, 617–19.

FRIDAY MARCH 25TH [1864]

... Capt Postlethwaite has issued an order for all slaveholders to report the number of their slaves on pain of fine not less than $100. Enrolling commenced.

SATURDAY MARCH 26TH [1864]

Col Frank Wolford has been dismissed from the service by the President for violation of the 5th Article of War, by his treasonable speech in this city. . . .

MONDAY MARCH 28TH [1864]

. . . The sentence of the President expelling Wolford from the Army is said to have been revoked at the request of Gen Grant. . . . Gen Green Clay Smith spoke at the Court house tonight. He made quite a refreshing Union speech and used up the Copperheads badly.

WEDNESDAY MARCH 30TH [1864]

. . . It is said a loyal paper is to be edited here soon[1] It will be a good thing The Union men need a paper in which they can express their sentiments without having to send all the way to Cincinnati to do so. The [Lexington] Observer will go down rapidly after that paper begins, and if it is well conducted it will not want subscribers. . . .

1. In April 1864 the *Lexington National Unionist* began publication. Established to marshal support for Lincoln in the November election, the paper criticized Frank Wolford and Governor Bramlette for their opposition to the wholesale recruitment of black troops and other policies of the Lincoln administration. See John David Smith, "The Recruitment of Negro Soldiers in Kentucky, 1863–1865," *Register of the Kentucky Historical Society* 72 (October 1974): 381 n.

THURSDAY MARCH 31ST [1864]

. . . It is reported here that Camp Nelson was evacuated owing to a change of military base and the military stores taken to Nashville. This is another proof of the need we have of a loyal local paper. We citizens don't know the local news generally until we see the Cincinnati papers. We Union citizens, that is, for we dont like the 'Observer and Reporter.' Col. King is gone Most of the troops are gone & the city at present under command of a Lieut. Well, I suppose the rebels will try to come here. The secesh seem to expect them.

The rebel farmers are saving up all the provisions they can. The[y] wont bring any butter or fowls to market if they can help it & refuse to sell their grain unless they get three prices for it and often not then. Our mill being in a secesh neighborhood is rather bare of grain just now. Well, so much the better if the rebels come—they won't find as much to steal from Pa as last time. . . . My hopeful secesh uncle-in-law Mr. Robb[1] who lives near Georgetown on the Cincinnati road is also gone to the Southern part of the state ostensibly to buy cattle but I would not be surprised if it was to help the rebels.

1. William N. Robb was the husband of Letitia Preston Dallam, younger sister of the diarist's mother. They lived at "Winton," the country estate of Letitia's mother. Robb assisted General William Preston, determined to make his way from Lexington to join the Confederate army, in avoiding capture by Federal soldiers. See Evans Papers.

Saturday April 2 [1864]

The Gazette is down on the Cin. Commercial, Louisville Journal, & Frankfort Commonwealth for denying that Gov. Bramlette had a proclamation in type against negro enrollments & asks if they will attempt to impeach Dr R.J. Breckenridge at the meeting in Boyle County (where he gave the people to understand that the Governor had two proclamations prepared, one of which he had in second thought concluded not to issue) & gives the following copy of the Gov's dispatch to the Provost Marshal of Boyle Co. "If the President does not upon my demand, stop the Negro enrollment, I will. I am waiting his answer". . . .

Lieut Gov Jacobs[1] & Wolford said to be here today attended by a rabble rout of secesh to whom they made Copperhead speeches, the subjects of which were mostly abuse of the Govt. & Mr Lincoln & praise of McClellan.

1. Richard Taylor Jacob (1825–1903), an Oldham County politician, worked for neutrality early in the war, but eventually raised troops and fought for the Union. Elected lieutenant governor as a Union Democrat in November 1863, he unexpectedly supported Democratic candidate George B. McClellan against Lincoln in the 1864 presidential election. Like Frank Wolford, Jacob loudly opposed Lincoln's emancipation policy and the recruitment of black soldiers. As a result, General Burbridge banished Jacob to the Confederacy in November 1864. Lincoln allowed him to return to Kentucky in January 1865, hopeful "that there is less . . . misunderstanding among Union men now than there was at the time of the arrest." See Kleber, ed., *The Kentucky Encyclopedia*, 462, and Basler, ed., *The Collected Works of Abraham Lincoln*, 8:222.

Monday Apr 4th [1864]

Mrs. Duncan's house was discovered to be on fire this A.M. between 9 & 10. Pa and Mr. Gratz ran up at the first alarm & a crowd soon collected. The fire engine soon arrived and filled at the cistern by Mrs

Morgans but the hose was too short & by the time the other hose arrived the roof was burned off. The fire was soon put out when the engine began. The furniture was all saved. Mrs D. thought the roof caught from the chimney but the general opinion among the neighbors is that it was set fire to. There have been several fires lately. . . .

Index

Note: Italicized page numbers indicate illustrations.

Index

35th Massachusetts, 166, 176n. 1
36th Massachusetts, 1st Division, 9th
  Corps, 121n. 1, 121
40th Kentucky (U.S.), 166, 166n. 2
40th Kentucky Mounted Infantry
  (U.S.), 200, 200n. 1
42nd Ohio, 15, 15n. 1
43rd Alabama Regiment, 39n. 17
44th Ohio, 99
45th Kentucky Mounted Infantry, 189,
  189n. 1, 193
45th Ohio Volunteers, 106n. 1
48th Kentucky. *See* 52nd Kentucky
  Mounted Infantry (U.S.)
48th Pennsylvania Volunteers, 122–23,
  122–23n. 1, 124, 124n. 1, 125–26,
  138, 141n. 1, 171–72n. 2, 183; band,
  133, 151; camped in Little College
  Lot, 152, 153n. 1; death of Gen.
  Nelson, 155; drunk and fighting,
  137; Medical Hall fire, 129
52nd Kentucky Mounted Infantry
  (U.S.), 188, 189n. 1
52nd Ohio, 28, 28n. 2
54th Indiana, 23, 25, 25n. 2
79th New York, 157, 161–62, 162n. 1
83rd Indiana, 112n. 1
93rd Ohio Infantry, 28, 28n. 1
117th Illinois, 104, 104n. 1
129th Illinois, 113

abolition, 98, 108; Abolition stand, 175
abolitionists, xviii, xx, 82, 85, 102, 182;
  Beecher, Henry Ward, 169–70;
  Cravens, James H., 112n. 1;
  Radicals, 187
Adams, Charles Francis, 162n. 1
Adams, T.B., 111, 124
Adams Express cars, 113, 137
Agricultural and Mechanical Associa-
  tion, 36n. 1
Agricultural and Mechanical College,
  71n. 1
Aid Society, xxiii, 5, 7, 7n. 1, 32, 93;
  concerts, 16–17, 74, 81; loses
  supplies to rebels, 29–30, 70; makes
  bandages, 29; supper for sick and
  wounded, 35; tableaux, xvii, xxxn. 7,
  16, 81, 106
Alexander, Edward Porter, 84, 84n. 2

Alexander (rebel officer), 114
Alexandra (ship), 144, 162n. 1
Allen, B.E. "Buck," 47, 48n. 1
Allen and Boyd, 44, 46, 47n. 3
Alston, R.A., 139, 139n. 1, 140
Alton, Ill., 148
amateur concerts. *See* concerts, amateur
Amateur Musical Association, xvii, 14,
  16–17
ambulances, 45, 47, 49, 74, 88; detained
  by rebels, 47; fired upon, 25; under
  flag of truce, 34; Morgan riding in
  rebel ambulance, 64; stage coaches
  as, 53
ammunition, 40, 40n. 1, 44
Amnesty and Reconstruction, Procla-
  mation of, 176–77n. 1
amnesty oath, 192, 194
Antietam, Md., battle of, 39n. 23,
  131n. 1
Ariol, Ky., 177n. 2
Army of Kentucky, 75n. 1
Army of Northern Virginia, 39n. 23
Army of the Cumberland, 111n. 2
Army of the Ohio, 10n. 3, 65n. 1
Army of the Potomac, 39n. 23, 117–
  18n. 1, 161
Army of the Tennessee, 119n. 2
Ashbury, Capt., 99, 101, 103, 127, 133
Ashland, 66, 67n. 1, 138, 160, 161n. 1
Athens, Ky., 100
Atkinson, William P., 141n. 1
Augusta, Ky., 35, 39n. 24, 196

Bain, Nannie, 40–41, 41n. 3
Bain family, 160n. 2
band, military, 74, 122; 48th Pennsylva-
  nia Volunteers, 133, 150, 151; 7th
  Rhode Island, 171, 172–73
bandages, making of, 29
Baptist Church, 88, 95, 177n. 1
Baptist Female Seminary, 7n. 2
Bardstown, Ky., 74, 75n. 2, 168–69, 193
Barkley, "Beau," 62
Barnes, B.F., 144
Barnes, Joshua, 197, 197n. 2
Bath County, 191–92
Beard's stable, 62
Beauford, Col., 196
Beauregard, P.G.T., 108n. 1

Index

Peter, Frances Dallam: burial lot and bill for

Burkham, J.H., 141, 142n. 2

Burnett, Henry C., 110n. 5

Burnside, Ambrose Everett, 117, 117–18n. 1, 126; attacking Morgan, 140; censorship, 122n. 1, 124, 131, 132; Cumberland Gap, 162, 163n. 1; Fort Saunders, Knoxville, Tenn., battle of, 171n. 1, 175n. 1; at Kingston, Tenn., 159–60, 160n. 1; martial law, 147, 149, 152; parties, 120, 178; and southern sympathizers, women, 121–22; in Lexington, 133, 150–51

Bush, Dudley, 14

Bush, James H.G., 103

Bush, James M., 14, 15, 15n. 1, 79, 117, 177; Louisville Medical College, 163; trip to Europe, 178n. 3

Bush, Thomas J., 15, 15n. 5

butternuts. *See* rebel soldiers; southern sympathizers

Butters (guerrilla), 113

Byrd, Mrs. Col., 171

Cahill, Edward, 184, 185n. 1

Cairo, Ill., 118

Camelite Church, 88

Campbell and Cochran carpet store, 44, 44n. 3

Camp Burnside, 131n. 2

Camp Chase, Ohio, 21, 94, 119, 121, 192, 197n. 1

Camp Dick Robinson, 62, 63n. 5, 121n. 1, 126n. 2, 154–55

Camp Nelson, 6n. 1, 149, 177, 177n. 2, 181, 183, 193, 201

camps, 95, 123, 132; convalescent, 124; medical care in, 82, 85–86; organization and instruction of troops, 63n. 5, 133. *See also under specific camps*

Camp Wild Cat, 14n. 1

Canada, 86, 86n. 1, 94, 161n. 1

Carr, Judge, 100

Carter, Samuel P., 111, 111n. 1, 132

Casey, Samuel Lewis, 109, 110n. 5

Cashin, Joan E., xxvi

Cassell, John L., 45n. 1

Castleman, John B., 72, 72n. 3

Castleman, Mrs., 48, 72

Catholics, 74, 75n. 2, 84–85, 135, 138

cemeteries, 136

cemetery plot, Frances Peter. *See* Peter, Frances Dallam: burial lot and bill for

censorship: books, 131; mail, southern, 122n. 1; newspapers, 56, 124, 131, 132; Union mail, 35

Central Christian Church, 20

Chattanooga, Tenn., battle of, 164n. 2, 171n. 1, 172, 173n. 1, 175n. 1

Cheapside, 120, 138, 175

Cheatham, Mary Ready, 148, 148n. 2

Cheatham, William A., 148n. 2

cheer ("hurra"), 188; for Jeff Davis, 11; for Lincoln, 31

Chenault, D.W., 140, 141n. 2

Chicago Times, 131, 131n. 1, 132

Chickamauga, battle of, 97n. 1, 111n. 2, 164, 164nn. 1, 2, 175n. 1, 189

Christ Church, 36, 39n. 27, 62, 63n. 4, 117, 150

Christiansburg, Ky., 137

Church, Dr., 154

churches, 36, 39n. 27; African American, 177, 177n. 1; observance of fast days, 117, 125; Thanksgiving, 150. *See also under specific churches*

Churchill, Thomas James, 42, 42n. 2

Cincinnati Commercial, 109, 110n. 4, 173, 181, 202

Cincinnati Enquirer, xxvi, 124

Cincinnati Gazette, 35, 120, 158, 175, 184–85, 202; and Beecher, Henry Ward, 169; Frances Peter as reader of, 107n. 3; on Morgan, John Hunt, 97, 142, 148, 174; on Prentice, George D., 189–90, 193

Cincinnati police force, 20–21, 21n. 4, 23n. 1

Cincinnati Times, xxv, 158

Clarke (southern emissary), 16

Clay, Brutus J., 96n. 1, 146, 149

Clay, Cassius Marcellus, 28, 28n. 2

Clay, Henry, 12, 86n. 1, 161n. 1, 190

Clay, James B., 66, 86, 86n. 1, 104, 161n. 1

Clay, Mrs. James B., 21n. 2

Clay, Thomas, 56, 58n. 1

Index

Index

Davidson, James T., 134, 134n. 2
Davis, Garrett, xviii, xxxn. 3, 182–83, 183nn. 1, 2
Davis, Jefferson, 11, 38n. 3, 48n. 1, 101, 164n. 2; declares fast day, 117; letter to France, 120
Davis, Jefferson C., 68–69, 70n. 1
Davis, Lieut., 74
Davis, William C., ix–x
Dayton Journal, 148
Dead Rabbits. *See* Irish-Americans (New York)
DeCourcy, Col., 7, 15, 22, 136, 136n. 2
Democratic Peace meeting, 98
Department of Southwestern Virginia, 12n. 1
Department of the Ohio, 5n. 4, 117–18n. 1, 131n. 1, 190n. 1
desertions, Confederate, 50, 71–72, 72n. 1
Desha, Mrs., 4
diaries, American women, xvii, xxx–xxxin. 8
Didlake, George, 17, 17n. 1
dinners. *See* entertainments
diptheria, 91, 94–95, 101n. 3
District of Indiana, 145n. 1
District of Kentucky, 193, 193n. 2
"Dixie" (song), 17, 122
dogs, 144
Dolan, Tom, 147
Doolittle, Mrs. Charles C., 81, 81n. 1
dormitory, Transylvania College, 33
Doroughty, William, 139
draft: escaping from, 143; exemptions, 178, 178n. 1; Kentucky, 133n. 3, 182; New York riots, 151, 152n. 1, 156, 162. *See also* enrollment, military, of blacks; recruitment, blacks
Driggs, S., 115, 115n. 3
Dudley, Benjamin, xiii
Dudley, Ethelbert L., 9n. 1, 9–10
Dudley, James, 93
Dudley, John, 14, 15, 61, 69, 192
Dudley, Mrs. John, 8, 9n. 3, 70
Dudley, Tom, 192
Dudley, W.A., 119
Dudley, Will, Jr., 4
Duke, Basil Wilson, 4n. 2, 30, 38n. 3, 39n. 24, 64n. 2, 67n. 1; prisoner,

196, 197n. 1; reported death of, 89, 89n. 1, 95
Duke, Mrs. Basil (Henrietta), xix, 11, 12n. 2, 40; leaves Lexington, 63, 64; visits penitentiary, 160
Dumont, Ebenezer, 65, 65n. 1
Duncan, Eliza, 80n. 1
Duncan, Ella, xxiii, 121–22
Duncan, F.S., 79, 80n. 1
Duncan, Henry, 65, 66, 66n. 1, 121, 144
Duncan, Henry, Jr., 66n. 1, 132
Duncan, Mrs., 202
Dyas, Robert J., 166, 166n. 2

Eastern Lunatic Asylum, 101n. 2
Edwards, Don, xxxn. 3
election of 1863, 146–48, 151–52; Federal military interference, 146, 146n. 2, 148n. 1, 148–49, 150n. 1
Elliot, J.M., 11, 12n. 3, 58, 188–89
Elrod, E.W., 35, 39n. 20
Elrod, T.B.E., 35, 39n. 20
Emancipation Proclamation, xviii, 93, 93n. 2, 98n. 1, 118, 143, 190n. 1
England, 144, 157, 162, 162n. 1
enlistment: escape from, 26; reenlistment, 183, 186, 188
Ennis, John, 38n. 5
Enrollment Act, 152n. 1
enrollment, military, of blacks, 194, 194n. 3, 197, 200–201
entertainments: ball at Frankfort, Ky., 100; bonfire, 147; Burnside reception, 120, 121–22; dances, 128–29, 130, 178; dinner, Thanksgiving, 150, 172–73, 175–76; dinner at Short Street hospital, 16; dinner for Kentucky veterans, 190, 191; opera, 91; strawberry party, 18; tableaux, 16. *See also* concerts, amateur
epilepsy, xxxn. 6; treatment, xiii
Episcopal church. *See* Christ Church
Estil County, 117
Estil steam furnace, 32, 38n. 10, 40
Evans, Catherine Peter, xxxn. 5
Everett, Peter, 134, 134n. 1, 136, 136n. 2
Eversman, D.H., 43, 127, 132, 138, 139, 153, 169; Hospital No. 2, 29, 33, 39n. 15, 74, 79, 134

Index

exemptions from military service, 178, 178n. 1

Falmouth, Ky., 166
fast days: Confederate, 117; Union, 125, 126n. 1
Faust, Drew Gilpin, xxi, xxii, xxvi–xxvii, xxxin. 12
feminist theorists, xxi
Ferrie, Capt., 67–68
fires, 87–88, 126–27, 129, 135, 150, 154, 169, 171, 203; Harrodsburg, Ky., 193; Lebanon, Ky., 143n. 1; Mount Sterling, Ky., 113–15, 115n. 1, 117; during rebel occupation, 32, 42, 45, 46, 48, 52, 55
Fisher's Dye shop. *See* J. Fisher Dyeing and Tailoring Establishment
Fisk, John F., 26n. 1
Fitch, Frank, 63, 63n. 6, 66
Fitch, Fred, 63, 63n. 6
flag, "Wild Cat," 14
flag of truce, 34, 42, 194
flags, Confederate, 8–9, 30, 52, 62, 65, 67, 78, 116
flags, Union, 49, 73–74, 81, 91, 143; dragged behind horses, 33, 62; regimental flags, 126, 135; taken down, 60–61, 62, 66
Flanagan, Teddy, 117
Fleming, Dr., 114
Fleming, William R., 87, 87n. 1
Flemingsburg, Ky., 160
Fletcher, Samuel M., 94, 95n. 1
Florida, soldiers from, 33, 35–36, 39n. 26
Flournoy, Victor M., 179, 179n. 1
Floyd, John B., 158, 158n. 1
Foley (southern mail carrier), 22
Foley, Maj., 136
Fort Clay, 138
Fort Delaware, 5n. 3, 196n. 1
Fort Donelson, 8n. 1, 12n. 1, 135, 158n. 1
fortifications, 114, 119, 120, 127
Fort Pickens, 41
Fortress Monroe, 124, 124n. 1
Fort Saunders, Knoxville, Tenn., battle of, 160n. 1, 174, 175n. 1
Fort Scott, Ks., 97n. 2
Fort Sumter, 41

Fox, Dr., 47, 74, 80–81
France, 120–21
Frankfort, Ky., 21, 22, 49, 52, 62, 95, 100, 125; inauguration of governor, 159; inauguration of governor, provisional, 50, 51, 56, 58n. 2; Kentucky States Rights Party convention, 98, 98n. 1, 99, 108, 110n. 2
Frankfort Commonwealth, 103, 104n. 1, 191, 199, 202
Frazer, John W., 162, 163, 163n. 1
Fredericksburg, Va., battle of, 117–18n. 1
Freedmen's Bureau, 97n. 3
Fremantle, Arthur, xx, xxxin. 10
Frenchman (Union soldier), 74, 75
Friedman, Jean E., xxxin. 11
Fry, James B., 194n. 3
Fry, Speed Smith, 5n. 5, 6, 6n. 1, 10, 135; and impressed slave labor, 149, 151, 162; Union Democrat speech, 107, 109
Fry, Tom, 135
fugitive slaves. *See* slaves, fugitive
Fullerton, J., 87
funerals: rebel, 11–12, 78; Union, 9n. 1, 9–10, 91, 102
furloughs, 183, 186, 188

Galt House, 163, 164n. 1
Gano's Regiment, 4n. 1
Garibaldi, 101n. 2
Garrard, Col., 114
gender identity, xxi–xii, xxvi–xxvii, xxxn. 2
General Order No. 38, 122n. 1, 124, 131, 132
General Order No. 87, 131
General Order No. 100, 147–48, 148n. 2
Georgetown, Ky., 22, 23, 39–40, 42–43, 50
German-Americans (Missouri), 166, 166n. 3
Gettysburg, battle of, 130, 136, 136n. 1
Gibbons, Mrs., 94
Gibson, Mrs. M.D. "Hart," xxiii, 79, 80n. 1, 121–22
Gibson, Randal, 111n. 1
Gilbert, Abijah, 123, 123n. 1
Gilbert, E.A., 99, 108, 110n. 2
Gilbert, John, 12, 123

Index

Home Guards, 18, 20, 21n. 4, 39n. 18, 48; Bath County, 191–92; Mount Sterling, Ky., 25; Richmond, Ky., 27

hoops, 76

Hoover, Mr., 60

Hopkins, Lieut., 84

horse stealing, 61, 62, 72, 102, 103, 106, 124

Hospital No. 1, 20, 20n. 2, 26, 29, 79, 85, 88, 115; during Confederate occupation of Lexington, 30, 32, 33, 64; and deaths of patients, 74, 81; diptheria, 94–95

Hospital No. 2, 18, 26, 29, 74–75, 88, 115, 125, 127, 129; during Confederate occupation of Lexington, 33, 39n. 15, 50, 51, 52, 57, 60; and deaths of patients, 45, 70, 74, 79, 83; garden, 134; and Union reoccupation of Lexington, 71, 74

Hospital No. 3, 163

hospitals, 14, 16, 18, 20, 26, 29, 118, 122, 177, 191; buildings taken over to serve as, 17–18, 82, 87, 88, 90, 95; cleaning of, 62, 70, 71, 173; during Confederate occupation of Lexington, 41, 59, 63; convalescents used to guard, 103; Dr. Watson as medical director of, 153–54; inspection of, 178; Invalid Reserve Corps' service in, 193, 193n. 3; Thanksgiving dinner held at, 172–73. See also under specific hospitals

Hulett, Mr., 43

Hunt, Drummond, 169

Hunt, F.W. "Frank," 99, 101n. 1, 119

Hunt, John Wesley, 4n. 2, 12n. 1

Hunter, David, 96n. 1

Hunter, Gen., 46

Hurlbard, Capt., 89

Hurlbut, Stephen Augustus, 118, 119n. 2

Hutchcraft, Capt., 141

inauguration: of governor, 159; of provisional governor, 50, 51, 52, 56, 58n. 2

Independent African Church, 177n. 1

Indianapolis Journal, 175

Indian mound, 120, 120n. 1

Indians, 32–33, 39n. 20, 75

Invalid Reserve Corps, 193, 193n. 3

Irish-Americans (New York), 108, 151, 152n. 1, 157n. 2, 162, 167

ironclads, 144, 162, 162n. 1

iron industry, 38n. 10

Island No. 10, 118, 119nn. 2, 3

J. Fisher Dyeing and Tailoring Establishment, 46, 47n. 1

Jackson, Dr., 138

Jackson, James S., 28, 28n. 2, 29

Jackson, Misses, 46

Jackson, Thomas J. "Stonewall," 35, 39n. 23

Jackson (wagon master), 47

Jacob, Richard Taylor, 107n. 2, 142, 143n. 2, 202, 202n. 1

Jamison, Mr., 47, 56, 62, 132, 173; and Dr. Watson, 153–54; on meeting Abraham Lincoln, 159

Jeffrey, Rosa Vertner, 181, 181n. 1

Johnson, Madison C., 70, 71n. 1

Johnson, Maj., 196

Johnson, Robert F., 79, 79n. 1

Johnston, Albert Sidney, 8n. 1, 14

Johnston, George W., 49n. 2

Journal (Providence, R.I.), 176

July Fourth celebrations, 138

Kansas elections, 149, 150n. 2

Kansas-Nebraska Act, 150n. 2

Keen, Edward, 11–12, 12n. 1

Keesler, Jacob, 7, 7n. 3

Keiser, Jack, xix, 65, 67, 69

Keiser, Jim, 33, 69, 79, 82

Keiser Coach Makers, 87

Keiser's Boarding House, 82

Kennedy, Matthew, 23

Kenton bar, 95

Kentucky: Confederate invasion of, 25n. 2, 26n. 1, 28n. 1, 49n. 3, 115; neutrality of, 47n. 2, 63n. 5, 197n. 1, 202n. 1; recruitment in, 133n. 3; and secession, question of, 49, 49n. 2, 95, 97, 97n. 1, 99–100

Kentucky Agricultural and Mechanical College, 7n. 2, 9n. 2

Kentucky legislature, 95, 98, 98n. 1, 99: Conscription Act of, 104; and neutrality crisis, 26n. 1; and

Index

recruitment, 186, 188n. 1; resolution on Mississippi convention, 107, 107n. 3; resolutions on Federal relations, 190, 191n. 1
Kentucky Loyalist, 140, 141n. 1
Kentucky States Rights Party, 98, 99, 110n. 2
Kentucky Statesman, 15, 15nn. 3, 4, 34, 35, 40, 48, 141n. 1
Kentucky University, 193, 193n. 4
Kessler, Jacob. *See* Keesler, Jacob
Key, Frank, 4n. 2
King, Capt., 84
King, William S., 166–67, 176, 176n. 1, 194, 201
Kingston, Tenn., 159–60
Kirby Smith, Edmund. *See* Smith, Edmund Kirby
Know-Nothing Party, 125n. 1
Knoxville, Tenn., 60, 61, 160n. 1, 174, 175n. 1

Lady, Claudia Lynn, xxxn. 3
Lancaster, George, 31–32, 38n. 5, 44, 160
Lancaster, M.P., 160, 160n. 1
Lancaster, Mrs. M.P., 160
Lancaster, Maggie, 106, 160
Lanckhart and Mentelle Iron Foundry, 38n. 9. *See also* Montell, Mr.
Lanphere, Charles H., 16, 16n. 1
Lanphiger, Capt. *See* Lanphere, Charles H.
Laschelles, Mr., 178
Laurenceberg, Ky. *See* Lawrenceburg, Ky.
Lawless, R.C., 32, 38n. 12
Lawrenceburg, Ky., 52, 138
Lebanon, Ky., 8, 108, 193; capture of R.A. Alston in, 139; death of Thomas H. Morgan in, 139, 139n. 2; Morgan's raids on, 20, 141n. 3, 142, 143, 143n. 1; rebels in, 140–41
Lee, John W., 116, 116n. 3
Lee, Robert E., 39n. 23, 136n. 1
Leonard, Elizabeth D., xxi, xxii
Lexington, Ky., ix, x, 56n. 1, 100; Confederate occupation of, 15n. 4, 29–61, 78–79; defense of, 23n. 1; fortification of, 114, 127; housing, lack of, 171–72; Union evacuation from, 29, 34, 39n. 18, 106n. 3;

Union reoccupation of, 63n. 1, 65, 71
Lexington Blues, 10, 10n. 4
Lexington Brewery, 38n. 12
Lexington Chasseurs, 10n. 5, 12n. 1, 15n. 5, 27n. 1, 35, 38n. 5, 72n. 3
Lexington Fairground, 15, 15n. 2, 29, 36n. 1
Lexington National Unionist, 201, 201n. 1
Lexington Observer and Reporter, 15, 16nn. 6, 7, 71, 71n. 2, 85, 104, 123, 185; Copperhead endorsements by, xxv, 137; on election of 1863, 148–49; on Frank Wolford, 197; letters to, 86, 157, 173, 174; Wickliffe, Daniel Carmichael (owner/editor), 110n. 6
Lexington Rifles, 12n. 1, 25n. 1, 38n. 3, 38n. 5
Libby Prison, 175, 175n. 1, 188n. 2, 189
Lincoln, Abraham, xviii, xix, 6n. 2, 21n. 4, 109–10, 116; blacks, military enrollment of, 185n. 1, 191, 197, 201; censorship of newspapers, 132; and Copperheads, 107n. 1, 157nn. 1, 2, 183n. 1; declares fast day,125, 126n. 1; described by Mr. Jamison, 159; Emancipation Proclamation, 93, 93n. 2, 98n. 1, 118, 143, 190nn. 1, 2; and Frank Wolford, 151, 195, 195–96n. 2, 198, 201; General Order No. 100 protecting black soldiers, 147–48; Proclamation of Amnesty and Reconstruction, 176, 176–77n. 1
Lindsay, Daniel W., 15, 15n. 3
liquor, destroyed by Union soldiers, 125
Litchfield, Ky., 142
Little College Lot, ix, xiii, xvii, xxiv, xxv, 80n. 2; 1st Missouri Cavalry encampment, 73, 92, 93; 48th Pennsylvania Volunteers encampment, 123, 133, 152; 79th New York encampment, 157, 161; citizen guard encampment, 23; as Lexington Rifles' drilling grounds, 25n. 1; maps of, xxxn. 1, 23, 24, 151n. 1; Morgan's encampment, 51; and rebel troops, xx, 31, 32, 43; as Union convalescents' drilling

Index

grounds, 103; and Union troops, 29, 127, 188, 200
Logwood, Thomas S., 141, 142n. 3
London, Ky., 5, 5n. 1, 71n. 2
Longstreet, James, 197, 200; Fort Saunders, Knoxville, Tenn., battle of, 171n. 1, 174, 175, 175n. 1; and prisoners, 183–84; pursuit of Grant, 179, 182
Louisville, Ky.: theater, 129, 131; Union State Convention, 111–12
Louisville Democrat, 45
Louisville Journal, 10, 35, 168, 188, 191, 202; editors, 194nn. 1, 2; ownership, 190, 193–94
Louisville Medical College, 163, 164n. 2
Love, John, 141, 142n. 2
Lunatic Asylum, Washington, D.C., 159
Lusby's Mill, 18
Lusby, William H., 144
Lyon, Capt., 138

Magoffin, Beriah, 15n. 3, 26n. 1, 197, 197n. 1
mail, southern. *See* southern mail
Mailbag, 186
Major, Dr., 42, 73, 114
Major, Tom, 67
Maloy, James, 144
Manson, Mahlon, 28n. 2
market, 33; difficulty in reaching, 75; high prices of, 198; withholding of goods from, 201
Marshall (guerrilla), 123
Marshall, Humphrey, 43, 44, 44n. 1, 45, 50, 52, 53
Marshall, Martin P., 93, 93n. 1
Marshall, Thornton F., 93, 93n. 1
martial law, 21–22, 26, 115–16, 141, 145; during 1863 Kentucky election, 147, 148–49; in Nicholasville, Ky., 146
Martin, Mr., 99
Martin, Mrs., xxiii, 57–58
Masonic Hall, 20, 76, 77n. 1, 190, 192
Mathews, J.D., 36, 39n. 28
Matthews (Presbyterian clergy), 150
Maxwell, Cicero, 193, 193n. 1
May, Andrew Jackson, 123, 123n. 2
Maysville, Ky., 35, 134, 134n. 1, 136

Mc——, John (wagon driver), 34, 39–40, 45, 49, 51, 97
McAllister, Sarah, 120, 120n. 1, 173
McCauly, John, 92n. 2
McCauly, Mrs. John, 91
McCaw, Mrs. Thomas D., 184
McCaw, Thomas D., 94, 94n. 1
McClellan, George B., 35, 39n. 23, 80, 85, 202, 202n. 1
McCook, Col., 28
McCracken, William, 62, 63n. 3
McCullough, David, 73, 73n. 2
McEwing, Mrs., 172
McFarland, Mrs. John, 132, 133n. 1
McGowan, Mrs., 42
McGowan's Hotel. *See* Megowan's Hotel
McMurtry, John, 116–17n. 6
McWhiney, Grady, 64n. 2
Meacham, Dr., 191, 193
measles, 23, 85
Medical Hall, x, xiii, 15n. 1, 17–18, 32, 115, 122; burned down, 129; engravings of, 19; used for hospital, 90, 95
Megowan's Hotel, 82, 82n. 1, 87
Megowan, T.B., 82n. 1
Melodeon Hall, 127, 159, 195–96n. 2
Meredith (estate), 120n. 1
Metcalfe, Leonidas, 20, 20n. 1, 27, 28, 28n. 1
Methodist Church, 87, 187
Micham, Dr. *See* Meacham, Dr.
Midway, Ky., 100, 116–17n. 6
military discipline, 5, 7, 28, 90–91, 176, 195
Miller, Linda Patterson, xvii
Miller, Mrs., 76
Miller, Randall M., xvii
Miller, Sarah Jane, 155
Mill Springs, Ky., battle of, 5n. 3, 5n. 5, 6, 10n. 3, 14n. 1, 52n. 1, 195–96n. 2
Milward, H.K., 188, 189n. 1
Milward, Joseph Usher, 102, 102n. 1
Missionary Ridge, battle of, 97n. 1
Mississippi Convention, 107, 107–8n. 3, 109, 110
"Miss Nancy," 163
Missouri Cavalry, 84, 92, 93
Mitchell, Mrs., 46
Monmollin, Mrs., 17n. 1, 17

Index

Monroe, Thomas B., Jr., 15, 15n. 3
Montell, Mr., 32, 40, 44, 46. *See also* Lanckhart and Mentelle Iron Foundry
Montmullin's mill, 40
Moon, Virginia "Jennie," 121, 122n. 1
Moore, C.C., 120n. 1
Moore, Shelton, 120
More, Col., 200n. 1
Morgan, Alex, 99
Morgan, Calvin C. "Caley," 3, 4n. 2, 6, 140, 142
Morgan, Charlton H., 4n. 2, 99, 101, 101n. 2, 102
Morgan, E. *See* Morgan, George / N. (blacksmith)
Morgan, Frank Key, 8–9, 9n. 1
Morgan, George/N. (blacksmith), 83n. 1
Morgan, George W. (U.S.), 18, 44n. 2, 46n. 1
Morgan, George Washington "Wash" (C.S. Maj.), 34, 39n. 20
Morgan, Henrietta, xix, 4n. 2, 11, 21, 21n. 2, 86; and arrest of Teddy Flanagan, 116, 117; coal delivered to, 49; house of, 161; house searched, 8–9, 88, 127; houses rebels, 3–4, 64, 66–68, 79–80; and injury to Basil Wilson Duke, 89; leaves Lexington, 52, 55, 63; and Morgan, Charlton H. (son), 101; Morgan, John Hunt (son), 30, 145, 160; and Morgan, Thomas H. (son), 139; and networks of communication, xxv, 51, 179; and southern mail, 22, 87
Morgan, John Hunt, xviii, xix–xx, 4, 4n. 2, 12n. 1, 140n. 1; and Alston, R.A., 139n. 1; and Bragg, Braxton, 64, 64n. 2; at Corydon, Ind., 140; as "favorite son," 186–87, 188n. 2; at Harrodsburg, Ky., 142; at Lebanon, Ky., 141n. 3, 142, 190n. 1; in Lexington, Ky., 30, 32, 43, 55, 71, 71n. 1; and Lexington Rifles, 38n. 3, 104, 116–17n. 6; marriage of, *13*, 148; Morgan, Thomas H. (brother), 139n. 2; Ohio Penitentiary, imprisoned in, 145, 145nn. 1, 2, 160; Ohio Penitentiary, escape from,

137–38n. 1, 145n. 2, 174, 174n. 1, 179; at Orleans, Ind., 140; at Paris, Ky., 25n. 3; proclamation issued by, 20–21, 21n. 1; publishes *Vidette*, 85, 85n. 1; reports of, 8, 20–21, 22, 63, 64, 88, 97, 100, 128–29; and southern mail, 87; at Vernon, Ind., 141, 142n. 2; and Wolford, Frank, 197. *See also* Morgan's cavalry; Morgan's guerrillas; Morgan's raids
Morgan, Martha Ready "Mattie," *13*, 148, 148nn. 1, 2
Morgan, N. *See* Morgan, George/N. (blacksmith)
Morgan, Nash, 66–67
Morgan, Richard C., 4n. 2
Morgan's cavalry, 4n. 1, 30, 39n. 21, 68n. 1, 94, 185; capture of Mount Sterling, Ky., 134, 134nn. 1, 2
Morgan's guerrillas, 38n. 6, 45, 55, 88; at Athens, Ky., 100; camped in Little College Lot, 51, 52; at Georgetown, Ky., 22, 23; and Gratz, Benjamin, 55; at Lawrenceburg, Ky., 138; at Mount Sterling, Ky., 113–15; and railroad vandalism, 27, 113, 113n. 1; Wilgus, Mrs. J., 68. *See also* Cluke's guerrillas
Morgan's raids, 12n. 1; Christmas Raid, 89n. 1; First Kentucky raid, 20n. 1, 20–21, 21n. 1, 25, 25n. 2, 116–17n. 6; Ohio and Indiana raids, xxv, 38n. 3, 137–38n. 1, 137–45, 145n. 2, 148; Second Kentucky raid, 64n. 2, 64–68, 72
Morgan, Thomas H., 4n. 2, 139, 139n. 2, 140
morphine, 121
Morris, James C., 143, 143n. 1
Morrison College, x, 18
Morrison Hall, *19, 83*
Mount Sterling, Ky., 25, 42, 43, 44, 134, 183n. 1, 199; fire and battle of, 113–15, 115n. 1, 117, 126; guerrillas at, 175, 189; Morgan's cavalry at, 134, 134n. 1; rebel soldiers at, 102, 103, 105, 178
Mundy, Marcellus, 3, 4, 4n. 1, 5, 7
Munfordville, 35
Murfreesboro, Tenn., battle of, 6n. 1, 148

Index

Index

Peter, Frances Paca Dallam (mother), x, xi; on seeing rebel officer, 14; talks with drover, 158; talks with guerrilla, 139; talks with Mr. Martin and son, 99; talks with rebel soldiers, 35–36, 40, 41, 42, 43; talks with Union soldiers, 73, 152–53, 182, 183

Peter, "Frank." *See* Peter, Frances Dallam

Peter, Hugh (brother), 7n. 1

Peter, Johanna (sister), xxv, 7n. 1, 41, 128, 151, 159, 171, 182; dance card of, *130*

Peter, Letitia "Lettie" (sister), xi, xxv, 7, 7n. 1, 151, 159, 171, 182; and amateur concerts, 37, 84; nurses sick and wounded, 118; talks with rebel soldiers, 32, 58; talks with Union soldiers, 73–74, 182; and "Uncle Tom," 163; and Willcox dance, 128

Peter, Robert (brother), 7n. 1, 91

Peter, Robert (father), x, xi, xii, *165*; as assistant surgeon, 16, 17–18; and Ben Peter, 26; in charge of hospitals, 18, 29, 80–81, 84, 85, 122, 169, 176, 191; and Dr. Watson, 153–54; and excavation of Indian mound, 120n. 1; on faculty of college, 90, 163, 178n. 3; and Frances Peter, xviii, xxiii; on Frank Wolford, 197; letter by, xxix; and Lettie Peter, 32; as Lexington citizen, 33–34, 97n. 4, 105, 133, 143, 155, 202; mill of (*see* Peter's mill); and news of war, 43, 119, 126, 174; and newspapers, 157, 173, 174; and rebel soldiers, 14, 178; reports of happenings in Lexington, xxv, 51, 56, 57, 104; talks with guerrilla, 45; talks with rebel soldiers, 40, 42

Peter, Sarah (sister), 7n. 1

Peter, William (brother), xi, 7n. 1

Peter diary, ix–x, xiii, xvii–xxi, xxiv, xxvii, xxxn. 4, 38n. 14

Peter family estate, 120n. 1

Peter family home, x, xiii, 19, 32, 80n. 2, 133, 158, 182

Petersburg, Va., battle of, 39n. 17, 122–23n. 1

Peter's mill, 22, 34, 41, 60, 180n. 1,

201–2; payment for use of, 39–40, 43–44, 45; taken by rebels, 22

Phoenix Hotel, 56, 57, 60, 60n. 1, 62, 63, 120, 122, 178, 182n. 1

Picket, Ann, 87, 87n. 1

Pike, Samuel N., 91n. 1

Pittsburg Landing, battle of. *See* Shiloh, battle of

Pleasants, Henry, 138, 138n. 1

Plug Uglies. *See* 2nd Maryland V.I.

Poe, Col., 132

Polk, Charles E., 62, 63n. 2

Pope, John, 119n. 3

Port Royal, S.C., 96, 96n. 1

Postlethwaite, Louis, 23, 66, 200n. 1

Prairie, Mr., 172–73

Prentice, George D., 190n. 1, 190, 193–94

Prentiss, Gen., 14

Presbyterian churches, 10n. 2, 150

Preston, Caroline H. "Carrie," 33, 38n. 13, 138n. 2

Preston, Jessie Fremont, 138n. 2

Preston, Margaret H., 138n. 2

Preston, Margaret Wickliffe, 38n. 13, 78, 80, 82, 86, 164

Preston, Mary Owen, 138n. 2

Preston, Susan C., 138n. 2

Preston, William, 38n. 13, 48, 48n. 1, 164n. 1, 202n. 1; daughters of, 137, 138n. 2

Prewitt, Richard H., 105, 105n. 1

prisoners, rebel, xxiv, 11, 77, 99, 118, 132, 181; from Cumberland Gap, 162–64; escape, attempted, 144, 150; in Federal uniform, 104, 105; from Louisiana, 147; Morgan's guerrillas, 89, 101, 113; at Mount Sterling, Ky., 122; sick and wounded, 75; from Somerset, Ky., 133; from Texas, 147; at Vernon, Ind., 141. *See also* Ohio Penitentiary

prisoners, Union, 32, 196, 197; at Bell Island Prison, 175n. 1, 175; at Lebanon, Ky., 142; at Libby Prison, 175, 175n. 1, 188n. 2, 189; paroled, 30, 50, 60, 67, 101, 115n. 1, 117; threatened with hanging, 70; threatened with shooting, 48

Proclamation of Amnesty and

Index

Index

Index

Warfield Woods, 143
Warner, William A., 15, 15n. 1, 16, 18, 23, 25, 26, 29, 91, 188
Washington, Ky., 28
Washington's birthday, 9, 99
Waters, Frank, 6, 6n. 1
Watkins, Louis D., 194, 195n. 1
Watson, Dr., 153–54
Watson, William, 59, 59n. 3, 77–78
weather: rain, 103, 156; severe cold, 181; snow, 90, 95
Welter, Barbara, xxi
Werts, John H., 32, 38n. 7
Wheeler's cavalry, 175
Wheeler & Wilson sewing machine shop, 5, 5n. 2, 32
whiskey, destroyed by Union soldiers, 125
whiskey, gunpowder, 170–71
White, Paul, 152–53
White's. *See* Thomas W. White and Brother
Whites, Lee Ann, xxi, xxii
Whittaker, Walter C., 112, 113n. 3
Wickliffe, Carmichael, 14
Wickliffe, Charles A., 148n. 1
Wickliffe, Daniel Carmichael, 16n. 7, 26, 71, 109, 110n. 6, 119, 137, 149
Wickliffe, Robert, 38n. 13
Wild Cat, battle of, 10n. 3, 14
Wileman, Abram G., 166, 166n. 1
Wilgris, John B., 10n. 4, 10
Wilgus, J., 66, 68
Wilgus, Mrs. J., xxiii, 68, 68n. 2
Wilkins, Ross, 132
Willcox, Orlando Bolivar, 80n. 2, 125n. 2; censorship of newspapers, 124; dance for Unionists, 128–29, 129n. 1, 130; in Indiana, 135; in Lexington, 122–23, 126, 131, 132; at Medical Hall fire, 129; and southern sympathizers, women, 125n. 1
Williams, James M., 97n. 2
Williams, John T., 105
Williams, Mary, 102
Williams, S.R., 63, 64n. 1

Wilson, Henry, 182, 183n. 2
Wilson, John S., 63, 63n. 6
Winchester, Ky., 100, 103, 114, 125, 126, 146, 175–76
Winchester Pike, 45
Window on the War, x, xxxn. 3
Winton (estate), 202n. 1
Wirts. *See* Werts, John H.
Wise, Gen., 120
Wisener, Moses, 89, 90n. 1
Wolf County, 123
Wolford, Frank, xviii, 142, 151, 194, 195, 195–96n. 2, 196, 197, 198, 201
Wolley, Mrs. George, 40, 41n. 2, 43, 115
women, northern, xxii–xxiii, xxxiin. 16
women, southern white: Confederate, xxi, xxii, xxxiin. 15, 28, 174, 184–85; nursing of sick and wounded, 50, 51, 74, 79, 92, 118; shoplifting by, 167; Union, xxxin. 13, 31, 36; Union, dinner for veterans, 190, 191–92; Union, Thanksgiving dinner, 172–73. *See also under specific names*; Aid Society; southern sympathizers, women
women's history, xxii–xxiii, xxvi, xxxin. 12, xxxi–xxxiinn. 14, 15
Wood, Fernando, 156, 157n. 2
Wood, Mrs., 32
Woolley, Mrs. *See* Wolley, Mrs. George
Worley, C.T., 21n. 4, 27n. 1, 57, 60–61, 66, 67, 67n. 2
Worley, J.T., 67n. 2
Worley, James W., 67n. 2
wounded. *See* soldiers, sick and wounded
Wright, Horatio Gouverneur, 29, 69, 75, 96, 105–6, 106nn. 2, 3, 117; and southern sympathizers, women, 116

Yeaman, George Helm, 112, 112–13n. 2
Yeiser, P.E., 171, 171n. 1
Young, E., 72

Zollicoffer, Felix, 5, 5n. 5, 6–7, 8, 10, 14n. 1

D